MY FAMILY

A Window into the Secrets, Successes, and Sins of Early New Orleans and Beyond

Michelle Freret Prather

Legacy Book Press, LLC
Camanche, Iowa

Copyright © 2023 Michelle Prather

Cover Images: front top, Salazar y Mendoza, Vincent Rillieux, (Private collection); Norbert Rillieux, (courtesy of the Louisiana State Museum accession no. 11223); William Freret, (courtesy of The Historic New Orleans Collection, accession no. 1969.12.8); front bottom, Jay Dearborn Edwards, Freret's Cotton Press, Poydras Street, (courtesy of The Historic New Orleans Collection, accession no. 1982.32.7); back cover, Street scene in the Faubourg Marigny, several houses including the Marigny plantation house, Félix Achille Saint-Aulaire, Vue d'une Rue du Faubourg Marigny, Nelle. Orléans, (courtesy of The Historic New Orleans Collection, accession no. 1937.2.2).
Cover design by Kaitlea Toohey (kaitleatoohey.com)

All rights reserved. No part of this book may be used or reproduced by any means, graphic, electronic, or mechanical, including photocopying, recording, taping or by any information storage retrieval system without the written permission of the publisher except in the case of brief quotations embodied in critical articles and reviews.

ISBN: 978-1-7375926-8-6
Library of Congress Case Number: 1-11690636251

Acknowledgements

I am forever grateful to my family for their encouragement and support: to my husband, James Prather, for listening to my ideas and asking great questions, to Amélie Prather for her keen eye for the conventions of writing, and to Sarah Prather for the family tree images that she created.

Special thanks go to Professor Emeritus of History at Tulane University, Lawrence Powell, who encouraged me to broaden my research and shake my family tree to find the stories that are in this book. He also helped connect me to academics who graciously answered my questions.

Many thanks go to historian, writer, publisher, and my uncle, Christian Garcia, for guiding me during the research and writing process and giving me advice on how to make my manuscript better; to Gervais Favrot Jr. for helping me decipher old family documents and filling in some gaps; to John and Lesleyanne Wolvett, my distant relatives whom I discovered through ancestry.com, for meeting with me in London and giving me new information about the Frerets; and to Doug Gruse and Jan Risher, my writing coaches, for believing in my work and helping me hone my writing skills.

I am truly fortunate to live in an area that has preserved so many artifacts from the past. The resources available at The Historic New Orleans Collection, The Louisiana State Museum, and the archives and special collections at Tulane University and Louisiana State University were invaluable.

I appreciate the following scholars and writers for sharing their knowledge with me: Tara Dudley, The University of Texas at Austin; Emily Clark, Tulane University; Richard Follett, The University of Sussex; Calvin Schermerhorn, Arizona State University and Fulbright Senior Scholar at the University of Nottingham; John Stauffer, Harvard University; Craig Bauer, University of Holy Cross; Melinda Nelson-Hurst, Tulane University; William de Marigny Hyland, Parish Historian/Site Manager, Los Isleños Museum Complex; Art historian and Author Cybèle Gontar; Sharon Bertsch McGrayne, author of several books about scientific discoveries and the scientists who made them; bestselling author Edward Ball; and especially Christopher Benfey, Mount Holyoke College, whose book, *Degas in New Orleans,* inspired me.

To my family—past, present, and future.

CONTENTS

Preface i
Author's Note iv

The Rillieux Family 1

    Vincent Rillieux Sr. 1740-1800 2
    Vincent Rillieux Jr. 1778-1833 8
    Constance Vivant 1788-1868 12
    Bernard Noel "Manuel" Andry 1758-1839 17
    Norbert Rillieux 1806-1894 22
    Edmond Rillieux Sr. 1810-1897 52
    Edgar Degas 1834-1917 67

The Cantrelle Family 73

    Jacques Cantrelle 1697-1778 74
    Michel Bernard Cantrelle 1750-1814 82

The Verret Family 89

    Nicolas Pierre Verret 1725-1775 90

The Jones Family 95

    Evan Jones 1739-1813 96

The Bringier Family 121

    Emmanuel "Marius Pons" Bringier 1752-1820 122

Michel "Doradou" Bringier 1789-1847	127
Duncan Farrar Kenner 1813-1887	129
Paul "Louis" Bringier "Don Louis" 1784-1860	132

The Freret Family 145

James Freret Sr. 1773-1834	146
William Freret Sr. 1803-1864	153

Index 166
Bibliography 169
About the Author..215
End Notes..216

PREFACE

My Family: A Window into the Secrets, Successes, and Sins of Early New Orleans and Beyond is the unvarnished story of my ancestors and how they navigated the ever-changing destiny of Louisiana and its citizens in the eighteenth and nineteenth centuries. I grew up hearing stories of the Revolutionary War hero Vincent Rillieux, the efficient Mayor of New Orleans, William Freret, and even the somewhat distantly related artist, Edgar Degas. The images I conjured up were static, and I realized that I knew little about the rest of their lives or the times in which they lived. I began to add flesh to their skeletons by reading Christopher Benfey's book *Degas in New Orleans: Encounters in the Creole World of Kate Chopin and George Washington Cable*. Benfey's book chronicled Edgar Degas' five-month visit to New Orleans from the fall of 1872 until the spring of 1873. Benfey included information about the city of New Orleans and some of Degas' relatives. I researched every relative of Degas who was mentioned in the book to see if we were related. I was immediately taken with one in particular - Norbert Rillieux. The once famous engineer was my first cousin five times removed, yet I had never heard of him in family lore. My interest was piqued when Benfey referred to him as "a closely guarded secret." The "secret" was that the man who revolutionized the sugar industry all over the world was a free man of color. I'm not sure he was actually a secret, but he was not mentioned when my ancestors were discussed. I wondered who else would fall out my family tree if I shook it hard enough. As I mined archives and read works by scholars, I discovered free men and women of color, war heroes, inventors, a Cuban filibuster, a universal suffrage activist, spies, founders, philanthropists, entrepreneurs, sugar barons, cotton factors, and slave traders.

In writing about my family, I tried to resist the urge to tell incomplete stories by omitting painful realities to produce idealized versions of people and events. Time, place, culture, events, and personalities steep together to produce the potent concoction that is our human story. If one of those ingredients is left out, we risk contorting the retelling to fit our own ideas about the order of things. Human beings are afraid of disorder, so we create false order by telling stories with contrived plots. We sometimes crop the truth to produce a snapshot of the past that makes us feel comfortable in the realm we have created. As we grow and evolve as humans, it is natural that our sense of justice is offended by practices of the past like slavery, the lack of agency for women, slave holding free people of color, and shifting loyalties. We must use our past to inform our present, but we must tell the whole story, which is messy and rife with contradictions. It is in the contradictions that we develop acceptance and clarity.

The truth is elusive but couching the particular in the context of the whole gets us closer. History is not a series of discursive facts, but a synergy of complex stories that interweave and meander through a particular time and place. If accounts are populated by archetypes – the evil slave owner, the noble enslaved person, the father who uses his daughters as business assets, or the mixed-race man who heroically defies the odds – we reduce the stories of real lives to myth. While the moral lessons may survive, our ability to see ourselves in the story is diminished. We see each character in the myth as other from ourselves, or we over identify with an idea of a person and fail to see the whole. If left unexamined, the story that is told of our progress can be skewed and result in a contrived, shallow awakening that is reactive and judgmental. We become unable to see beyond the reality we have built despite voices raised against it. If those from the past who participated in things we now find objectionable are seen only as villains, then we fail to understand that we too can become encapsulated by our own time and become part of collective justifications. Conversely, if we lionize those who have done remarkable things or blazed trails of enlightenment and reduce them to symbols, our heroes aren't authentically human, but are stiff, one-dimensional portraits.

Author's Note

My Family: A Window into the Secrets, Successes, and Sins of Early New Orleans and Beyond is not meant to be an exhaustive retelling of history. It is the story of my family's journey that gives added depth to the story of Louisiana. I am honored to be a witness to their struggles and successes. I hope I have done them justice. I regret that I was not able to tell the story of many of the women in my family as there are few primary documents that shed light on their personal lives. Regrettably, their stories are largely told within the context of their fathers, husbands, and sons.

Some of the biographies included in the book are much longer than others due to differences in availability of information and the complexity of the events. The people I included in the book intrigued me in some way or another and gave me new insight into Louisiana's multi-layered history. I did not go into detail about the life of Edgar Degas because he was so famous that his story has been told by countless biographers. I included details of his life that connected him to New Orleans and my family. Historian Craig Bauer wrote entire books about the Bringiers and Duncan Kenner. His research was invaluable and provided a basis for my work on the Bringiers, but I tried to make new connections and observations. I discovered mixed-race ancestors who were of enormous importance to the city, but who had all but been erased from my family tree. I discovered Norbert Rillieux, a free man of color who was one of the most respected scientists and engineers of the mid-1800s. He has been included in several books, but I wanted to know more than the same thin facts repeated in almost every source and list of African American scientists. I wanted to know more about the man whose understanding of the new field of thermodynamics gave us the technology to produce snow white sugar crystals, desalinate water, and manufacture soap and glue, condensed milk, and pharmaceuticals in usable concentrated forms.

The term Creole means many various things to different people. For the purposes of this book, it is used as it was in the eighteenth and nineteenth centuries – native born Louisianians whose parents were of French or Spanish descent. The term was used to distinguish them from Anglo-Americans who moved to Louisiana after the purchase by America in 1803. In the nineteenth century, it was also used to differentiate them from new immigrants from Germany and Ireland.

Rillieux Family

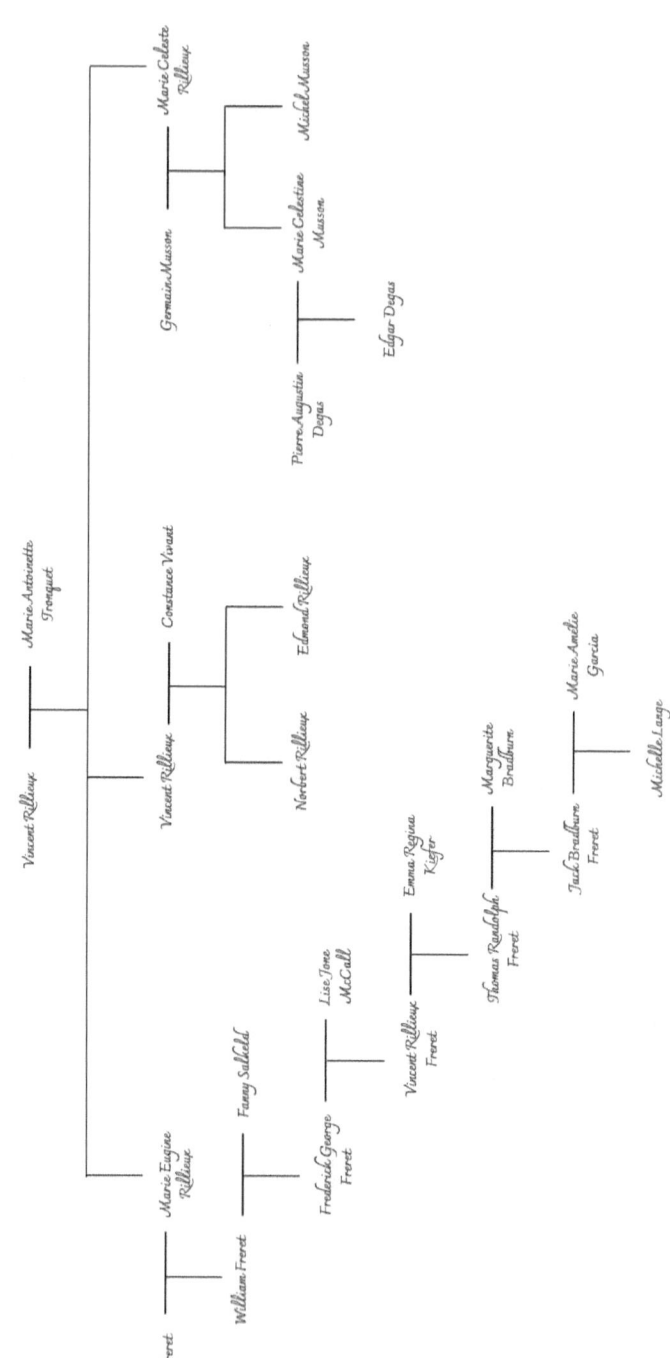

The Rillieux Family

Vincent Rillieux Sr.
1740-1800

    Eight generations ago, as early as 1727, François Rillieux was living in the Pascagoula area of the Louisiana Territory.[1] In 1738, he and his wife Marie Marguerite Chenet and their young children settled on Bayou Bonfouca near present day Slidell, Louisiana, just across Lake Pontchartrain from New Orleans.[2] Their family grew to include four daughters and five sons. At the time, the Louisiana Territory was under French control, although it would change hands many times before it became part of the United States in 1803. When François and his wife settled in Louisiana, there were very few French settlers living in what is now East St. Tammany Parish. Only five non-native families lived in the area: LaPointes, Gravelines, Krebs, Rillieuxs, and Chaumonts.[3] The settlers looked to the Tunica-Biloxi tribe to show them how to harness the area's natural resources, raise and breed cattle, and farm the land.[4] Supplies were often scarce, so the French relied on the tribe for necessities like salt, rice, cattle, and horses.[5] The Tunica-Biloxi Nation also helped protect the colonists from attacks from rival tribes like the Natchez and Chickasaw.

    After François's death in 1760, his widow, Marie Marguerite, bought a huge tract of land from the Tunica-Biloxi tribe. It was situated between the land she owned and the Pearl River. Marie Chenet Rillieux needed the land for pasture for her approximately one hundred cows, which encompassed approximately 100,000 acres between Bayou Bonfouca and the Pearl River in what is now St. Tammany Parish.

François's oldest son, François, was killed in a hunting accident in 1759, so the Widow Rillieux sold the land in 1769 to Vincent, the next eldest son.[6] He took over the family home and business and lived there for many years.[7]

In 1777, Vincent Rillieux married Marie Antoinette Tronquet de La Rose, a native of New Orleans.[8] They raised their large family on the plantation in St. Tammany Parish and at a home across Lake Pontchartrain in New Orleans. Vincent Rillieux and Marie Tronquet had nine children together, but only seven lived to adulthood.[9] Vincent Rillieux proved to be a savvy businessman. The Rillieux family continued to manufacture tar and pitch and raised cattle on their country property on the Pearl River. France, Spain, and Great Britain encouraged colonial settlers to take advantage of the area's natural resources to produce materials like tar and pitch that were used in the shipping industry.[10] During this time, meat was scarce in New Orleans, and consequently, raising cattle was extremely profitable. Previously, it was only the Native Americans in the area who provided people in the city with meat, so Rillieux seized the opportunity to capitalize on the lack of supply.[11] He developed a shipping business to transport his goods to New Orleans and beyond.

Conflict in Europe ultimately altered the borders of the Spanish, French, and British colonies in North America and changed the colonists' lives. As land changed hands, colonists like Vincent Rillieux and his family became subjects of foreign realms who were once considered enemies. In 1762, the Louisiana Territory and the Isle of Orleans were ceded to Spain by France in the secret Treaty of Fontainebleau during the Seven Years War. Initially, the Spanish wanted to keep the transfer quiet because they were afraid that Great Britain would attack and seize control of the nearby territory before Spain could get forces there to defend it. France was locked in a bitter conflict with Great Britain and used the offer of the Louisiana Territory to entice Spain to support them in the conflict. Spain wanted the territory to act as a buffer between the British colonies and New Spain. When Great Britain found out about the deal, they attacked Spain. In 1763, in the Treaty of Paris that ended the war, France and Great Britain openly recognized Spain's ownership of the territory, but the treaty granted Great Britain unfettered access to the entire Mississippi River. The vast, sparsely settled Louisiana Territory then came under the governance of the Captain General of Cuba. The war proved very costly for Spain and France. France lost all its holdings in North America, while Spain ceded Florida to Great Britain in exchange for Havana and Manila, two of its main trading centers. Frenchman Vincent Rillieux's St. Tammany Parish property was in British controlled West Florida, and his New Orleans shipping business was in Spanish New Orleans. When he crossed Lake Pontchartrain carrying goods from his farm to the city, he crossed from one country to another.

Spain and France watched with interest as Great Britain's American colonies grew more defiant and rumblings of rebellion surfaced. The two countries bitterly resented the outcome of the Seven Years War and were eager to retaliate against the world power. On one hand, they saw the American colonial trouble with Great Britain as an opportunity to swoop in and gain control of the weakened colonies. However, world politics complicated things. Spain did not want to upset Portugal, its close neighbor and ally of Great Britain. In addition, Spain did not want to openly support rebellion for fear that the idea of separating from the mother country would spread throughout its own colonies. Bourbon monarchs, King Carlos III of Spain and King Louis XVI of France, were cousins and tied together by the Bourbon Family Compact. They quietly joined forces to rebuild their navies into a single fighting force capable of challenging the formidable British fleet.[12] Spain began covertly supporting the American colonies in their fight for independence even before fighting broke out between the colonists and Great Britain.[13] Through a network of smugglers and strawmen,[14] Spain, under local control, clandestinely supplied the Continental Army in the upper Mississippi Valley with gunpowder and medical supplies.[15]

The relationship between Spain and Great Britain was strained, yet they traded openly at Fort Bute, a British fortification at the point at which Bayou Manchac and the Mississippi River meet. According to historian Lawrence Powell, the area surrounding Bayou Manchac was populated by British merchants and was a base of operations for British smugglers and pirates. This network provided the region's residents with needed supplies and luxuries and allowed merchants like Vincent Rillieux to do business with other traders from foreign colonies.[16] As tensions between the two countries mounted, there were skirmishes between Spanish and British ships in the area. In 1778, the Spanish governor, Bernardo de Gálvez, learned that King Carlos III aimed to drive the British from the Gulf of Mexico and the banks of the Mississippi. Considering his King's objective, Gálvez changed the rules of the tacit trade arrangements and refused to allow a British ship, the *West Florida*, to enter Bayou St. John, a waterway that connected Lake Pontchartrain to the Mississippi River. In retaliation, the *West Florida* captured two boats anchored in Spanish waters in New Orleans, one of which belonged to Vincent Rillieux.[17]

The next year, Vincent Rillieux avenged the seizure of his vessel. He was the commander of a sloop of war for the Louisiana Militia under the flag of Spain. Rillieux received intelligence that a well-armed British ship planned to enter Bayou Manchac, which served as a shortcut from the Mississippi River to the Gulf of Mexico. He formulated a plan to capture the barque and its men with his small contingent of fourteen citizen soldiers. Rillieux and his men built entrenchments and hid themselves until the vessel was nearby. Screaming and yelling, they fired upon the ship in unison and created such a ruckus that the British sailors thought a large force was attacking them. The British crew was so alarmed by the attack that they dashed below deck. Rillieux and his men seized the opportunity to race to the ship and seal the hatches shut and captured all on board. According to the *Madrid Gazette*, the prisoners were a captain, a first lieutenant, two second lieutenants, fifty-four grenadiers of the Waldeck regiment, and ten to twelve sailors.[18] Rillieux was hailed as a hero and was instrumental in keeping the British from gaining control of the Mississippi River.

As Vincent Rillieux's reputation as a civic and military leader grew, so did his assets. In 1795, Vincent Rillieux built several structures in the French Quarter. The houses were part of the building boom that took place because of two devastating fires. In 1788, the Good Friday fire destroyed most of the public buildings in the city and over 900 residences. Another fire in 1794 destroyed another 200 properties. After the fires, the architecture of the French Quarter became predominately Spanish, and officials enacted new fireproofing guidelines for all new construction that required either brick construction or wood to be covered with at least one inch of cement. One of the buildings built by Rillieux was at 417 Royal Street. The pink stucco building is now the home of the famous Brennan's Restaurant. Its low-pitched roof and plaster covered brick walls were signatures of Spanish colonial style.[19] The Rillieux family owned the house on Royal Street until Vincent Sr. died in 1800. Vincent Rillieux also commissioned the building of a mansion at 343 Royal Street. Don Vincent Rillieux died on February 10, 1800. He left his family a small fortune that included so many assets that it took 400 pages to list the inventory of his estate.

In 1805, the Widow Rillieux purchased a house and large piece of land on Bayou St. John as her country home. She made significant changes to the magnificent house that fronted the bayou and added several buildings. She sold the house in 1810 to James Pitot who was a successful importer and exporter as well as the first elected mayor of New Orleans.[20] The home is now called Pitot House and is a Louisiana Landmark and a National Trust Historic Site. It was completely renovated in the 1960s and is the only Creole colonial country house in New Orleans that is open to the public.[21]

Marie Tronquet endured two more heartbreaking losses after her husband Vincent died. Her daughter, Eugenie, died in 1808 and left behind three young sons and a daughter. Two years later, her twenty-two-year-old son, Michel Vincent Rillieux, was killed in a duel.[22] These tragedies did not stop the incisive Widow Rillieux. Marie Tronquet continued to grow her assets after her husband's death. She was a shrewd businesswoman involved in many real estate deals in the French Quarter and beyond between 1803 and 1820.[23] She maintained her own records of transactions concerning the plantation on Bayou Bonfouca as well as mortgages, notes, bank statements, and receipts for land improvements and buildings. She even kept a secret stash of gold and silver in her home. The Widow Rillieux eventually bought a house on Chartres Street between Conti and Bienville and continued to live in lavish style. Shortly before she died, she moved to her daughter's large home in Faubourg St. Marie.[24] Faubourg St. Marie, later called Faubourg St. Mary, was the first suburb of New Orleans and is now the Central Business District of the city.[25]

After Marie Tronquet Rillieux's death, her heirs sold 4,400 acres of the St. Tammany Parish land to Bartholomew Martin, the overseer who worked for the Rillieux family. The remainder of the land's ownership was in dispute more than ninety years later, and rights to it were determined by the United States Supreme Court in 1852. The heirs of Vincent Rillieux filed a petition against the United States that alleged that they were the rightful owners of land in St. Tammany Parish. The plaintiffs claimed that Vincent Rillieux purchased the land from the Biloxi tribe with the consent of the French government, so it belonged to them. As a result of the Treaty of 1763, the land in question passed from France to Great Britain, and the certificate of two French officers from 1765, certifying that the claimant had been for a long time in possession, furnished no evidence of title. It was determined that no application was made to the British government for a grant; therefore, the Rillieux family lost ownership of the land despite having lived on and worked it for nearly seventy years.[26]

Vincent Rillieux Jr.
1778-1833

After the death of his father, Vincent Jr., the eldest of the Rillieux children, sued his father's estate to receive 1,000 pesos as payment for administering his home and enslaved people for three years without pay. Amazingly, Vincent Jr. managed his father's 640-acre farm, 1,000 head of cattle, and eighty enslaved people from the time he was sixteen years old. The Rillieux family, under Vincent's leadership, continued in the pitch and tar business until 1824 when his mother Marie Tronquet died and the estate was divided. In addition to managing his family's large plantation, Vincent Rillieux Jr. was a planter, engineer, inventor, and a family man. He had a long-standing relationship with Constance Vivant, a free woman of color.[27] They had seven children together and lived as husband and wife.[28]

Vincent Jr., like his parents, had a keen mind for business as well as agricultural expertise. In 1806, he erected fireproof cotton presses and tobacco warehouses in New Orleans in Faubourg St. Marie at the corner of Tchoupitoulas and Poydras Streets, having fronts on both streets and Magazine. Fire was of constant concern in early New Orleans, so it was particularly important that the presses were fireproof and listed as such in the property description. Six years earlier, Vincent's brother-in-law, James Freret, built the first cotton press in the city. The Freret Cotton Press operated by hand, whereas the one Vincent Rillieux Jr. invented was a steam operated cotton baling press or cotton compress. Prior to Eli Whitney's invention of the cotton gin in 1794, some cotton was grown in Louisiana, but the invention of the mechanical method of separating cotton seeds from the fiber catapulted cotton production into a new era.[29] Technological gains in the cotton industry were watched worldwide as cotton was such a large part of global commerce. A German trade journal reported that Vincent Rillieux sought to use horses rather than enslaved people and wanted to use two presses and interrelate them. The new press could do twice the work in half the amount of time.[30]

Vincent Rillieux Jr. knew that New Orleans had to make some changes to become the city of its potential. When New Orleans was bought by the United States in 1803 as part of the Louisiana Purchase, the streets were unpaved and had no drainage except for ditches or wooden gutters that ran alongside the streets.[31] Consequently, the streets were filthy and turned into breeding grounds for disease. When it rained, it created muck from a mixture of cow and horse manure, human waste, and mud.[32] Yellow fever, malaria, and cholera were common adversaries for the early citizenry. Mosquitos bred in the stagnant water that collected in the streets and ditches. It was difficult to be outdoors at dusk, and people had to sleep with mosquito netting around their beds so they would not be attacked by the blood sucking pests. At the time, scientists did not know that yellow fever and malaria were mosquito-borne illnesses, so mosquito control was not a top priority, even though it impacted the city inhabitants' quality of life. The city leaders were so consumed with maintaining the levees around New Orleans that they had little time to address anything else in terms of infrastructure.[33] The unsanitary conditions also led to intestinal problems and dysentery.[34] People used the streets to get from place to place when necessary. Elegantly dressed New Orleans ladies sometimes went barefoot until they arrived at their destinations.[35] Rillieux understood that improving the condition of the streets was paramount to moving the city forward. He set to work and fabricated stone pavers in his press yard. He put down the first paved streets in front of his presses on the corner of Poydras and Magazine not far from his home at the corner of Baronne Street. Vincent Rillieux Jr. might not have realized that the unsanitary conditions were the reason for epidemics, but he knew that paved streets were important for commerce in that they provided stable ground for the transportation of goods and a safe, clean passage between his presses and his residence.[36] It wasn't until years later that Benjamin Morgan, a prominent businessman, decided that based on Rillieux's example, the whole city should be paved. In 1818, Morgan laid down an experimental swath of pavement on Gravier Street between Magazine and Tchoupitoulas. The section of street was chosen because it was well traveled and near the main dock coming from the river. The small section of pavement was a welcome relief to those carrying loads across the spongy, muddy city routes. By 1822, Morgan convinced the mayor and city council to begin paving all the streets. Between 1822 and 1823, all of Chartres Street and parts of Conde, St. Peter, and St. Ann were completed.[37]

The Rillieux family was committed to serving the city and Louisiana. The early nineteenth century was a particularly challenging time for New Orleans as well as the nation. The War of 1812 once again pitted Americans against the British. The fight over the strategically situated city of New Orleans and control of the Mississippi River occurred at what is now Chalmette, just below the city. Vincent Rillieux Jr. served his country at the Battle of New Orleans as a corporal in Captain Chauveau's Company of the Louisiana Militia.[38] Unbeknownst to both sides, peace had already been negotiated between the two nations prior to the Battle of New Orleans. Engagement between the two forces lasted from December 14, 1814, to January of 1815. When General Andrew Jackson realized that the British were near Lake Borgne and could gain access to New Orleans, he ordered a surprise attack at Chalmette. Jackson gathered as many troops as he could, but his force of 4,500 was greatly outnumbered by British troops. Vincent Rillieux Jr. fought alongside family members and other aristocrats as well as "army regulars, frontier militiamen, free blacks, and Choctaw tribesmen."[39] His "wife's" brother, Charles Vivant, was a second lieutenant and fought with the First Battalion of Free Men of Color.[40] The battalion was led by white officers and included some lower ranking line officers who were free men of color. Louisiana was the first state in the Union to commission non-white military officers.[41]

The Americans soundly beat the British and suffered relatively few casualties. The victory ushered in a new era of national pride and unity and put an end to British aggression toward America. Anglo-Americans who settled in Louisiana after the Louisiana Purchase and Creole-Americans fought together against a common enemy. This alliance against a mutual adversary began to chip away at the rivalry between the groups.

Vincent Rillieux Jr., along with his brothers-in-law, James Freret, married to Eugenie Rillieux, and Honoré Landreaux, married to Melicerte Rillieux, were city councilmen or aldermen during the Augustin Macarty (sometimes spelled McCarty) administration from 1815 to 1820. Rillieux served with Macarty at the Battle of New Orleans and would continue to fight for New Orleans as the city encountered further adversity. During Vincent Jr.'s tenure on the council, New Orleans saw an outbreak of yellow fever, and the disease killed 1,142 people in five months. On May 5, 1816, the city's administration and its residents faced one of its constant foes – floodwaters. Water inundated New Orleans because of a breach in the levee six miles above New Orleans at the Macarty plantation, present-day Carrollton area. The break allowed water to flood the land between the city and Faubourg St. Marie. Much of what is now Downtown New Orleans was covered with floodwaters three to five feet deep.[42] The water remained in the city until emergency trenches were dug through Metairie Ridge and channels were cut connecting to Bayou St. John. Rillieux worked as part of the administration to help the city recover after the devastation.[43] Undoubtedly, Vincent Rillieux Jr.'s formidable engineering skills helped steer the emergency response.

Vincent Rillieux died suddenly from a stroke at age 50. He left behind seven children, some of whom were still minors, and his companion Constance Vivant.

Constance Vivant
1788-1868

Constance Vivant was the long-time companion of Vincent Rillieux Jr. and the mother of his seven children. She was one quarter white, or a quadroon, as she was the child of a half African American mother, Louison Cheval, and a white, French father, Charles Vivant.[44] Louison was born an enslaved person but was purchased out of slavery. She was the daughter of white landowner François Cheval and an enslaved woman named Maria Juana.[45] Constance Vivant's father fully acknowledged his and Louison's five children by giving them his last name and providing for them in his will.[46] Upon Charles' death, Louison inherited 1,000 pesos, and each child received 200 pesos. Charles' mother and sister inherited the remainder of the estate.[47] In addition, Louison was sometimes referred to as Louison Vivant in real estate transactions, and that they presented themselves as a committed couple.

The arrangement between Constance Vivant and Vincent Rillieux Jr. was like that of Constance's parents; however, their relationship is often inaccurately referred to as a plaçage. Plaçage is an arrangement between a white man, usually French, and a mulatto or mixed-race female. Lore has it that the agreement, often facilitated by the young woman's mother, stipulated that the young woman and children resulting from the liaison would be taken care of for life. The woman was relegated to the role of mistress, not partner.[48] Typically, the white man would eventually leave his paramour to marry a white woman and start a "legitimate" family. Many historians have debunked the idea of the placée, or contracted wife, yet it continues to be repeated and believed by many people. Historian Charles Chamberlain stated that as far as he knew, no one has ever found a plaçage contract. However, he said that long-term relationships like common-law marriages did exist.[49] In Louison's will, Constance is listed as Constance Vivant-alias Rillieux.[50] This reference shows that the community clearly saw Vincent and her as married as was the case with Constance's parents.[51] The idea of plaçage is more closely tied to the mixed-race women who came to New Orleans after the revolution in Saint-Domingue. In 1809, more than 9,000 black and white refugees arrived in New Orleans from Cuba. They originally fled the French colony of Saint-Domingue to Cuba because of the slave revolution there.[52] The Saint-Domingue refugee population included French-speaking white plantation owners, free people of color, and enslaved people.

Emily Clark, a professor of American Colonial history at Tulane University calls this "the plaçage-complex."[53] Clark explains, "The myth has some basis in fact, but is really attributed to the sad plight of the mixed-race refugee women from Saint-Domingue. These refugee women did have relationships with white men and bore their children. They were looking for security anywhere they could find it. And so, for a brief, really tragic moment in this city's history, there were a lot of free women of color who were available for short-term relationships, and maybe even for prostitution. But what I think is really important is to recognize that it was time limited, but it created a reputation for the city."[54]

Constance Vivant was born in Louisiana, and her family had close ties to the white Rillieux family as well as to other affluent Creole families. Her place in society was more elevated than the newly arrived mixed-race women from Saint-Domingue. In colonial Louisiana, the term Creole was used to describe a person who was born in the new world, but whose parents were born in either France or Spain.[55] Relationships among white families and families of mixed race were not uncommon in late eighteenth and early nineteenth century New Orleans. Eulalie Mezange, Constance's half-sister, had a relationship with Jean Soulié who was also white and a close friend of Vincent Rillieux Jr. Eulalie was born into slavery when her mother was still enslaved but was freed in 1784. Vincent and Jean served together in the New Orleans Militia, and Soulié served as recorder for Mayor McCarty's administration at the same time as Vincent Jr. served as an alderman.[56] The relationship was so close that the couples served as godparents to each other's children.[57] There is also evidence that Jean Soulié and Charles Vivant, Constance Vivant's father, were business partners.[58] Jean Soulié was named the executor of Charles' estate on October 14, 1808.[59] In addition, Vincent Rillieux Jr. was connected through business with Jean Baptiste Meullion, Louison's brother and Constance's uncle.[60] Norbert Soulié and Edmond Rillieux, two of the couples' sons, were business partners. This interconnectedness speaks to the unconstrained interaction in the social and business worlds among free people of color and white people and gives evidence of the close family ties among white people and free people of color in New Orleans. In her book, *The Strange History of the American Quadroon Free Women of Color in the Revolutionary Atlantic World*, Emily Clark asserts, "New Orleans-born and – descended free women of color met husbands and made partnerships with white men by means of long-established networks of sociability and kinship."[61] "Partnerships between Orleanian women of color and white men were not uncommon in New Orleans."[62]

The plaçage myth helped create a one-dimensional, flawed picture of free women of color in New Orleans. Free women of color often seeded their business investments with money they inherited from their white fathers or their mixed-race mothers. Some formed business partnerships with their white husbands or other free people of color in the community.[63] Free women of color were far more involved in the real estate market than their white counterparts.[64] Such was the case with Constance Vivant. As early as 1805, she engaged in real estate transactions. Constance Vivant owned property in New Orleans as well as a plantation and enslaved people, as did her siblings. Her sister, Adelaide, owned many properties in the Vieux Carré.[65] Another sister, Lucille Vivant Litou, and her husband once owned a mansion designed by famous architect Henry Howard in what is today the Garden District of New Orleans.[66] The home is now referred to as the Grinnan-Henderson-Reily House and would presently be worth well over three million dollars.

Free women of color made up about twelve percent of slave owners in New Orleans.[67] Louisiana Slave Records from 1818 indicate that Constance Vivant bought half interest in a sugar plantation and its forty-one enslaved people in St. Bernard Parish on Bayou Terre aux Boeufs.[68] The plantation consisted of a dwelling house, a store, and a sugar house.[69] She bought the property from Jean Chauveau who commanded her husband Vincent Rillieux's regiment at the Battle of New Orleans and later became his business partner.[70] Property records of what is today known as Kenilworth Plantation in St. Bernard Parish indicate that Jean Chauveau once owned the property with Vincent Rillieux. Was the property Constance Vivant bought from Chauveau the site of Kenilworth Plantation? Did Chauveau facilitate Constance Rillieux and Vincent Rillieux owning property together? This might have been a way to circumvent inheritance laws. The total cost of Vivant's investment was $50,000. She paid Chauveau $6,000 in cash and $19,000 in property that included enslaved people.[71]

The fertile land and warm climate in this southernmost part of Louisiana were ideal for yielding needed produce, fish, and poultry that the settlers sold at the market in New Orleans.[72] Sugar cane grew relatively well in these subtropical conditions, though not as ideal as tropical Cuba or Saint-Domingue to the south. The sugar industry in Louisiana developed rapidly after sugar cane juice was successfully granulated on a commercial scale. In 1795, planter Etienne de Boré and sugar chemist Antoine Morin from Saint-Domingue proved that cane sugar syrup from Louisiana would granulate. Astute investors and plantation owners like Constance Vivant recognized the potential of sugar as a cash crop. They bought southern Louisiana land, which was at the northern most point for successful sugar cultivation and created Louisiana's Sugar Bowl. At the time of her death in 1868, Constance Vivant had cash and real estate holdings that totaled $4,102 (over $120,000 in today's dollars), even after the decimation of Louisiana's economy due to the Civil War. Vivant left her small fortune to her unmarried daughter, Marie Heloise Rillieux, even though she had three surviving sons. She undoubtedly understood that although her sons faced racial hurdles, her daughter also confronted the limits placed on women, especially unmarried women of mixed race.

The white men who fathered children with free women of color like Constance Vivant often acknowledged their children who were products of their relationships. Many men signed the baptismal record when their children were baptized in St. Louis Cathedral, as was the case with Vincent Rillieux Jr. It was probably Constance Vivant who was an active member of the congregation at St. Louis Cathedral when their seven children were baptized. In 1800, records from St. Louis Cathedral indicate that seventy-two percent of the 792 baptisms there were of people of African descent and free people of color.[73] This was partly due to Spanish laws and customs that were put in place in Louisiana in 1762 when France ceded the Louisiana territory to Spain. After 1769, the number of French people who attended the Catholic Church began to drop off as Spanish clergy were installed. At the same time, the percentage of free women of color attending the Catholic Church greatly increased. According to Lain Kapplan-Levenson, "Free women of color were the most pious people in New Orleans in the colonial period. They're the ones who were filling St. Louis Cathedral, literally filling it."[74] By 1803, when the United States bought the Louisiana colony from France, women of color dominated the congregation at St. Louis Cathedral, with very few men attending church except on special occasions. The Roman Catholic Church under Spain accepted these women and their children as testament to their charge and belief that they should be and are the religion for all people.[75] It is also for this reason that the Roman Catholic Church baptized children of so-called illegitimate unions. Despite this seeming acceptance of mixed-race relationships, the clergy had to tread lightly as to not criticize colonial laws prohibiting interracial marriages. When Louisiana became part of America, the European city had to begin to adopt new cultural norms to fit into the politics and Anglo-American culture of the United States.[76] The Territorial Legislature of Louisiana passed The Black Codes of 1806 and 1808 which restricted the rights of free people of color.[77] By 1807, marriage between a white person and a person of color was not permitted.[78]

Bernard Noel "Manuel" Andry
1758-1839

In 1811, the largest slave revolt in American history took place in Louisiana. The uprising began in St. John the Baptist Parish, about forty miles northwest of New Orleans at the Andry plantation, later called Woodland Plantation. This was the home of Vincent Rillieux Sr.'s niece, Marie Anne Marguerite Rillieux Thomassin, and her husband, Bernard Noel "Manuel" Andry. The local militia's arsenal had at one time been located at the home of Manuel Andry, as he was the first commandant of the German Coast. The German Coast was an area about twenty-five miles upriver from New Orleans that was established in 1721. Swedes of German heritage and Germans settled in the area and were indentured servants charged with supplying the colony with needed staples produced on their farms. They contracted with John Law's Company of the Indies that oversaw the colony's finances. When Law's company went bankrupt, they were no longer obliged to honor their contracts as indentured servants, but they remained in the area and continued to supply New Orleans and the surrounding area with timber and food.[79]

Manuel Andry was a native Louisianian of French heritage. Andry and his sons grew and processed sugar on their plantation. He was one of the largest slave holders in the parish. There were eighty-six enslaved people who worked the Andry's land. Andry represented the German Coast in the Territorial Legislature, and Governor Claiborne endorsed him as a worthy candidate to serve as a member of the House of Representatives for the Louisiana Territory. In a letter to President James Madison, Claiborne wrote, "Mr. Andry is a man of integrity; has reciy'd (sic) a good education, and is much esteemed by his neighbours (sic)."[80]

Conditions were difficult and sometimes grueling for the enslaved people who worked on sugar plantations. It was hot much of the year and they had to contend with mosquitos and snakes as they worked the land. Their duties included planting and cutting cane, maintaining levees, digging ditches, and logging cypress.[81] The successful slave insurrection in Saint-Domingue that took place from 1791 to 1804 emboldened the enslaved people of southern Louisiana to revolt against their masters in hope of a life of freedom. Many of the planters from Saint-Domingue relocated to Louisiana and brought enslaved people with them. The newcomers spread the story of the successful rebellion.

One of the leaders of the German Coast revolt was Charles Deslondes, a slave driver who belonged to the Widow Deslondes but worked at the nearby Andry sugar plantation. Because of his position as a slave driver, Charles had more freedom to move about than most enslaved people. Charles traveled on errands for Andry and was permitted to visit his companion on the Trépagnier estate. He conspired with Quamana from the plantation of James Brown and Harry Kenner from the Kenner and Henderson plantations.[82] They planned to lead a group of enslaved men and maroons to liberate fellow captives along the Mississippi River and establish a black settlement.[83] The three held a secret meeting at the Andry plantation on January 8, during the Epiphany season. The Epiphany began on January 6, the twelfth night after Christmas. The traditional parties and visiting of the season distracted the planters.[84] The rebels chose the Epiphany in hopes that their masters would not notice their absence because of the celebrations. That windy and stormy night, a band of enslaved men snuck into the Andry home and severely injured Manuel Andry with an axe and fatally wounded his son, Gilbert Thomassin Andry. The rebels stole guns, ammunition, horses, and militia uniforms from the Andrys. There is evidence that there were few weapons left in the arsenal when the rebels got there. They had to make do with farm tools and makeshift weapons. Many wore the pilfered uniforms as the rebels had in Saint-Domingue.

The band of enslaved men left the Andry home and headed down the east bank levee toward New Orleans and gathered more enslaved people as they went. Accounts vary as to how many joined the uprising.[85] It was somewhere between 150 to as many as 500 enslaved people who marched toward New Orleans and burned plantations along the river as they went. The army of insurrectionists made their way to the Trépagnier plantation and killed François Trépagnier with an axe. They continued down River Road to adjacent St. Charles Parish attacking, pillaging, and burning other plantations as they made their way toward New Orleans. Their plan was to make it to New Orleans, join other revolutionaries who were already in the city, and free as many enslaved people as possible.

Even in his wounded state, Manuel Andry managed to make it across the river to the west bank to the plantation of Pierre Bauchet St. Martin to spread the word and gather forces to stop the insurgents.[86] The women and children of the plantations fled to New Orleans for protection. As word spread of the approaching rebels, fear and panic gripped the city. Governor Claiborne issued an order that all cabarets in the city and suburbs of New Orleans were to be closed and enforced a 6:00 p.m. curfew for all male negroes (sic).[87]

The rebels did not count on Manuel Andry gathering a fighting unit so quickly. Andry pulled together a militia of eighty men and set out to capture the rebels and crush the insurrection. General Wade Hampton, Commander-in-Chief of the United States Southern forces, was in New Orleans on his way to assist with a conflict with Spain over West Florida. Governor Claiborne had nightmarish visions of the plantation slave army joining forces with the city's large slave population.[88] The substantially smaller white population would not be able to defend the city and could fall victim to the same atrocities as their counterparts in Saint-Domingue.[89] At Claiborne's request, General Hampton gathered two companies of volunteer militia and thirty regular army troops.[90] On January 11, Manuel Andry wrote a letter to Governor Claiborne informing him of the insurrection and asking for troops to help protect the coast. In the letter, Andry told the governor of his son's death. He went on to tell Claiborne that his forces "made considerable slaughter," but many rebels had escaped into the woods. Andry was particularly interested in apprehending the leaders and making an example of them. Andry and his men captured three of the leaders, including Charles Deslondes. Andry and several of the other white landowners in the area held an inquiry and pronounced Deslondes guilty of leading the insurrection. His punishment was brutal. First his hands were cut off. He was then shot in the thighs, which broke both of his legs. Finally, Charles Deslondes was burned to death.[91]

Hampton's troops met and defeated the remaining rebels at the plantation of Jacques Fortier.[92] About thirty enslaved people were killed in action and about forty-five more were put to death.[93] The St. Charles Parish District Court spent about a week interrogating the captives. Judge Pierre Bauchet St. Martin appointed a tribunal of five planters to decide the fate of those held for trial. The tribunal met at the home of Noel Destrehan. Destrehan, Alexandre Labranch, Pierre-Marie Cabaret de Trepy, Adelard Fortier, and Edmond Fortier comprised the tribunal. After a day of deliberation, eighteen enslaved people were condemned to death.[84] Each was to be taken to their respective plantations and executed in front of the enslaved people who lived there.[95] Many of the dead rebels had their heads severed and put on poles along the river as a warning.[96]

The revolt had far-reaching implications, but authorities and planters down-played it as an isolated incident rather than a widespread problem that foreboded future unrest among the enslaved. Those in power did not want to embolden enslaved people in other parts of Louisiana or the South. Governor Claiborne used the insurrection to push the idea of a more organized militia. The Territorial Legislature also enacted more restrictive laws for free people of color as well as enslaved people.[97] In an address to the legislature, Governor Claiborne lamented the great financial losses suffered by some planters at the hands of the rebels. At the governor's request, the legislature passed an act that compensated the plantation owners for their damage: one-third of the appraised value of each dwelling house destroyed and three hundred dollars for each enslaved person who was executed.[98]

Ironically, Woodland Plantation, the home where the revolt began, was also the birthplace of the great Edward "Kid" Ory, trombonist and jazz band leader. Ory was the leader of the first black jazz band to make a recording. Ory's father was white, and his mother was Afro-Spanish and Native American.

Norbert Rillieux
1806-1894

In 1806, Vincent Rillieux and Constance Vivant had the first of their seven children. On March 17, Constance gave birth to Norbert. He was baptized in St. Louis Cathedral by Padre Antonio de Sedella, or Père Antoine as he was called by the locals. Three more boys and three girls followed between 1808 and 1821.[99] Norbert proved to have his mother's drive and his father's inventive spirit. It was common for young men of means, who were the products of interracial relationships, to be sent abroad to study, but because of his precociousness, Norbert was sent away at a particularly early age. He was sent to Paris in 1817 when he was just eleven years old.[100] This must have been difficult for his parents, but they knew their young son needed to leave a changing social and political climate in New Orleans and embrace what Europe had to offer in terms of education and opportunity.

Travel from North America to Europe was difficult and dangerous. Steamships were not yet crossing the Atlantic Ocean, and a trip could take as long as six weeks if conditions were harsh. Those traveling to Europe bought passage on cargo ships that were not equipped for the comfort of their passengers. It was quite possible that treacherous seas could wash people overboard or render them seasick for much of the journey. Sinking was an ever-present possibility in the sometimes turbulent Atlantic.[101]

Conditions in New Orleans were not much safer. In 1817, a new epidemic of yellow fever struck New Orleans and eighty people died.[102]

Possibly the biggest concern Vincent Rillieux Jr. and Constance Vivant had for the future of their biracial children, especially a savant like Norbert, was the restrictions put on people of color after the Louisiana Purchase. Up until the Louisiana Purchase in 1803, New Orleans had been under either French or Spanish control. Spain had a long history of allowing slave masters to release their enslaved people or for them to eventually purchase their own freedom. This created a large group of free people of color who contributed to the development of New Spain and were considered an integral part of the growth of Spain's colonies in the New World. Many free people of color were able to amass great fortunes and often participated in the more erudite pursuits of their upper class white counterparts.[103] They attended the theater and opera but were relegated to a separate tier from white patrons.[104] "Respectable free people of color" sat in the Bragnoire or box seats, while free blacks and enslaved people sat in the gallery.[105] According to Michael Taylor, curator of books for Louisiana State University Libraries, the French saw class as more important than race, which is why in pre-American Louisiana, free people of color who were well educated and came from affluent families, intermingled and cohabitated with whites without social or legal repercussions.[106] The social status of free people of color was more closely tied to wealth and education, rather than race.[107] Taylor further asserts that race for the British was far more important than class. Racial discrimination was largely nonexistent in nineteenth century France.[108] People of color in British colonies faced social and legal restrictions that far exceeded conditions in other European settlements.[109] America inherited this way of thinking, and after the Louisiana Purchase, these ideas began to shape policies regarding people of color.

The *gens de couleur libres*, the free people of color, were a liminal group who, according to historian Rudolphe Desdunes, "shared neither the privileges of the master class nor the degradation of the slave. They stood between – or rather apart – sharing the cultivated tastes of the upper caste and the painful humiliation attached to the race of the enslaved."[110] Vincent Rillieux and Constance Vivant hoped that by sending him to France, Norbert could be educated in France's superior schools without the prejudice that existed in America. Their wish for all their children was for them to be raised as cultured, intelligent young French gentlemen and ladies. Even though Louisiana was under Spanish control for nearly forty years from 1762-1802, Louisianans of French descent never gave up their French identities.[111] French continued to be spoken, with Spanish used almost solely for official documents.

When Norbert arrived in Paris in 1817, there were few Americans there, less than a thousand; however, Norbert must have felt at home.[112] He probably viewed himself as a French New Orleanian or Creole, rather than an American or person of color, even though the Louisiana Territory had been part of the United States since 1803. New Orleans was culturally more like a European city than an American city. In New Orleans, shops, markets, and taverns remained open on Sundays, and the elite entertained in grand style. New Orleanians threw large parties and indulged in European imported goods such as olive oil, brandied fruit, anchovies, coffee, and French milled soap.[113] Some of the less desirable aspects of Paris like rat infested, mucky streets were also reminiscent of New Orleans.

Vincent Rillieux Jr. made sure his son was looked after and encouraged in his studies. He arranged for Norbert to be in the care of his former business partner and inventor, Maurice Poirot de Valcourt. Valcourt made the introductions for Norbert at the prestigious L'École Centrale, specifically École Polytechnique, and recommended his admittance. Jean Baptiste Dumas, one of the founders of the school, was impressed with the fact that Norbert came from a French family that helped establish the United States.[114] The school was highly selective. Not only was ability an important criterion, but family ties and social rank were as well. Norbert did not disappoint his father nor his mentor. Tenacity and ingenuity were in Norbert Rillieux's DNA. This and his remarkable intellect propelled him to develop ideas that furthered scientists' understanding of thermodynamics and to invent an apparatus that revolutionized nineteenth century sugar production all over the world.

By 1826, at the age of twenty, Norbert was granted his first patent.[115] His invention used compressed hydrogen gas in iron cylinders to power a steam engine with large footboards. Although he held the patent, he was not able to capitalize on his idea because he did not have the financial backing to do so. The idea was later developed as the compound engine.[116] Samuel Brown, a British engineer, is widely credited with inventing the internal combustion engine. However, some in the scientific world recognize Norbert Rillieux's work on combustion engines to be the seminal step in developing the invention. J. Renaux, a writer for *L'Echo de la Fabrique*, an industrial journal, asserted that Brown was not in fact the inventor of the internal combustion engine. Renaux claimed that Brown owed the success of his machine to the machine patented by Norbert Rillieux in 1826.[117]

While at École Centrale, Norbert continued to experiment with steam engines. Together with Dumas and Peter Seguier, son of the first president of the Royal Court, Norbert tested most of the one hundred steam engines that existed in Paris and gave the owners advice as to how to make them run more efficiently.[118] In 1830, Norbert Rillieux published a series of articles about his work in the journal *Le Temps*. His ideas caused quite a stir in the scientific community. According to an article in *Scientific American Supplement*, these writings "showed him at twenty-four years as the strongest mechanical engineer of his time."[119] The articles discussed his theory on multiple-effect evaporation that was to become the basis for his groundbreaking invention, and what Charles Brown, a sugar chemist with the United States Department of Agriculture, called "the greatest invention in the history of American chemical engineering."[120]

Norbert Rillieux's early time in Paris was marked by political unrest, as was much of the nineteenth century in France. Many students and other intellectuals were involved in the republican movement aimed at toppling the French monarchy. Some were Bonapartists and favored a strong military leader, others sought a constitutional monarchy, radicals advocated for a true republic, while monarchists wanted the status quo to remain. Revolutionaries were called to action in response to policies put forth by King Charles X that restricted the rights of the French people. Since Napoleon Bonaparte's abdication in 1814, the French people had become accustomed to having somewhat of a say in government, even though they were ruled by King Louis XVIII. He was a moderate ruler but was disliked by some of the nobility for giving too much power to the people. Under King Louis XVIII, the French people had some limited voting rights and there was a legislative body. When the king died in 1824, his brother ascended to the throne. Charles X was a much different ruler than his brother. He sided with the ultra-royalists and envisioned a monarchy similar to prerevolutionary times and put in place policies that restricted the press and gave more power to the Roman Catholic Church.[121] Tempers boiled over when the July Ordinances were issued by the king without the input of the Chamber of Deputies, the lower house of the legislative body. The ordinances were extreme and shocked and angered those who favored a constitutional monarchy. The ordinances dissolved the Chamber of Deputies, severely curtailed voting rights, and restricted the freedom of the press. Newspapers could not be published without government consent. The students of the L'École Polytechnique took on leading the resistance, and soon others in the schools of medicine and law joined them. The newspapers refused to be silenced and published articles railing against the ordinances and incited the public.[122]

On the night after the ordinances were published, a small group of leaders from L'École Polytechnique met with the celebrated Marquis de Lafayette at La Grange, his estate outside of Paris. Norbert Rillieux was almost certainly there, as he was one of the principals of the group. In addition, his grandfather, Vincent Rillieux, was Lafayette's friend.[123] Lafayette dreamed of the idea of a republic in France and was one of the leaders of the French Revolution in 1789. He was enraged when he read Charles X's July Ordinances in the *Moniteur*, France's official newspaper. Lafayette had a long history of fighting for the rights of people to participate in their own government and held fast to the idea that all men are equal. Decades before, Lafayette was instrumental in helping the Americans defeat the British in the American Revolutionary War. He became a close friend and confidant of George Washington and was celebrated in America as a Revolutionary War hero.[124] The young students who were involved in the new resistance knew that Lafayette's fame and respect would give credence to their movement.

Shortly after their meeting, on the morning of the 27th of July 1830, barricades went up on the streets of Paris and the bloodshed began. The July Revolution lasted three days and occupation of the Hotel de Ville, the seat of government in Paris, changed hands several times between the patriots and the royal troops. Paris was in chaos with average citizens joining forces against the royal troops. The population became increasingly concerned about the state of Paris and dreaded anarchy. The people were losing faith in the patriots and many in the National Guard abandoned their posts. The patriots knew they had to do something to reignite their cause and regain the confidence of the people. Upon Lafayette's and a few other prominent patriots' suggestion, a provisional government was formed. As a result, the national guardsmen reappeared in uniform and fighting forces were created, commanded by the students of L'École Polytechnique, while Lafayette controlled the military forces. Charles X abdicated and fled to England, and the Chamber of Deputies was reinstated. Lafayette and some of his compatriots realized that a republic was out of reach considering the vastly different political factions in France, so they were willing to settle for a constitutional monarchy.[125]

Through Lafayette's support, the Duke of Orleans was placed on the throne and dubbed King Louis-Philippe. It is understandable that Lafayette would find the Duke a suitable compromise. As a young man, the Duke had supported the 1789 Revolution; however, he fled France during the Reign of Terror in 1793. Like Lafayette, he had a close connection to America. During his exile, he lived in the United States and visited George Washington at Mount Vernon.[126] The victory of the patriots and the abdication of Charles X were enthusiastically celebrated in the United States. Parades were held in New York, Baltimore, Philadelphia, Richmond, Boston, Charleston, and New Orleans. The citizens of New Orleans even sent a flag to Paris that hung in the Hotel de Ville.[127]

Republicans opposed anything less than a true republican form of government. Secret societies were immediately formed. One such group was the *Société des Amis du Peuple* (Society of the Friends of the People). Norbert Rillieux was among the leaders of the group and a member of the publications committee. The society held public and private meetings at their headquarters at the Peltier Riding School on the Rue Montmartre. Members were students, out-of-work young men, and those who had been members of previous social protests and organizations. The organization tested the newly formed government's limits through political meetings, marches, and provocative publications. They organized demonstrations, printed propaganda pamphlets, and published a newspaper called the *Tribune*. In August following the July Revolution, the group succeeded in spearheading a demonstration of more than 3,000 men to demand that new elections take place. They contended that because of the July Revolution, the ordinances prohibiting such freedoms had been nullified. The march was eventually disbanded at Lafayette's request. The leaders of the Friends of the People maintained that they were well within their rights to assemble and publish their ideas. Because their headquarters was near factories and small businesses, the group began to take on advocating for workers' rights. Riots and strikes interrupted commerce in Paris, destroying some factories. Finally, the Friends of the People pushed too far when they produced placards that demanded overthrowing the Chambers.[128] The leaders of the publication committee, including Norbert Rillieux, were arrested and put on trial. Arrests began in the summer of 1831 for a trial to be held in January 1832. There was a hearing on December 10, 1831, and all the accused were present. During the investigation, Rillieux's apartment was searched, and objectionable publications were seized. According to the testimony, Rillieux was back in America by the time the trial took place in January 1832.[129] All the accused were acquitted but were sentenced for what appears to be contempt, and the group was officially dissolved. Rillieux was sentenced to four years in prison, and a 4,000-franc fine was levied against him. There is no evidence that he paid the fine or served any time in prison.

Norbert Rillieux's revolutionary spirit did not end with politics. His scientific pursuits were revolutionary as well. Norbert's voracious hunger for innovative ideas in the infant field of thermodynamics drove him to seek out others who were groundbreaking in their thinking. Rillieux attended a course of lectures on applied physics at the Conservatoire des Arts et Métiers in Paris by noted chemist and French industrialist, Nicolas Clément.[130] Clément was focused not on the mechanics of steam engines, but on their optimum use of energy. Norbert cited these ideas as critical to the formation of his own theories. Rillieux realized that collaboration among scientists was essential and led to further inventions and discoveries. Because of his passion and aptitude, Norbert Rillieux became an instructor of applied mechanics at L'École Centrale. At twenty-four, he was the youngest to have ever held such a position at the prestigious school.

Rillieux was captivated by the physics of steam and its potential benefit to industry. Shortly after the July Revolution, while he was still in France, Rillieux developed his theory of multiple-effect evaporation as applied to sugar refining. His process proposed harnessing the latent energy of steam in a way that would forever change sugar manufacturing all over the world.[131] At the time, raw sugar from the West Indies and Louisiana was refined in Russia, England, Holland, France, and some parts of the northern United States.[132] France was the hub for sugar technology in the early nineteenth century. Very few refineries existed in the West Indies or Louisiana. Rillieux's pioneering principles were met with skepticism by French manufacturers because his method was thought to be too complicated and untested.

Prior to the development of Rillieux's apparatus, sugar refining in Louisiana and the Caribbean was primitive and unreliable. The process was labor intensive, dangerous, and required vast amounts of fuel to evaporate the liquid from cane juice to form white sugar crystals. The Jamaica Train method of sugar refining required many enslaved people, and spilled juice could produce severe burns. It also took meticulous timing and great skill to recognize the exact moment to strike the sugar to make crystals. The process was unpredictable and often produced a ruined or unsatisfactory product.

Norbert Rillieux knew that efficient and effective evaporation was crucial to the production of fine, white sugar crystals.[133] Rillieux's invention employed a closed evaporator with three evaporators for sugar juice, in which he used the successive use of steam energy from the evaporating juice to fuel evaporation. The invention conserved fuel and energy and made manufacturing sugar more efficient and less expensive, and production was more reliable and predicable. Rillieux built on the ideas of his predecessors who developed vacuum pans for use in sugar refining.

Although Rillieux's multiple effects apparatus in a vacuum would go on to revolutionize the sugar industry and form the basis for all future industrial evaporation processes, he had a difficult time finding patrons to fund experiments and production. It is possible that Rillieux's enthusiasm for his watershed ideas overwhelmed his would-be investors in terms of scope and innovation. Earlier in his career, Norbert Rillieux faced a similar situation when he partnered with a company in Nantes to produce a steamboat using his principles. The company thought Rillieux had overstated the promise of his invention and withdrew its support. In an interview, Jean-Baptiste Dumas, one of the scientists who founded L'École Centrale, described Rillieux as "a young man of great activity of mind."[134] But his eagerness to see his ideas come to fruition and his investors' lack of patience with disappointment and experimentation led Rillieux to leave France to pursue investors in America. Dumas recalled, "He had a handsome carriage in front of him in France, but he wished to promise very well without being able to keep all that he had promised, and ultimately the boat on which he counted on to make his reputation, compromised him. In consequence of embarrassment of money, finding no more credit, he returned to America."[135]

Norbert Rillieux returned to America sometime after December 10, 1831, and before his January 1832 trial in France. Edmond Forstall, a friend and business associate of Vincent Rillieux Jr., asked Norbert Rillieux to get his new sugar refinery up and running. This would have been a lucrative and prestigious position for Norbert and would have provided him with the contacts and resources to further his own work on his multiple-effects evaporator. Vincent Rillieux Jr. and Edmond Forstall had a falling out before Norbert could take the position. The rift was likely due to a disagreement over the performance of Edmond Rillieux, Norbert's younger brother, as one of the builders of Forstall's refinery.[136] Vincent Rillieux Jr. demanded that Norbert turn down Forstall's offer.

Norbert Rillieux then had to scramble to find financial backing and a place to conduct real-world experiments on his apparatus. He first approached Thomas Morgan, an innovative sugar planter from Plaquemine Parish, in late 1831 or early 1832. Morgan erected a vacuum pan at his sugarhouse in 1830 and was the first planter in Louisiana to use a vacuum pan for sugar production.[137] Rillieux asked Morgan to allow him to conduct experiments on his estate, but he declined. Norbert Rillieux also visited the estate of his cousin, William Freret. William and his brothers were trained in engineering in Liverpool and were a logical choice for Norbert. William Freret was also uninterested in sponsoring his invention or allowing him to do experiments on his estate.[138]

Rillieux experienced further heartbreak when his father, a young man of fifty, died suddenly of a stroke on July 17, 1833.[139] Even though Norbert's father was a wealthy cotton press proprietor and plantation owner, neither Norbert, his siblings, nor his mother inherited anything from him as he died intestate. The probate documents stated that the deceased, Vincent Rillieux, was not married. Prior to 1808, white men were able to name their mixed-race children as heirs. The Civil Code of 1808 made inheritance by children of interracial couples more complicated. The law defined natural children as illegitimate children who had been acknowledged by their fathers. According to historian Emily Clark, "Their [natural children] capacity to inherit was always vulnerable to the claims of more-distant white relatives".[140] A law passed in 1831 stated that children of mixed blood could not be legitimate and could not inherit from their parents.[141] It is possible that had Vincent Rillieux not died prematurely, he would have provided for his children and Constance Vivant through donations of money and property. It was not unheard of for this to be done, especially if there was not another legitimate family. Ironically, William Freret, who turned down Norbert Rillieux's request for help in developing his multiple-effect evaporator, inherited part of Vincent Rillieux's estate. William Freret's mother, Eugenie Rillieux Freret, died before her brother, Vincent; therefore, William and his siblings inherited their mother's portion of his estate.[142]

Despite setbacks, Norbert Rillieux did not give up on his dream of perfecting and selling his multiple-effect evaporator. In 1834 or 1835, he erected his evaporator at the plantation of Zenon Ramon.[143] According to Rillieux, this apparatus was made by Mr. Donet, the owner of a small foundry in the lower part of the Faubourg Marigny. Donet died during the trials and the apparatus was never tried. It was taken down a year or two after Donet's death.[144] Norbert's brother, Edmond Rillieux, returned to New Orleans after a mysterious absence sometime after his father's death, and the two went into business together.[145] The Rillieux brothers placed an ad in the *New Orleans Bee* on May 19, 1834, that stated, "N. & E. Rilleux [sic], Civil Engineers and Architects, are ready to excecute [sic] with neatness, dispatch, and at moderate prices, all kinds of maps and plots of cities, borghs [sic], lots, houses, factories and of machineries of every description. They will also attend to measurements for and such estimates as may be required when undertaking workmen. 72 Camp St. Nearly opposite the Theater."

Norbert also sought out other business opportunities and associated with Emile Barthe, an attorney, as well as Claudot Dumont and was highly successful in real estate speculation. Sadly, his financial success was short-lived. He lost most of his assets in the Panic of 1837.[146] The Panic of 1837 was a major fiscal crisis for the United States, but it hit New Orleans particularly hard. Some of the Jackson administration's policies had the unintended consequence of destabilizing large banks. To make matters worse, the Bank of England raised interest rates to slow down the pace at which money was leaving the country. At the same time, there was a drop in the price of cotton, a major cash crop in and around New Orleans. This spiraled into economic devastation for many in New Orleans after one of the major cotton brokers folded under the financial pressure.[147]

Rillieux continued to try to persuade investors and sugar planters to back him in his effort to perfect his sugar refining apparatus even in the unstable economic climate. In 1842, he approached Andrew Durnford who was the owner of St. Rosalie Plantation in Plaquemines Parish and a free man of color like Rillieux. Rillieux offered Durnford $50,000 to have use of his sugar plant. In addition, he offered him fair market value of the sugar produced. In return, Durnford would supply the raw cane sugar. Durnford rejected the offer and stated, "I do not want to lose control of my people. (His 75 enslaved people.)" Dunford's was not an unusual sentiment. Some planters, white as well as people of color, feared giving enslaved people too much knowledge because they would become restless and unsatisfied.

Having been turned down by Durnford, Rillieux approached sugar planter Jean-Baptiste Letorey of St. Emma Plantation on Bayou Lafourche. Rillieux contracted with Leeds Foundry to build the apparatus using his drawings and under his direction. The equipment was not ready until the end of the rolling of the crop when the cane was cut, and the juice was extracted. Letorey allowed Rillieux to conduct a trial of his equipment and agreed to buy the Rillieux apparatus if it performed as promised. According to Rillieux, Letorey told him that he wanted to stop the initial trial after seeing that the apparatus worked well. Letorey claimed that it was because he wanted to wait until the next crop. He explained that he intended to build a new sugar house closer to his plantation to reduce the cost of hauling his cane. The apparatus was dismantled, but the parts remained at the plantation. Rillieux was shocked and furious to find out the next year that Letorey had attempted to steal his invention and patent it under his own name. Letorey's plan was not successful because Rillieux had not left a copy of his plans, so Letorey was unable to construct it correctly.[148]

Frustrated and anxious to get his multiple-effect evaporator into production, Rillieux lamented, "After these two experiments, seeing I could do nothing with the Creole or French planters, I addressed myself to Mr. Theo. [sic] Packwood."[149] Packwood's father, Samuel, and his mother, Alice Eliza, were from Connecticut and were Anglo-American.[150] This is significant because Rillieux was from a French Creole family. As late as the 1830s, thirty years after Louisiana became part of America, Creoles often referred to non-Creoles as Americans or foreigners.[151] Creoles jealously guarded their French heritage and resented what they saw as the American invasion and assault on their culture.[152] Anglo-American planters were characteristically forward thinking, capitalists willing to take calculated financial risks. They leveraged the contacts that they had from their former homes on the eastern seaboard and developed a network of national connections. Conversely, Creole planters typically preferred to deal within the local sphere of business and social networks.

Despite the American-Creole divide, the Packwoods and Norbert Rillieux were a logical alliance. Samuel Packwood was known as an innovator in the sugar and cotton industries. He introduced the use of bagasse, the dried husks of sugar cane, for fuel in boiling sugar.[153] Pioneering Louisiana planters like the Packwoods often consulted French trained scientists like Rillieux for new techniques that would improve sugar production because there were no institutions in America that provided training in sugar production. The early 1840s saw a vast increase in the profitability of sugar as a cash crop. The tariff of 1842 added an extra two and a half cents per pound for foreign sugar.[154] Many planters used the additional income to improve their production equipment. This new-found profit caused some planters to reexamine traditional methods of sugar production and investigate more modern techniques. However, Rillieux's apparatus was so groundbreaking that many in the industry viewed it as untested, too expensive, and too complicated. Rillieux's ideas were so state-of-the-art that even the scientists at the United States Patent Office did not fully understand that this apparatus was a novel invention. When Rillieux first applied for a U.S. patent in 1840, his initial application was denied on the basis that an apparatus of multiple-effect already existed. However, the previously designed apparatuses were multiple-effect in open air. Rillieux's patent agent finally convinced the patent office that "open air was not a precedent for an apparatus of the multiple-effect in vacuo."[155] The vacuum employed by Rillieux was the addition that allowed for drastic improvement in fuel economy. Norbert Rillieux's patent was finally granted in 1843.

The Rillieux apparatus constructed at Packwood's Scarsdale Planation, later called Myrtle Grove, was wildly successful. One thousand hogsheads of sugar were made instead of 800 that would previously have been produced with the same amount of cane. The sugar was much finer and of better quality, so it sold for seven cents a pound instead of four cents.[156] Sugar was such a large part of the economic engine of Louisiana, that it was of concern to planters and merchants as well as those who were not directly involved in the industry. Newspapers reported on the sugar crop's status, advances in production, and agricultural methods. In 1844, Theodore Packwood wrote a letter of reply to the editor of the *New Orleans Bee* praising the merits of the Rillieux apparatus. Packwood reported that every aspect of his contract was met by Rillieux, and the apparatus delivered as promised. Packwood used his poorest cane to try out the new equipment and was still pleased with the results concerning the produced sugar's quality, ease of use, and fuel consumption. In closing, he declared, "I had many opportunities of admiring the ability and ingenuity of M. R. [Mr. Rillieux], and I do not hesitate to declare that he is highly deserving of credit, and in every respect entitled to the full confidence of the sugar planters of Louisiana."[157] Soon afterward, the system was installed at Bellechasse, a plantation that Packwood owned with Judah P. Benjamin.

Norbert Rillieux's brilliant mind was never satisfied. He continued to work on perfecting his apparatus and in 1846 received US patent 4879 A for *New and Useful Improvements in the Method of Heating, Evaporating, and Cooling Liquids*, especially intended for the manufacture of sugar.[158] The popularity of the Rillieux apparatus continued to grow, but because of the considerable initial investment, it was most often used on large plantations.[159] During the late 1840s, Edmund Forstall actively campaigned against the Rillieux apparatus. Forstall claimed that "Rillieux was an engineer but no planter and did not know the need of the Louisiana sugar industry and that it was useless to pay such a high price for a Rillieux apparatus when the open kettle answered as well."[160] Forstall ignored the fact that Rillieux's mother owned a sugar plantation. Although there were naysayers and sceptics, the Rillieux apparatus, manufactured by Merrick and Towne of Philadelphia, delivered astounding results. The device helped to produce sugar of superior quality and dramatically lowered fuel costs. Sugar chemist Professor R. S. McCulloh described the sugar produced using the Rillieux apparatus in his report to the United States Congress: "In Rillieux's apparatus the use of the latent heat is carried out more perfectly and fully than in any other system known... The sugar made with this apparatus is of a beautiful light straw color, of fine, large crystal, and free from unpleasant odor, and commanding a good price and ready sale."[161]

Judah Benjamin became one of Norbert Rillieux's chief supporters among Louisiana planters. Benjamin was an attorney but became captivated by the sugar industry. He wrote articles about sugar production and took trips to France to learn about improved techniques for producing superior sugar. Judah Benjamin and Norbert Rillieux developed quite a close relationship. They both maintained offices in New Orleans. Benjamin practiced law in New Orleans except for the years between 1845 and 1847 when he had difficulty with his vision, and Rillieux maintained a civil engineering office at 57 St. Peter Street.[162]

Norbert Rillieux sometimes stayed at the Benjamins' Bellechasse Plantation for weeks at a time. Visitors and nearby planters listened to Rillieux's impromptu seminars on the chemistry of sugar or the working of his apparatus.[163] Rillieux had the reputation of being somewhat blunt and mercurial as some geniuses are, but he was also a gifted storyteller and enthralled his listeners.[164] The relationship between Benjamin and Rillieux contradicts the stereotypical, one-dimensional view of the Antebellum South that depicts a world with strict racial divisions. There were prejudices to be sure; however, in Louisiana, the lines were often blurred. A limited understanding of Colonial and Antebellum Louisiana makes the close bond between Norbert Rillieux, a free man of color, and Judah Benjamin - lawyer, sugar planter, Jew, and future Attorney General, Minister of War and the Secretary of State for the Confederacy - seem unlikely, even shocking. Although Benjamin was an integral part of the Confederate hierarchy, he did not assert that slavery was the divine order of things as some proponents of slavery did. The primary bond between Rillieux and Benjamin was sugar. They were highly educated, brilliant men who realized the potential benefits of their alliance to the sugar industry. Both men had family ties to the aristocracy of southern Louisiana, Rillieux through his white family and Benjamin through his Creole wife's family, the St. Martins. Yet, they were not completely accepted as social equals in Creole and American society because of their ethnic and racial heritages. It is not hard to imagine that their shared adversarial relationship with Edmund Forstall and their liminal social status strengthened their connection. Benjamin represented two free men of color in a lawsuit against Forstall's Citizen's Bank.

In 1851, the levee protecting Plaquemines and Ascension Parishes had fifteen to eighteen breaches, and many of the sugar planters suffered devastating losses that year, including Benjamin. The sugar crop at Bellechasse was completely wiped out as well as some of the refining equipment.[165] The following year, Judah Benjamin was elected to the United States Senate. He had to sell his half interest in Bellechasse to his partner, Theodore Packwood.[166] Benjamin was unable to recover from the loss because he was too busy with his new life as a senator, and he had suffered a large financial setback due to nonpayment of a debt that he had endorsed.[167] Norbert Rillieux lost one of his most ardent patrons when Judah Benjamin moved to Washington D.C.

In addition to his work on his invention, Norbert was devoted to the city of New Orleans and Louisiana just as his father and grandfather had been. Norbert Rillieux, like his father Vincent, realized the importance of drainage for the city and devised an innovative plan. Rillieux enlisted the support of J. J. Mercier, an attorney for the city, to ask the Louisiana Legislature for a drainage law for the city and state. Rillieux then presented his plans for evaluation. He saw drainage as such a critical issue that he proposed that the city should take care of it if the state would not. Rillieux approached wealthy capitalists in the city like his father's friend, Laurent Milladon, and property owners in Faubourg Tremé who stood to benefit from new drainage. The would-be investors were not interested, and the idea of a drainage company for New Orleans had to be pitched to the state as a joint effort with the city.[168]

On March 19, 1835, the Louisiana Legislature passed a law establishing the New Orleans Draining Company. The plan was to drain and reclaim all the land between the upper limits of Faubourg Livaudais, the line of the New Canal, to Lake Pontchartrain.[169] The act authorized the sale of 10,000 shares to raise one million dollars in capital. The law provided for a twelve-member board of directors. Four members were to be appointed by the mayor with the approval of the City Council, two by the governor with the approval of the Senate, while the remaining six were to be selected by the stockholders. Board members included James P. Freret, cousin of Norbert Rillieux, and Edmond Forstall, sworn enemy of the Rillieux family.[170] Forstall was elected president of the board and used his position to appoint another engineer to oversee the project, so Norbert Rillieux was not given credit for the plans. The bitterness between the Rillieux family and Edmund Forstall plagued Norbert and affected his ability to get work as a civil engineer on government projects.[171]

Years later, Rillieux's ideas were stolen again, but this time on a much larger scale. There was fierce competition in Louisiana's lucrative sugar industry. The production of "white gold" grew exponentially from its meager beginnings in 1802 through the Antebellum period. Colonial Louisiana sugar planters produced approximately 5,000 hogsheads of sugar in the early 1800s.[172] That amount skyrocketed to 449,000 hogsheads by 1853, with Louisiana producing one-fourth to one-half of all the sugar consumed in the United States.[173] Investors, engineers, manufacturers, and planters from all over the world wanted to be part of the booming sugar business. By 1849, thirteen sugar plantations employed the new and improved Rillieux multiple-effect evaporator.[174] The success of Rillieux's revolutionary invention made it a target for industrial espionage. Sometime between 1849 and 1850, a German named Brami Androea arrived in Philadelphia and approached Merrick and Towne, the manufacturers of the Rillieux apparatus, about building a Dégrand steam sugar apparatus that was used at a factory in Magdebourg, Germany, and throughout much of Europe. Androea had at one time worked as an assistant to Rillieux in America and as engineer at Buckau Maschinenfabrik, a manufacturing plant in Germany. Androea was impressed with the Rillieux apparatus and quickly realized that it was superior to those presently used by European sugar manufacturers. He stole the plans and sold them to Tischbein, director of the Buckau Maschinenfabrik for 20,000 Marks. Tischbein then took out a patent in his own name and installed the first Tischbein apparatus at a sugar beet factory of Jacob Hennige in Magdebourg. Tischbein then resold the plans to the firm of Cail & Company of Paris, and soon Rillieux's pirated apparatus was all over Europe.[175] Cail and Company, under the leadership of Charles Dérosne, installed their first version of the apparatus at the Coincy Sugar Factory at Douai, France. Neither Tischbein nor Cail and Company completely understood the intricacies of Rillieux's apparatus as he intended it to be constructed. It is possible that Androea did not give Tischbein all the necessary information as to the working of the apparatus.[176] Tishcbein promoted his system as a triple-effect evaporator, but it actually functioned as a double-effect and therefore, didn't produce the promised results. This infuriated the European manufacturers as coal was their greatest expense, and they had purchased the new equipment so they could substantially cut down on fuel consumption. The triple-effect evaporator was dubbed the "triste-effect," which means sad or dismal. Most of the factories in Germany returned to double-effect evaporators and trade journals and books drew erroneous conclusions about the merits of multiple-effect evaporators.

Later in life, amidst continued controversy about the proprietary rights to the triple-effect apparatus, Rillieux railed, "Dérosne never built an apparatus of triple effect; he never invented anything. He was a man who appropriated to himself the invention of others and used them without paying the inventor anything." He then explained that after the death of Dérosne in 1844, his partner Cail, who Rillieux claimed could neither read nor write, took over the business. Cail, according to Rillieux, began as a wheelwright, learned to be a coppersmith, became the foreman and eventually Dérosne's partner. Rillieux claimed that Cail stole the rights to his apparatus and patented it in France under his own name. Rillieux defended the merits of his invention and declared, "You have copied my invention, but lack the mind to understand my principle."[177]

In the 1840s, sugar was a valuable global commodity, much like oil is today. Specious claims were often made by equipment manufacturers and sugar refiners to sell their products. In 1846, the United States Treasury Department commissioned a study to examine chemical and manufacturing issues in the sugar industry.[178] Richard S. McCulloh, a former professor of natural philosophy, mechanics, and chemistry at Jefferson College in Pennsylvania, conducted the analysis.[179] McCulloh unequivocally endorsed the Rillieux apparatus as the best method for evaporation in vacuo.

Even with international acclaim as an engineer and inventor, in his home state of Louisiana, Norbert Rillieux was subject to humiliating laws regarding free people of color. However, his grey eyes, light skin, and Creole parentage spared him some of the indignities suffered by some free blacks. Up until 1830, when registration of free blacks was imposed, people of mixed-race were often unquestioned about their racial identities unless there was overt evidence that they were of African descent. When registration codes for free blacks were enacted in 1830, those who lived in Louisiana prior to 1812 were exempt. This was a nod to their Creole heritage as descendants of the white European settlers who established Louisiana.[180] But as abolitionist rumblings increased in the North and some free blacks in Louisiana publicly advocated for these ideas, Louisiana's white population became more and more concerned about maintaining what they saw as the economic necessity of slavery. In the mid-to-late1850s, even more restrictive laws were passed regarding free people of color. They were banned from forming any new organizations or churches, could not assemble even for religious services without the supervision of a white person, were required to have a permit proving their free status, and enslaved people could no longer be emancipated.[181] As mixed racial heritage became more of a liability in New Orleans, there were fewer economic opportunities for free people of color. Banks were reticent to lend money to them, so entrepreneurial ventures were often out of reach.[182] There were some exceptions, and a few people of color were very wealthy capitalists. Albin and Bernard Soulié, Norbert Rillieux's cousins, amassed a fortune worth over $500,000 and lent capital to other free people of color.[183]

Fear that the status quo of an economy based on the labor of enslaved people might be disrupted, propelled many southerners to wield racialized science as a weapon in their arsenal to justify the subservience of blacks and to give credence to the concept that slavery was the natural order of things. Anyone of mixed racial heritage became even more marginalized. The American School of Ethnology, the first school of scientific racial anthropology, supported the idea of polygenesis, the theory that the races had separate origins and set out to prove that there were significant differences among the races.[184] American Egyptologist and former United States Consul for the city of Cairo, George R. Gliddon, supplied physician and scientist, Samuel Morton, with one hundred skulls from the inhabitants of ancient Egypt to prove his claim that the races had different crania sizes, thus different brain capacities.[185] Gliddon decided to reach beyond the scientific world and introduced the everyday citizen to Morton's theory of white supremacy and promulgated the idea that true Egyptians were not Negro (sic), but Caucasian. Gliddon arranged to take four mummies along with various antiquities from Egypt and began his lecture series and mummy unwrapping exhibitions in Boston in June of 1850. More than 1,500 people attended his Boston lecture. This first opportunity that most Americans had to view a mummy spawned a fervent interest in all things Egyptian.[186] Gliddon then took his show on the road to Philadelphia and finally to New Orleans in January of 1852. Large crowds of New Orleanians attended the much-anticipated unwrapping of the last of Gliddon's mummies at Lyceum Hall. Lyceums were learning centers intended to promote adult education and sponsor debates and lectures on topics of the day.

Gliddon masterfully included Drs. Jones, Wedderburn, and Chilton of the Medical Department of the University of Louisiana in his unwrapping ceremony to add to the scientific legitimacy of his claims. The local physicians were tasked with removing the linen gauze.[187] In his series of twelve lectures, Gliddon expounded on the art, culture, writing, and science of ancient Egypt, telling the audience that, "Egypt was the cradle of science."[188] This understanding of ancient Egypt was unsettling to many whites and created a quandary for those who justified slavery on the basis of black inferiority and fitness for servitude. They needed to believe that the white race was responsible for such advances. Slavery proponents were predisposed to accepting the pseudoscience of Gliddon and others because of their need to preserve the socioeconomic structure of their world. From New Orleans, Gliddon went to Mobile to deliver more lectures.[189] It was there that he enlisted the help of his friend Dr. Josiah Nott, a Mobile physician who started a hospital for "free Negroes" and enslaved people, treated many of Mobile's elite citizens, and was considered an expert on the differences among races given his experience with white and black patients.[190]

Nott delivered two speeches to the Louisiana Legislature in December of 1847 at the request of J.D.B. DeBow, professor at the University of Louisiana and creator and editor of the magazine *Commercial Review of the South and West*. De Bow was an ardent supporter of slavery and proponent of Nott's theories. However, years later, DeBow championed Rillieux and his apparatus as a superior invention.[191] The speeches, entitled the "Connection Between the Biblical and Physical History of Man Together," outlined Nott's scientific reasons for his support of polygenesis theory and explained his opinion concerning the inferiority of those of the Negro (sic) race and of aboriginal Americans.[192] In his speeches, Nott averred, "I shall however, be able to show satisfactorily, that recent investigations have overthrown all previously received opinions on the subject, and that the Egyptians were a Caucasian race." In 1854, in *Types of Mankind*, Nott and George Gliddon reasserted the position on Mulattos as hybrids of two distinct species. Nott proposed, among other things, that Mulattos were intermediate in intelligence between blacks and the whites and were physically delicate.[193] Subsequently, Josiah Nott became the Chair of Anatomy at the University of Louisiana, later Tulane University. Nott and Gliddon donated the two mummies to the university where they remain today. The debate about racial origin and differences landed squarely in New Orleans during the 1850s.

Nott and Gliddon's claims about ancient Egyptians must have fascinated and frustrated a learned man such as Norbert Rillieux. Having been educated in Paris, Norbert Rillieux would have been part of the European obsession with all things Egyptian that began when Napoleon Bonaparte invaded Egypt in 1798 and his troops unearthed the Rosetta Stone which held the key to deciphering ancient Egyptian hieroglyphics. Frenchman Jean Jacques Champollion eventually cracked the code that allowed the hieroglyphics' hidden meaning to be revealed. Champollion was dubbed the Father of Egyptology. In the early 1820s, Champollion published *Précis du Système Hiéroglyphique des Anciens Égyptiens* or *Hieroglyphic and Hieratic Elements of the Rosetta Stone*. This was the same period in which Norbert Rillieux was studying in Paris. It is likely then, while a student in Paris, that Rillieux became interested in Egyptian hieroglyphics.

In addition to his work in thermodynamics, Rillieux was a noted Egyptologist. His work was known among archeologists of the day as evidenced by the mention of his work by Charles Étienne Brasseur de Bourbourg in *Quatre Letters Sur le Mexique*. Brasseur de Bourbourg referenced Norbert Rillieux's work on the *Book of the Dead* and stated that he had met Rillieux in Mexico during his travels there in 1851 and again later in Paris. Brasseur de Bourbourg was a French Roman Catholic priest, linguistic scholar, and archeologist who specialized in Mesoamerican studies. In his work, Brasseur de Bourbourg credited Rillieux's work on the translation of the *Egyptian Book of the Dead*, with his understanding of Mayan language and his translation of the *Popol Vuh*, the sacred book of the Quiches of Guatemala.[194] Brasseur de Bourbourg claimed that Rillieux helped him understand, "the duplicity of meaning in Mexican texts."[195]

Although his contemporaries and historians largely discredited many of Brasseur de Bourbourg's conclusions about the Mayan language and his contention that Atlantis was the seat of all civilization, he was lauded for the amazing volume of information he amassed on the cultures and history of Mesoamerican tribes. Brasseur de Bourbourg maintained some contact with Norbert Rillieux when he returned to Paris from Guatemala. Rillieux conveyed to Brasseur de Bourbourg that he could see a similarity in the geological and geographical myths existing in *Popol Vuh*, and in the *Book of the Dead* that Rillieux was translating. It is possible that Rillieux was delving into Egyptian texts to find the history of Atlantis as well. Rillieux wrote a letter to the prestigious Académie des Inscriptions et Belle-Letters in Paris about a discovery he made in Egyptian texts about the formation of Atlantis or a root civilization.[196]

Were pseudoscientific theories about race put forth by the American School of Ethnography the impetus for Norbert's interest in Egypt and Atlantis? Myths were often used to explain scientific phenomena. Did Rillieux set out to understand Egyptian history to prove Nott, Gliddon, and others wrong? Rillieux believed that the ancient texts of Egypt contained stories that inspired Plato's creation of the story of Atlantis, the lost continent. For several decades, he continued the research he started in America.[197] Rillieux participated in the Exposition Universelles in Paris in 1878. The report from the exposition indicates that Rillieux believed that Atlantis was a reality and not a fable. He presented a summation of the scholarship in this area. If a connection between the Old World and the New World could be proved, and if monogenesis, a common ancestry of all people was documented in ancient texts, then the assertion that the races were separate species could not possibly be true. This would disprove the theories of the American Ethnologists about the hierarchy and origin of the races.

Many in the South justified slavery based on the "science" of Gliddon and Nott. Norbert Rillieux and other free people of color must have feared that this would eventually render their education and social standing useless, and they would be judged solely on their race as enslaved people were. Rillieux realized that he could no longer stay in Louisiana in such a climate and created a new home for himself in New York City.[198] Even though he left the South, he was still subject to the prejudices that existed throughout the United States. In 1857, Rillieux's petition for reissuance of his patent was initially denied on the basis that he was not a United States citizen because he was a slave. The patent office erroneously thought he was an enslaved person because of his race. Therefore, under the laws of the United

States, he was not a citizen. Rillieux was incensed and wrote back stating that he was the inventor and a citizen of the United States and had stated such in his original affidavit. He continued, "How could the commissioner arrive at such a monstrous conclusion against the expressed declaration to the contrary?"[199] His petition was eventually granted on March 17, 1857.

Eleven days earlier, the question of black citizenship had been decided by the U.S. Supreme Court. In *Dred Scott v Sanford*, the court held that blacks/mulattos were not citizens, nor could they be.[200] It is possible that the patent official had been given no direct orders as of yet, but prior to the decision, some federal officials, such as those in the U.S. Patent Office and the State Department did not want to grant patents or passports to people of color because it would indicate that the U.S. government deemed them citizens. Rillieux's application was no doubt in process prior to the decision; however, the controversy over black citizenship was not new.[201] The patent official might have referred to Rillieux as a slave due to his race but meant that race was the true determinant of citizenship. Up until this time, free people of color had been granted U.S. patents; however, Rillieux had no way of knowing if this would continue given the recent court decision and the increasingly divisive discourse concerning race, especially in the South.

Norbert Rillieux likely chose New York as his new home because of its sugar refining industry, enclaves of intellectuals, voting rights for free blacks, and its lack of laws against interracial marriage. New York was not without racial prejudice, and debate often raged over the rights of free blacks, but it provided a more tolerable climate than some other northern states like neighboring Pennsylvania and Ohio.[202] While in New York, Norbert married a young white woman named Matilda Jane Duff Van Leer (also spelled Van Lear) on April 18, 1857. The Rev. William Adams officiated at the prestigious Madison Square Presbyterian Church.[203] Norbert Rillieux might have passed for white when he married Matilda Van Leer to avoid controversy. Their marriage was announced in the *New York Daily Times* with no mention of Rillieux's race.[204] The couple had certainly heard about the riot over a mixed-race couple in Fulton, New York, four years earlier and might have feared the same would happen to them. In

1853, a mob in Fulton set out to attack and murder William G. Allen because he was of mixed race and was engaged to a white woman. Allen escaped with his life, but he and his wife had to leave America and resettle in England.

Matilda was the widow of Isaac Van Leer, a horse trainer and breeder. It is possible that part of Rillieux's motivation for moving to New York was so that he could marry Mathilda. It is unclear whether they met in New Orleans or New York; however, Matilda was living in New York as early as 1853.[205] Matilda Van Leer and Norbert Rillieux probably met through Norbert's close colleague, Duncan Kenner, who in addition to being a wealthy Louisiana sugar planter, was also an avid horse racer and breeder. Kenner and Isaac Van Leer both sold horses in New Orleans and participated in the some of the same races around the country.[206]

When Matilda Van Leer and Norbert Rillieux married, he became the stepfather of Sarah age nine and Isaac age eight. Matilda's mother also lived with them at No. 36 West Ninth Street in New York. Matilda Van Leer Rillieux had a fascinating background. She was the daughter of Mary Ann Dyke and John R. Duff, both of whom were stage actors. Together they had thirteen children, but only seven survived Mary Ann. Mary Ann's husband died in 1831 when Matilda was only thirteen. Mrs. Duff went on to become one of the most famous actresses of her time.

Mary Ann Dyke Duff, Rillieux's mother-in-law, gave Norbert and Matilda an entrée into the world of nineteenth century New York literati. Mrs. Duff entertained many famous literary figures at Matilda and Norbert Rillieux's home in New York's Washington Square neighborhood. Among them were Elizabeth Oakes Smith and Bayard Taylor.[207] Smith was an early feminist, novelist, poet, editor, and theater critic.[208] Bayard Taylor was a poet and travel writer who published a book in 1869 about his journey to Egypt between 1851 and 1852 called *A Journey to Central Africa.*

Sadly, Norbert's marriage to Matilda was short lived. Matilda and her mother died in New York the same year as her marriage to Norbert. Matilda Duff Van Leer Rillieux died on July 19, 1857, after a lengthy illness. The obituary invited friends of the family to attend the funeral at her late residence. It was stated that her remains would be taken to Greenwood Cemetery for internment.[209] There was quite a mystery surrounding the burial of Matilda Rillieux and her mother, Mary Ann Duff (Sevie), who died later that year on August 31, 1857. According to an article from the *Brooklyn Sun*, reprinted in the *Times Picayune*,[210] friends and relatives, including her own son, Thomas Duff III of Quincy, had no idea what had happened to Mary Duff.

Norbert Rillieux went back to France from New York in 1862, never to return to Louisiana again.[211] He understood that he could no longer live in a country that did not recognize him as a citizen. Rillieux applied for a passport on July 19, 1862, for him and his wife, Emily, to travel abroad. He signed an affidavit in which he swore that he was a United States citizen and submitted a letter written by an official at the United States Patent Office attesting to the same.[212] It was a customary practice to submit a letter from another citizen confirming the applicant's citizenship. This is puzzling because there is no record of Norbert Rillieux marrying anyone named Emily until 1888 in Brighton, England, when he married British-born Emily Cuckow. On the application, Rillieux stated that his wife was born in 1830, which is about the same time as Emily Cuckow's birth. It is possible that because Emily was white, they chose to live together without being officially married, just as Norbert's parents had done. Norbert's skin and eyes were light, so Rillieux might have passed for white so he could live with Emily without recrimination.

It was not until 1861 that the United States required a passport to leave or enter the country, although Europe had such requirements years earlier. It was difficult for a free person of color to get a passport, even prior to the *Dred Scott* decision. Free people of color were often denied travel documents. Several court cases challenged this practice, but to no avail. Instead, free people of color were sometimes issued a "certificate of protection" that requested that foreign countries give the bearer "lawful aid and protection."[213] In his opinion in the *Dred Scott* decision, Chief Justice Taney cited the fact that the United States refused passports to free persons of color based on an 1821 court ruling that stated that "free persons of color were not citizens within the meaning of the Constitution."[214] Race was not a category on a passport application; however, physical characteristics like hair color, eye color, nose, chin, and complexion were part of the data collected.[215] These were used to help the State Department officials determine an applicant's race. Rillieux probably presented himself as white, or it was assumed he was white when he applied for a passport. It is unlikely that he would have been granted a passport in 1862 if it were known that he was of mixed-race.

It is not surprising that Rillieux chose to remain in Europe after he left the United States. The sugar industry in the United States was decimated during the Civil War. Losses exclusive of land depreciation were estimated to be nearly $70,000,000. Many sugar plantations had been heavily mortgaged at the war's onset and were sold for as low as six to ten percent of their prewar value. Fields and equipment were destroyed, and many plantations were left unprotected due to breaks in the levee system that held back the Mississippi River.[216] Rillieux continued his work in Egyptology and the study of Meso-America; however, none of his scholarly work in these areas has been found. Upon his return to Paris in the early 1860s, Rillieux began working with the brother of famous Egyptologist Jean Champollion, Jacques Joseph Champollion-Figeac, and his nephew, Aimé Louis Champollion-Figeac.[217] All that remains are programs from exhibitions that he attended such as the International Congress of Americanists in Nancy, France. Rillieux stayed away from the sugar industry because he was devastated over his stolen plans and embarrassed about his multiple-effect apparatus' damaged reputation. It is hard to imagine that Rillieux's innovative mind stopped thinking about the science of thermodynamics even if he had retreated from the scientific community.

To make matters worse for Rillieux, the proprietary rights to his apparatus were still questioned by some in Louisiana. Rillieux's indefatigable nature forced him to overcome his losses, and he once again began experimenting with innovative ideas for evaporation equipment sometime in the late 1870s. According to the *Commissioner of Patents Journal of Great Britain 1880*, on December 17, Norbert Rillieux was granted patent number 5296: *"Evaporating and boiling apparatus employed in the manufacture of sugar and application of bagasse as fuel partly applicable for evaporating and boiling other substances."*

In 1880, Rillieux was visited by his old friend and colleague, Duncan Kenner, who was the president of the Louisiana Sugar Planters Association. Kenner undoubtedly heard about Rillieux's recent work and wanted Louisiana sugar planters to have the benefit of the latest science regarding sugar production. Kenner's visit to see Norbert Rillieux was likely intended to get Rillieux to bring his knowledge and expertise to Louisiana Sugar Planters to rebuild the industry and give it a competitive edge in the world market.

Duncan Kenner continued to champion Norbert Rillieux's work throughout his life. Up until 1886, the debate persisted as to who deserved credit for inventing the process of multiple-effect evaporation: Norbert Rillieux or Dérosne and Cail, contractors of Dégrand. According to an article in the *Daily Picayune* from July 9, 1886, the Louisiana Sugar Planters Association, chaired by Duncan Kenner, decided to weigh in on the argument over proprietorship of the process. The debate became quite public and contentious as reflected in a series of articles in the *Daily Picayune*. The *Picayune* had previously published an article that the Rillieux apparatus was invented by the French engineer, Dérosne. This assertion was based on information from a "responsible source." However, in a follow-up article, the writer wrote, "Our correspondent has impugned the originality of the Louisiana inventor." The article then recanted the initial assertion and stated the case for Rillieux as the inventor. The reporter conceded that Dérosne and Cail employed many important new discoveries in their machinery, but that they had built on the ideas of others who came before them: Berry, Howard, Chaponais, D'Abouille, Cellier-Blumenthal, and Dumont. The newspaper consulted such sources as the writings of J. D. B. DeBow, the founder of *DeBow's Review*, a journal devoted to business and the economy. De Bow was a professor of commerce and statistics at the University of Louisiana.[218] DeBow was quoted as saying, "I consider the Rillieux plan of evaporation decidedly superior to that of Messrs. Dérosne and Caill (sic) in several important particulars." DeBow then went on at length to explain the differences between the inventions.

The committee created by the Sugar Planters Association ruled, and Judge W. M Bruwell of that committee reported, "Norbert Rillieux, a native of New Orleans, is entitled to the merit of having been the first to apply the principle of successive application of the same heat to vessels employed for boiling liquids in distillation or concentration, to the boiling and concentration of sugar, juice, or syrup in vacuo."[219] The *Picayune* followed up with another article entitled "Proposition to Erect Not One, but a Hundred Monuments to a Great Inventor." The article praised the sugar planters for approving the report given to them by Judge Bruwell but charged that it was not enough to pay homage to the past. The planters must now commit to using the apparatus to honor this great invention and inventor, the article concluded.[220]

Rillieux continued to work on improving multiple-effect evaporation. The new process combined his ideas and patents on the extensive uses of steam to power multiple vacuum evaporation and the heating of thin juices and vapor boiling techniques that did not damage syrups or sugars.[221] Rillieux was issued a patent for his latest invention, but ultimately lost his French patent rights to what was eventually called the "French Process" for sugar refining. Rillieux sued Delacourt and Dolignon for patent infringement for the apparatus they patented in 1882 on the basis that theirs was the same as he had invented. The engineers on the review committee appointed by the French courts cited lack of experimental evidence on a large scale and that those new results had not been achieved by Rillieux over existing methods. They also ruled that the arrangement of the Delacourt and Dolignon apparatus was not identical with Rillieux's patented apparatus. Finally, the committee found that Rillieux's new patent did not meet the standard for a novel invention.[222] Norbert Rillieux was again heartbroken over the loss of his latest patent in his adopted country.

At some point after September 1886 and September 1888, Rillieux temporarily moved to Brighton, England. Brighton is a coastal town that had a bustling industrial center, including sugar refineries near the newly constructed docks.[223] Rillieux could have had some involvement in the sugar industry there, or he might have wanted to retreat to a quiet seaside town. While living in Brighton, he married British citizen, Emily Ann Cuckow. On their marriage certificate of September 13, 1888, they gave the same address: 13 German Place (Now Madeira Place), Brighton in the County of Sussex. This is evidence that the couple lived together as husband and wife prior to getting married.[224] It is possible that as Norbert Rillieux reached the end of his life, he decided to marry Emily Cuckow so there would be no question as to her ability to inherit his substantial assets.

Not much is known about this period of Norbert Rillieux's life. There are no census records or directories that list him as having lived in Brighton. There is no evidence, other than the passport application in 1862, to explain how or when he met Emily, or why he decided to go to Britain. It is possible that in the wake of the humiliation and disappointment over losing the rights to his latest invention, he wanted the comfort of marriage and to retreat from the world that had disappointed him. There were no laws against interracial marriage in England.[225] However, attitudes in the United States against interracial marriage ensured that Norbert could not and would never return to Louisiana with his white wife. Even though anti-miscegenation laws were repealed during Reconstruction and were later reinstated, those who challenged the social taboos were often the victims of violence.[226] At the end of Rillieux's life, the couple lived in Paris and spent time at their property in Burgundy.[227]

Norbert Rillieux died in 1894 and is buried in Père Lachaise Cemetery in Paris. Paul Horsin-Deon, Rillieux's trusted colleague and friend, affectionately remembered him: "But Mr. Rillieux, this superior spirit, who so readily surpassed all others, had to battle without cessation against the jealousy, dishonesty, and mediocrity that overshadowed him. This was the cause of his difficulties in Louisiana, and the cause also of his difficulties in France. In fact, he had a process to maintain against his competitors. Experts were unwilling to recognize the validity of his invention, and Mr. Rillieux lost his process, which mortified him greatly. He was then eighty-five years old, but it seemed that age had not reduced his active temperament, in as much as he was still quick, active, and in full possession of his faculties. The loss of his process changed all this; he ceased from that day to devote himself to this work, which had been most dear to him; he died of a broken heart rather than from the weight of years."[228]

Horsin-Deon's son, Paul Horsin-Deon Jr. echoed this sentiment when he wrote about Rillieux. He added that some people thought Rillieux was a difficult person, but he contended that was not the whole picture. Rillieux could be blunt, but he was only defending his process against injustice. He remembered Rillieux as welcoming and well respected among the sugar manufacturers of his day. Norbert

Rillieux died without realizing that his systems would continue to be used in sugar production as well as in various other industries. Today, Rillieux's principles are used in producing salt and desalinating sea water, recycling on the International Space Station, and in manufacturing glue, evaporated milk, soap, and pharmaceuticals.[229] Emily Cuckow Rillieux lived until 1912. Her husband left her well taken care of financially. She remained in France, either in Portbail,[230] a small coastal town in France's Normandy region, or at the couple's property in Burgundy.[231]

EDMOND RILLIEUX SR.
1810-1897

Edmond Rillieux was the third son of Vincent Rillieux Jr. and Constance Vivant. He was sent to Paris for his education like his older brother, Norbert. Vincent Rillieux Jr. used his connections with other wealthy white planters and capitalists to help his son Edmond. Vincent Jr. helped Edmond and his cousin, Norbert Soulié, secure a contract with capitalists Gordon & Forstall to design and build the Louisiana Sugar Refinery. Norbert Soulié was also a free man of color and an architect. He was the son of Eulalie Vivant, a free woman of color and Constance Vivant's sister, and Jean Soulié, a white man and close friend of Vincent Rillieux Jr. Edmund Forstall, one of the principal investors in the refinery, was a sugar planter and business tycoon who traveled in the same social circles as Vincent Rillieux Jr. Forstall was one of the forerunners in the development of securities backed mortgages. Like many New Orleans businessmen, Edmond Forstall had international offices in other trade centers. In the mid-to early-1820s, Forstall was the managing partner of Gordon, Forstall, & Co. His partner, Alexander Gordon, headed the office in Liverpool, and they had a presence in Tampico, Mexico, as well.[232] By 1828, Gordon, Forstall, & Co. had developed into a formidable force in the merchant banking industry. The company had $250,000 worth of cotton consignment business in Liverpool. Forstall changed the banking industry all over the world and remained influential in Louisiana for decades.

Building stalled on the refinery and a scandal ensued over its completion. According to Christopher Benfey, Edmond Rillieux disappeared from New Orleans in 1832 before completing the Louisiana Sugar Refinery.[233] At the time, Edmond Rillieux lived with his parents in their Magazine Street home. Vincent Rillieux and Constance Vivant were shocked by their son's disappearance and were worried about what happened to him. Edmund Forstall was outraged and petitioned the court to get an accounting of Edmond Rillieux's estate. Ultimately, Edmund Forstall and Vincent Rillieux Jr. became bitter enemies over the incident. An inventory of Edmond's estate was made, and Bernard Soulié, his cousin and brother of Norbert Soulié, was named curator because Edmond Rillieux left the state without appointing anyone to take care of his business affairs. It is unknown whether Edmond Rillieux took off with the funds or got in over his head in terms of having the skills to finish the project. In the petition, Bernard Soulié asserted that Edmond had disappeared from his residence, usual avocations, and businesses, which indicated that Edmond Rillieux probably killed himself. Soulié told the court that he believed Edmond Rillieux to be dead. Edmond Rillieux's estate inventory showed that he was insolvent. Norbert Soulié claimed that Edmond had taken the final payment from Gordon and Forstall and had not turned it over to him as he was supposed to do. Rillieux had a warehouse full of building materials, but their sale would not cover what he owed his creditors. Vincent Rillieux Jr. testified that he had gone through his son's papers and found that Madame LaLaurie owed him 1,500 piastres (equivalent to $1,500). This was still not enough to cover his outstanding debts.

Madame Delphine McCarty LaLaurie was the mother-in-law of Edmund Forstall's brother. Madame Lalaurie's daughter, Maria Francisca de Borgia "Delphine" Lopez Y Angullo de Candelaria, and her husband, Placide Forstall, were investors in the sugar refinery. In 1831, Madame LaLaurie bought an unfinished townhouse at the corner of Royal and Hospital (Governor Nichols) Streets from Edmond Soniat Dufossat. Although Dufossat was supposed to finish the project before the sale, Edmond Rillieux must have been the builder or slater hired to do additional work. At the time, Edmond Rillieux was a partner in the firm of Walsh and Lyall, slaters. The tangled web of family and social connections between Edmond Rillieux and Madame Lalaurie was indicative of the interconnectedness of Louisiana's business, familial, and social networks. Delphine was the daughter of Louis Barthelomy Chevalier de McCarty and Marie Jeanne Lerable. Her cousin, Jean Baptiste Barthelemy de McCarty, had a long-term relationship with Henriette Prieto who was Edmond's aunt on his mother's side. Another cousin of Madame Lalaurie's was Augustin François de McCarty who was the mayor of New Orleans from 1815 to 1820. Vincent, Edmond's father, was an alderman in the McCarty administration. Delphine Lalaurie née McCarty became an infamous figure in the history of New Orleans. Over the years, her horrific treatment of her enslaved people was the subject of the TV drama, *American Horror Story*, starring Kathy Bates, and it is part of the script for countless French Quarter tour guides.

Edmond Rillieux eventually surfaced and returned to New Orleans. It is not known where he was when he was presumed dead. Upon his return, he went into business with his brother, Norbert. They speculated in land and worked as engineers and architects. Edmond remained in the city after Norbert left in the 1850s. Census data shows a steady decline in Louisiana's free black population between 1830 and the start of the Civil War. The rhetoric against free blacks in newspapers and government bodies increased, and a steady flood of white workers from Ireland and Germany took jobs otherwise held by free blacks. Many free people of color relocated to France, Haiti, Latin America, Africa, Mexico, or the northern United States. This was the case with the Soulié family who eventually relocated to France and never returned to Louisiana. In 1830, free people of color accounted for 7.7 percent of the population, but in the census taken just before the Civil War, free blacks made up only 2.6 percent of the population.[234] Some light-skinned free people of color passed as white and were classified as white in census data, therefore providing an inaccurate picture of the free black population. Edmond and Norbert Rillieux's mother, Constance Vivant, is listed as white in the Census of 1860, but in the Census of 1820, there is a female free person of color between the ages of 26 to 44 listed as living in Vincent Rillieux's home. The free woman of color was likely Constance Vivant. Vivant must have had white features as she was one-quarter black, so the census workers of 1860 might not have asked her race and assumed she was white. However, Constance Vivant is listed as a free woman of color in some real estate transactions and legal documents but with no race designation in others.[235] Edmond Rillieux and his eight family members living in his home were listed as white in the Census of 1850; however, his son's birth record in 1837 listed him as "colored."[236] Edmond was fair-skinned as well, as he was one-eighth black. The instructions to enumerators for the 1860 census specifically stated, "'Color,' in all cases where the person is white leave the space blank; in all cases where the person is black without a mixture insert the letter 'B'; if mulatto, or of mixed blood, write 'M'; if Indian, write 'Ind.' It is very desirable to have these directions carefully observed."[237] Clearly, the government was interested in correctly labeling race for the census count, so it is improbable that a person would be intentionally misclassified. Census takers might have assumed that many Afro-Creoles were white based on their appearances and counted them as such on the census. It is important to note that Edmond Rillieux never denied his race as he was a vocal Afro-Creole involved in post-Civil War politics.[238] In all probability, the population of free people of color did not decline as drastically as the data reflects. An unknown number of people of mixed race were classified as white in census data and in legal transactions.

Edmond Rillieux entered the rough and tumble world of Louisiana politics after the Civil War. He was active in the Republican Party as early as 1865 and was a delegate to the Republican Convention for that year.[239] He was approached by party leaders to run for elected office but declined, citing business responsibilities.[240] Edmond Rillieux fit the profile of many black political leaders in Reconstruction era New Orleans. He was free before the war, well educated, light skinned, of Creole decent, and spoke impeccable French as well as English and Spanish.[241] Edmond Rillieux was a builder, engineer, and businessman with considerable assets.[242] After the Civil War, the three-caste system of Antebellum New Orleans collapsed. Most whites grouped people who were free before the war with newly freed people. It is likely that Edmond became involved in the Republican party over his disgust over the 1864 Louisiana Constitution, a sentiment shared by most of his peers. While the new constitution adhered to the requirements laid out in President Lincoln's Ten Percent Plan, it failed to give blacks the right to vote. This outraged the elite free people of color. At first, they advocated that those requirements for voting established in the 1852 Louisiana Constitution should stand in terms of education and property ownership. They contended that they were taxpayers and part of the educated, property owners of the city and should have the right to vote.

A group of these men, along with whites who were referred to as radicals, formed the Friends of Universal Suffrage. Edmond Rillieux attended a group meeting that was held in mid-September of 1865. At the meeting, he was elected as an Orleans Parish delegate to the convention that was to be held later that month. The convention was held from September 25 - 27, 1865, with 111 delegates representing twelve parishes.[243] The pamphlet handed out at the convention and produced by the Central Executive Committee of the Friends Universal Suffrage pointed out that 300,000 enslaved people had been emancipated yet not given the right to vote, while 350,000 whites were enfranchised, many of whom were disloyal to their government and committed treason. The committee went on to advocate for voting rights for all men to form a political majority. Bernard Soulié was also a delegate from Orleans Parish and put forth a motion to rename and recast the party as the Republican Party of Louisiana. The resolution passed and the Louisiana Republican Party was born. Speeches were made, debates raged, and a united front was put forth. It was resolved that the new party would support the national Republican Party on federal issues.[244] Other resolutions reiterated the ideals of the Declaration of Independence, rejected the existing state constitution of 1864 and Louisiana's legitimacy as a state, and advocated for universal suffrage.[245] Opposition to the party was fierce. Amnesty had been granted to most Secessionists, and they began to regain political power over the Unionists who had populated the initial Reconstruction government. Originally, conservative Unionists opposed black suffrage, but they now had to embrace the movement to hold onto their political positions.

The Unionist white office holders decided to reconvene the Constitutional Convention of 1864 and write a new one that called for voting rights for all males, including blacks. The convention convened on

July 30, 1866, at the Mechanics' Institute in New Orleans. Twenty-five white radicals attended. Tensions were high and the newspapers had stirred up the population. Outside, between two and three hundred people of color paraded down the street waving American flags in support of the convention.[246] Mayor John Monroe led an opposition force of fellow ex-Confederates and police to prevent any disturbance that might occur. Violence erupted after an altercation between a black supporter and a white member of the taskforce. After a scuffle, a white man fired his gun at the black man. This lit the spark that ignited a melee. An enraged black activist fired on a newsboy who taunted the crowd. The police and sympathetic whites opened fire on the black marchers. Some marchers sought refuge in the building with the delegates, while others were gunned down in the streets. The radicals and their supporters knew they were outnumbered and outgunned. They tried to surrender several times and begged to be arrested, but the killing continued until thirty-four blacks were dead and one hundred nineteen were wounded. In addition, three white radicals were killed and seventeen were wounded.[247] The local press lamented the killing but stated that police had no choice but to take such measures. The national press, however, excoriated Louisianians who participated in the massacre. Martial law was reinstated and sweeping, and more severe Reconstruction acts were passed.[248] Edmond Rillieux did not let the threat of personal harm deter him from his goal of securing universal suffrage. He attended Republican rallies and served as a vice-president in the Louisiana Republican Party in 1868.[249] The Fifteenth Amendment was ratified in 1870 and all males obtained the right to vote.

By 1872, seven years after the Civil War ended, Louisiana was on the verge of anarchy, according to noted historian T. Harry Williams.[250] Republican William Kellogg and Democrat John McHenry each claimed victory in the gubernatorial election that year. Much to the horror of white native Louisianians, the federal government stepped in and declared William Kellogg governor of Louisiana after the election. Riots and mob actions broke out. An assassination attempt was made on Governor William Kellogg. As a result of the tumult in Louisiana, the state's reputation in the country and the world suffered, which in turn affected business and industry.

These dire circumstances prompted businessmen to come up with a plan to bring together the warring factions and end what they saw as the stranglehold put on their state by Reconstruction. They believed they could solve this problem without federal intervention. Powerful black and white businessmen came together to form what was to be the Unification Party. Edmond Rillieux became a leader in the movement aimed at alleviating racial unrest and improving Louisiana's business climate. Much healing needed to occur as Republicans who came from the North to Louisiana after the war were viewed by many in the South as carpetbaggers, unscrupulous and opportunistic people who went to the South to profit from Reconstruction. Local free people of color and whites who advocated for universal suffrage were seen as radical by many in both parties.

Most of the white people who led the Unification Movement were among the socially elite of New Orleans, and the people of color were well known and successful in the business community. Isaac N. Marks, a white New Orleans merchant, was the chairman, and P.G.T. Beauregard, revered Confederate general, was the head of the Committee on Resolutions.[251] The sponsors of the movement were known as the Committee of One Hundred, fifty white men and fifty black men. Edmond Rillieux and his son, E.J. Rillieux, and white businessman Michel Musson (Musson's mother, Celeste, was Vincent Rillieux's sister and Edmond's aunt) were among those on the committee. At first, meetings were held in secret until the plan was agreed upon and ready for publication. On March 29, 1873, the *New Orleans Times* announced the formation of the Unification Party. Many citizens of New Orleans and newspapers from in and around the city supported the movement. Writers of the *Times* called on whites to reject the racism of the past and to embrace a new era for the sake of Louisiana.[252] In addition to the *Times*, other newspapers also supported the movement: *The Herald*, an extreme Democrat publication, *L'Abeille* or *The Bee*, a French language newspaper with Whig leanings, and the *Picayune*, a newspaper known for its support of the Democrats.[253] Many in the community implored the movement to keep the political hacks and party bosses out. Local newspapers published the Committee of One Hundred report in June of 1873 in several issues during the next month. There was not much support for the movement in other parts of Louisiana, as demonstrated by articles and letters in newspapers outside of New Orleans and Baton Rouge. In its July 2, 1873, issue, *The Shreveport Times* called the New Orleans based movement "clap-trap." The paper warned that if given too much power, Negroes (sic) would rule the state. The *Ouachita Telegraph* opined, "As a specimen of satire, it [the report of the Committee of One Hundred] would rank high in the humorous literature of the day, did not the names of Beauregard, Gibson, and other well-known Southern men appear as endorsers. . ." The paper went on to declare, "The address is wrong, not only in theory, but recommends a practice which must prove destructive to all the ennobling virtues of our race and to every material interest of the state."[254] Other objections came from the Republicans for fear of losing their base of black support. *The Republican*, the state subsidized newspaper, accused the movement of subterfuge.[255] Another Republican publication pointed out that the Unification Party could not deliver the vote of African Americans because the African Americans in the party were the educated former free men of color who had no sway with those who were former enslaved people.

Prior to the public meeting that would be held to let the citizens know about the Committee of One Hundred's proposed plan, a letter to the editor of the *Daily Picayune* by a writer identified as A. Citizen listed the resolutions and asked the public for suggestions and criticism, as the resolutions were not meant to be ultimatums. Historian Justin Nystrom noted that the resolutions bore a striking resemblance to the Civil Rights Act of 1964.[256]

The Daily Picayune – June 18, 1873
Be it therefore resolved
FIRST-That henceforward we dedicate ourselves to the unification of our people.
SECOND-That by "our people," we mean all men, of whatever race, color, or religion, who are citizens of Louisiana, and who are willing to work for her prosperity.
THIRD-That we shall advocate, by speech, and pen, and deed, the equal and impartial exercise by every citizen of Louisiana of every civil and political right guaranteed [by the constitution and laws of

Louisiana],[257] by the constitution and laws of the United States, and by the laws of honor, brotherhood, and fair dealing.

FOURTH-That we shall maintain and advocate the right of every citizen of Louisiana, and of every citizen of the United States, to frequent at will all places of public resort, and to travel at will on all vehicles of public conveyance, upon terms of perfect equality with any and every other citizen; and we pledge ourselves, so far as our influence, counsel and example may go, to make this right a live and practical right, and that there may be no misunderstanding of our views on this point:

1. We shall recommend to the proprietors of all places of licensed public resort in the State of Louisiana, the opening of said places to the patronage of both races inhabiting our State.

2. And we shall further recommend that all railroads, steamboats, steamships, and other public conveyances pursue the same policy.

3. We shall further recommend that our banks, insurance offices, and other public corporations recognize and concede to our colored fellow-citizens, where they are stockholders in such institutions, the right of being represented in the direction thereof.

4. We shall further recommend that hereafter no distinction shall exist among citizens of Louisiana in any of our public schools or State institutions of education, or in any other public institutions supported by the State, city, or parishes.

5. We shall also recommend that the proprietors of all foundries, factories, and other industrial establishments, in employing mechanics or workmen, make no distinction between the two races.

6. We shall encourage, by every means in our power, our colored citizens in the rural districts to be/come the proprietors of the soil, thus enhancing the value of lands and adding to the productiveness of the State, while it will create a political conservatism which is the offspring of proprietorship: and we further more recommend to all landed proprietors in our State the policy of considering the question of breaking up the same into small farms, in order that the [our] colored citizens and white emigrants may become practical farmers and cultivators of the soil.

FIFTH-That we pledge our honor and good faith to exercise our moral influence, both through personal advice and personal example, to bring about the rapid removal of all prejudices heretofore existing against the colored citizens of Louisiana, in order that they may hereafter enjoy all the rights belonging to citizens of the United States.

Be it further resolved, That we earnestly appeal to the press of this State to join and cooperate with us in erecting this monument to unity, concord and justice, and like ourselves forever to bury beneath it all party prejudices [all past prejudices on the subject of race or color.

Resolved, also, That we deprecate and thoroughly condemn all acts of violence, from whatever source, and appeal to our people of both races to abide by the law in all their differences as the surest way to preserve to all the blessings of life, liberty, and property.

Resolved, That we pledge ourselves to the cultivation of a broad sentiment of nationality, which shall embrace the whole country, and uphold the flag [glory] of the Union.

Resolved, That as an earnest of our holy purpose, we hereby offer upon the altar of the common good, all party ties, and all prejudices of education which may tend to hinder the political unity of our people.

Resolved, That in view of numerical equality between the white and colored elements of our population, we shall advocate an equal distribution of the offices of trust and emolument in our State, demanding, as the only conditions of our suffrage, honesty, diligence, and ability; and we advocate this not because of the offices themselves, but simply as another earnest and proof upon our part, that the union we desire is an equal union and not an illusive (sic) conjunction brought about for the sole benefit of one or the other of the parties to the [that] union.

Over the podium from which speeches were made hung the American flag and the inscription: EQUAL RIGHTS – ONE FLAG – ONE COUNRY – ONE PEOPLE.

There were numerous speeches made by leaders in the organization.[257] Isaac N. Marks, chairman, began by stating that this was not a political gathering. He earnestly pled, "I hope and trust in God to lay upon the altar of our country the prejudices of the past to recognize all citizens of the United States as equals before the law."

Despite lack of support from other parts of the state and at the risk of alienating themselves from others in the community, the committee continued its work and held a public meeting in New Orleans on July 15, 1873. The meeting was well attended by both races, but there were more people of color than whites. Some white members of the committee were notably absent. Michel Musson, Edmond's white cousin, did not attend, neither did General Beauregard.[258] It was not stated why Beauregard, a leader in the movement, was not in attendance; however, he had taken some criticism from the community, especially when he advocated that children of all races attend school together. Father Abram J. Ryan, Catholic priest, poet, and publisher of the *Morning Star* and *Catholic Messenger* stirred up the large Catholic community in New Orleans when in the June 29, 1873, issue of the *Messenger* he questioned General Beauregard's Southern manhood and asked, "Would General Beauregard, who is Catholic as well as a Southern man, allow a child of his to go to school and associate there on terms of equality as a scholar with colored children?"[259] Williams suggested that Beauregard's participation in the movement was primarily political and pragmatic, as evidenced by his belief that "the whites could lead the Negroes to vote the right way."[260] Beauregard probably worried about expending political capital on a cause that was tenuous at best. It is evident though that some in the black community saw Beauregard as a genuine advocate for civil rights. After the general's death, a cousin of Edmond Rillieux, poet Victor Ernest Rillieux, wrote a poem in honor of the New Orleans icon.[261]

Chairman Marks was followed by Theophile Terrence Allain. Allain was born into slavery in West Baton Rouge, and at the time, he was a Republican in the Louisiana House of Representatives. Allain began by praising the United States Constitution and its framers. He stated that the addition of the 13th, 14th, and 15th Amendments made it an even more perfect document. He went on to state how these amendments had been largely ignored in Louisiana and the rest of the South. He specifically chastised country parishes for the practices and a devotion to racial division and suppression of rights of "colored people (sic)." However, he graciously acknowledged those who sought to right past disregard for the Constitutional rights of "colored people (sic)." He stated, "We claim these rights as being our due according to law and equity, while at the same time we tender our grateful acknowledgements to our Southern friends for their ample, though tardy recognition of them." He ended on a hopeful, somewhat conciliatory note saying, "We all know that there is no cloud so dark but that it has a silver lining and while we take encouragement from that, it is our bounden duty to make the most of the present movement."

After Allain came James Davidson Hill, one of the owners of the *Picayune*. He gave a brief introduction to remarks he would read for the absent William Randolph who sent word that he was ill. Davidson gave his endorsement of the movement and sited practical reasons why its success was important, mainly to get the federal government out of Louisiana's business.

J. Henri Burch, an African-American Louisiana state senator from Connecticut, who was considered by many to be a quintessential carpetbagger, spoke next. Burch's rhetoric inflamed the sensibilities of many when he said, "You white people of this state, if you had taken the proper course, would have easily acquired the confidence of the colored (sic) people and you would have had the government in your own hands, and the northern man who would have been placed in office would have been placed there because of his moral worth, and not as he has been, from necessity."

James Lewis, administrator of improvements for the city council and a noted black leader, spoke next. He read a pledge signed by a subgroup of the committee, a group of eight, who vowed that Negroes (sic) would not unite with whites to overthrow the "carpetbaggers" until "Negroes (sic) received full recognition of their civil and political rights."[262] The pledge was unexpected and was not sanctioned by the full Committee of One Hundred. One of the pledge signers was a Rillieux. The newspaper listed him as D. Rillieux, but there was not a D. Rillieux listed on the committee roster. Williams wrote that in the original article the first initial is difficult to make out.[263] It is likely that this was either Edmond or his son E.J. It is more likely that it was Edmond,[264] as he was active in the Republican Party and was a delegate to the Convention for Universal Suffrage. The pledge angered many committee and community members; it was seen as undermining the committee's original intent.

The *Daily Picayune* supported the ideas of the Unification Movement, but in the days following the public meeting, it sounded the death knell for the movement: "If we understand the great object of that meeting, it was to ratify the efforts of the committee of the One Hundred to harmonize the races and bring about a new election in which all would unite to banish forever from our soil bad government [carpetbaggers], establish good in its place, and to make peace, prosperity, and good will grow where now flourish only the noisome weeds of race antagonism, political persecution, and official corruption."[265] The paper laid the blame at the feet of Burch and Lewis for ruining the chance for unification to succeed. While the speeches and actions of Burch and Lewis were seen as inflammatory by many, the absence of General Beauregard, one of the most visible white leaders, the writings of Father Ryan, and the lack of support in the central and northern parts of the state cannot be ignored as having contributed to the breakdown of the short-lived effort.

Regrettably, the failure of the movement furthered the racial divide despite pleas from some in the community. A few, like Isaac Marks, continued to advocate for unification on moral, legal, and ethical grounds, but those ideals were often drowned out by propaganda that fed on the fears of white citizens. In a speech reported by *The New Orleans Times*, Marks vowed, "It is my determination to continue to battle against these abstract, absurd, and stupid prejudices, and to bring to bear the whole force of my character . . . to break them down. They must disappear; they will disappear."[266] Seasoned politicians seized the opportunity to solidify their bases and furthered the divide. Historians T. Harry Williams and Justin Nystrom contend that while many lauded the committee for not using political operatives, it is precisely the political missteps of the inexperienced leaders that contributed to the demise of the Unification Movement. Both assert that experienced political bosses who truly wanted the movement to succeed would not have allowed a controversial character such as Burch to speak, nor would they have allowed the group of eight to undermine the original committee.[267]

Michel Musson went on to join the Crescent City White League as one of its leaders, as did many whites who were motivated by economic and political reasons.[268] The White League began in rural parishes as a resistance to Kellogg's "illegitimate" governorship and federal intervention. The organization aimed to ensure white dominance in politics and restore local control in Louisiana. Leaders in the White League, in collusion with the *Picayune*, ginned up fears among whites with exaggerated stories of impending plans for people of color in the city to demand their civil rights and wreak havoc.[269] During the summer of 1874, a secret militia called the First Louisiana Regiment, or "Louisiana's Own" was formed. Members participated in drill practice and prepared to unite with the White League and take over the government by force.[270] Leaders bought inexpensive surplus Civil War arms and ammunition from northern dealers.[271] The White League platform that was published in the *Daily Picayune* declared, "We think the time has arrived for the white men of Louisiana to unite in defense of their families and civilization. And we believe that superiority in State affairs belongs to the white people from their superiority in wealth, in education, and in numbers."[272] The White League believed that blacks were given the right to vote prematurely, they were not ready to make wise decisions about government, and they were being manipulated by those in the National Republican Party. The League blamed the alliance between the Republican Party and blacks for ". . . our devastated fields, our waning commerce, our idle workshops, our decreasing population, our increasing taxes, our pauper multitudes, pensioners on alien charity..."[273]

The building animosity in the city culminated in a violent clash between the White League and the Metropolitan Police of New Orleans on September 14, 1874. White leaders called a mass meeting of the white citizenry and gathered 5,000 men at Clay Statue on Canal Street. Michel Musson was elected chairman and his son-in-law, Samuel Bell, was one of the vice-presidents.[274] The resolutions of the meeting included unseating Governor Kellogg. The White League directly addressed accusations by critics that claimed the aim of the league was to limit the rights of black people and stated, "That the white people of Louisiana have no right to deprive the colored people of their rights."[275] Under the direction of former Confederate General Fredrick Ogden, the militia seized control of key spots in the city, including City Hall. The fighting resulted in bloodshed on both sides. Eleven Metropolitans (police officers) were killed and sixty wounded, while the White League suffered twenty-one deaths and nineteen wounded.[276] The conflict ended in the surrender of the police station at Jackson Square and the state arsenal.[277] David Penn declared himself governor and was sworn in by the leaders of the White League on the basis that he had been duly elected lieutenant governor in the election of 1872. President Grant finally sent federal troops to support the skeleton crew that was already in New Orleans, and order was eventually restored. Kellogg was reinstated as governor of Louisiana, and federal troops took charge of New Orleans.[278] The conflict quickly became known as The Battle of Liberty Place, and the White League participants were honored with a monument that was erected in 1891 but has since been removed.

The battle increased polarization between the races and furthered delineation of the sometimes-nebulous racial lines of New Orleans. White Creoles, who a couple of generations before had done business with their mixed-race relatives, distanced themselves from them and often buried evidence of their family ties. This was hardly the environment for blacks or those of mixed racial heritage to attain the success they might otherwise have achieved under different conditions. Bernard Soulié, the last of the Souliés, left Louisiana and joined the rest of his family in Paris in 1872. Edmond reinvented himself; he went into the cigar business with his sons and became a retail dealer. In the 1880s, New Orleans was known as the nation's "Cigar Capital." Edmond lived a long life and died in 1897 at the age of eighty-six after a lengthy struggle with dementia.

Edgar Degas
1834-1917

Edgar Degas was a French Impressionist painter and sculptor who became famous during the late nineteenth and early twentieth centuries. When he arrived in New Orleans, Degas was on the verge of stardom in the art world. Edgar Degas traveled to Louisiana in October of 1872 to visit his mother's family, the Mussons, for respite after his stint in the French National Guard during the Franco-Prussian war.[279] The unrest started in July of 1870 when France declared war on Prussia. Once war was declared in July, most American tourists and those living in Paris returned home. The American colony which once boasted 4,500 people dwindled to only 150 by the end of the siege. By January 1871, conditions in Paris were so dire that the pet loving Parisians had begun eating cats and dogs along with the rats that roamed the streets.

Edgar Degas' mother, Célestine Musson, was born in New Orleans, but was taken to France by her father, Germain Musson, when her mother died in 1819, leaving behind five young children. Germain Musson was heartbroken at the death of his wife, Marie Célestine Rillieux, the daughter of Vincent Rillieux and Marie Tronquet. Overwhelmed by losing his wife and the prospect of caring for his five young children, Germain Musson moved back to Paris. Musson continued to do business in New Orleans and Mexico as a successful cotton broker and silver investor. At the age of eighteen, Célestine Musson fell in love with and married Augustin Degas.[280] The couple had the first of their five children, Hilaire Germain "Edgar" Degas, in 1834. The Degas family often had visitors from New Orleans, but Célestine never returned to the city of her birth, although she longed for the social life of New Orleans and the connection to family.[281] She died in 1847, when Edgar Degas was just thirteen years old.

Célestine's brother, Michel Musson, went to school in Liverpool, England, learned the cotton business, and eventually moved to New Orleans.[282] Like most French transplants to New Orleans, the Mussons kept in close contact with their family members and friends who remained in France. In 1863, Michel's daughters, Désirée and Estelle; his granddaughter, Joe Balfour; and his wife, Odile, fled Union-occupied New Orleans and settled in Bourge-en-Brasse, France, for three years. The Degas sons grew close to their Creole cousins while they were in France. The boys were devastated when their mother died, so getting to know their Louisiana family made them feel connected to their mother. The Degas brothers visited the Mussons often during their stay in France, and even thought of Odile as a second mother.[283] Rene, over his father's objections, decided to accompany his Louisiana family when they returned to New Orleans. He joined his Uncle Michel's cotton brokerage firm, and in 1869, married his cousin, Estelle. The second oldest Degas son, Achille, moved to New Orleans later that year and shared a home with René and Estelle on Esplanade Avenue.

Edgar Degas visited his family at their home in New Orleans from October 1872 until February 1873. When he arrived in the city, Degas expected to see a bustling example of American capitalism in New Orleans, as his brothers enthusiastically wrote to him about the cotton business. However, during his stay, Degas became bored by his brothers' business dealings and the incessant talk about cotton, agriculture, and labor shortages. After all, New Orleans was an urban center with many of the cultural aspects of European cities. He anticipated a more cosmopolitan, stimulating experience.[284] New Orleanians were obsessed with such topics because the cotton industry, as well as other industries like sugar, had suffered from a lack of labor and damage from the war.[285] Freedmen, formerly enslaved people, were unwilling to work for the low wages offered, and picking cotton became a symbol of the evils they had endured under slavery. New Orleans brokers, like Michel Musson, were keenly aware that if the growers they represented could not harvest their crops, there would be nothing for them to sell.

As was the case with many Europeans, prior to coming to New Orleans, Edgar Degas had a rather homogenous picture of America and did not grasp the vastness of its land, the diversity of its population, or the varied personalities of its towns and cities. Europeans often saw America as a modern and boundless incubator for entrepreneurial ideas without the conventional restraints of European business traditions.[286] Historian Christina Vella views Degas' painting of his Uncle Michel's cotton office in "A Cotton Office in New Orleans" as a depiction of this perceived ideal of entrepreneurship in America rather than the actual struggling post-war cotton industry or the city that would never regain its former glory as a center of commerce and culture.[287] Art historian Jean Sutherland Boggs suggests that the painting is a visual narrative in which viewers realize the interplay between the characters and the setting in telling a story. The painting depicts the aristocratic, white world of Creole businessmen in New Orleans and conveys their worries, pride, and personalities.[288]

While in New Orleans, Degas typically painted indoor subjects as his eyes were giving him trouble, and he was unable to spend long periods of time outdoors. He often asked family members to sit for him. However, between 1866 and 1868, a few years before coming to America, Degas focused on horses and completed his first of many paintings of racehorses entitled "The Parade," also known as "Race Horses in front of the *Tribune*." Ten years earlier, the famous racecourse, Longchamp, was built about an hour outside of Paris. Degas attended the races regularly and became fascinated with this aspect of modern life as well as the opportunity to capture the graceful animals in motion. Duncan Kenner, a close friend of the Musson, Degas, and Rillieux families, helped organize the Louisiana Jockey Club in New Orleans. Kenner and Degas undoubtedly attended horseraces together and talked about the artistic depictions of the noble animals. Before the Civil War, Kenner commissioned paintings of his treasured horses by artist Edward Troye and considered them to be among his prized possessions.[289]

Edgar Degas stayed in New Orleans until at least late February of 1873, although he had only intended to stay for two months.

During his extended visit, he painted his famous "A Cotton Office in New Orleans." It was the first painting Degas sold to a museum. The painting is still owned by Musee des Beaux-Arts in Pau, France.

Cantrelle Family

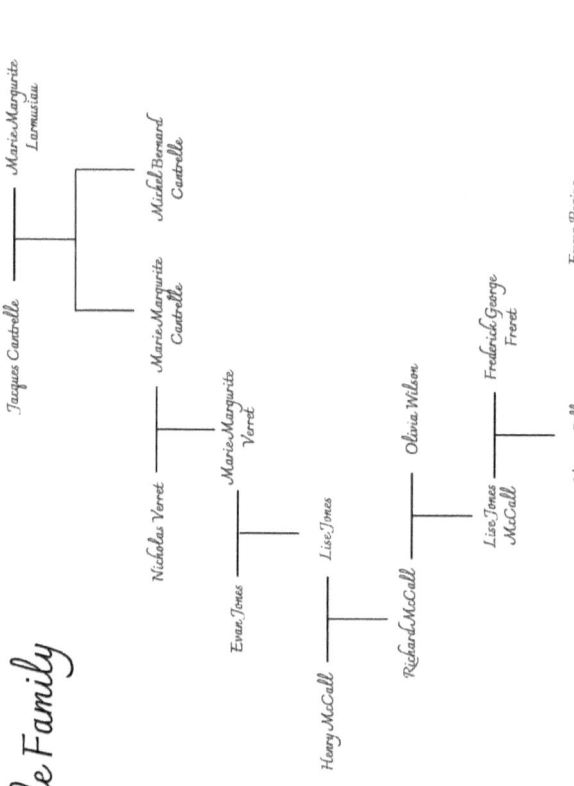

The Cantrelle Family

Jacques Cantrelle
1697-1778

Jacques Cantrelle was born in Picardie, France, in 1697. Jacques' parents and his sister died when he was about fifteen years old. He and his fourteen-year-old brother, Claude, were orphaned and destitute. They hatched a plan to get salt from Germany and sell it in France. Salt was a highly prized commodity and heavily taxed by the Crown. Their smuggling plot was exposed, and the brothers were arrested. Claude was released, but Jacques was sentenced to life in prison. When Jacques was twenty-one years old, the king gave him a reprieve on the condition that he was banished from France and could never return. Jacques accepted those terms and planned to go to Louisiana. Before he left, he married Marie Francienne Minquetz, and they had a son named Jean. The couple and their young son set sail for Louisiana on *Le Profound* in 1720. The trip was too difficult for their infant son, and Jean died on the trip across the ocean.

Jacques and Marie settled at the Arkansas Post in the Louisiana Territory. At the time, all commercial affairs of the French Territory were under the direction of John Law's Company of the Indies. Law was enlisted to help overhaul France's financial state and recruited French settlers like Jacques Cantrelle to build and populate the land that is present-day Arkansas. John Law was a Scottish financier who emigrated from London to Paris when his friend, the Duc d'Orléans, became the regent of France. Law's venture in Louisiana was part of a larger scheme to clean up the fiscal mess that rendered France nearly insolvent. His plan ultimately failed, the Arkansas Post was largely abandoned, and its settlers either returned to Europe or moved elsewhere in the territory. Jacques and Marie were among the settlers who relocated to the Terre Blanche Settlement at Fort Rosalie (present-day Natchez, Mississippi), a post established in 1716 by the governor of Louisiana, Jean-Baptiste Le Moyne de Bienville. Marie and Jacques built a home there, and Marie was one of the midwives for the colonists. Jacques probably farmed tobacco, the cash crop grown in the area. The fort was somewhat secure but had been attacked by the nearby Natchez tribe in the settlement's early years. By the late 1720s, there were about 600 non-native people living in the Natchez area, approximately 200 of whom were enslaved people.

Relations between the French settlers and their Natchez trading partners began to deteriorate in 1729 with the arrival of the new commandant, Chépart. He mistreated his officers and wanted to appropriate some of the Natchez's land for his personal plantation.[290] This infuriated the Natchez and caused them to be open to a more favorable trade arrangement with the British instead of the French.[291] Chépart dismissed the objections of the Natchez and underestimated their leaders' resolve and resourcefulness. He believed his thinly positioned garrison could protect the fort. He was so arrogant about his position of authority that he ignored rumors and warnings of an impending uprising.[292] On the morning of November 28, 1729, Natchez men arrived at the fort under the guise of trading corn and chickens for gunpowder and bullets. This was not at all an unusual occurrence, so no one was suspicious as the Natchez warriors surrounded the fort. On signal, the Natchez began killing the white males inside the fort. Many of the men were decapitated and their heads were brought to the chief, Great Sun. Pregnant women and small children were also killed. Other women were raped and enslaved along with their children.[293] The prisoners were held at the home of the ranking female chief.[294]

Jacques Cantrelle managed to escape the massacre. Some reports say that he was out hunting when the raid took place. Others claim that Jacques and his wife hid out in the corn house until dark and then tried to escape.[295] In this version of events, Jacques left his wife in hiding and went back to their house to gather some things, and when he returned, Marie was gone. Marie did not survive the attack and is listed among the dead.[296] After the attack, Jacques, a man named Guebo, and an infant they rescued made their way to New Orleans. The two men saved the infant son of Des Noyers, aide-Major of troops at Natchez and director of the concession, and Angelique Charison. Baby Antoine Laurent des Noyes survived with the help of a Native American woman who nursed him along the journey to New Orleans.[297]

It might have been Cantrelle and Guebo who first informed officials in New Orleans of the Natchez massacre. Governor Étienne Périer's first response was to strike out against the nearest group of Native Americans to ease the colonists' fears and to warn other tribes against similar actions. He ordered the nearby peaceful Chaouchas tribe destroyed.[298] The next February, a force led by Chevalier de Loubois, with the help of the Choctaw, attacked the Natchez and liberated the women and children who were taken in the raid. Several French children were killed when the Natchez hurled their bodies out of the fort. The retaliation by French troops against the Natchez people was brutal. A few escaped and eventually settled among the Chickasaws, while some were sold into slavery in Saint-Domingue. Four men and two women were burned to death in New Orleans as a warning to other would-be enemies.[299] The traumatized French women and children were taken to New Orleans and cared for by the Ursuline nuns.[300] Marie "Marguerite" Joseph Larmusiau, the widow of Pierre LeHoux who was killed in the Natchez attack, and her daughter, Marie Marguerite, were among the rescued. Marguerite and Pierre knew Jacques Cantrelle and his wife as they had also lived at the Arkansas post and relocated to Fort Rosalie.[301] A few months after the rescue, thirty-three-year-old Jacques Cantrelle and eighteen-year-old Marguerite Larmusiau were married in New Orleans and settled in what is now Gentilly Ridge in eastern New Orleans on Lake Pontchartrain. Marguerite was born in Avesnes-sur-Helpe, France, and arrived in Louisiana at the age of nine. Her father, Jean Baptiste Larmusiau, was the surgeon major to Governor Bienville.

The Cantrelles bought a home in the city and raised their seven children along with Marguerite's daughter. Jacques was well educated and employed as a notary. He was involved in or attended many social occasions, and he participated in countless business transactions in his role as notary. In 1762, before the Spanish possession of Louisiana,

Jacques Cantrelle received ten arpents that spanned the area near the present-day St. James Railway Station to the town of Donaldsonville. His sons-in-law, Nicolas Verret and Louis Judice, received grants on either side of Cantrelle. As Jacques was in his sixties at the time, he remained in New Orleans until Verret and Judice cleared the land for farming, constructed levees, and built houses. Jacques had a working indigo plantation on his land, but he did not build a home there until sometime between late 1764 and early 1765 after Louisiana was under Spanish authority, but before Spain had taken official control. His son-in-law, Nicolas Verret, who was married to his daughter, Marie Marguerite Joseph, oversaw the plantation's operation. Jacques named his plantation Cabahanoce, which was a Native American word meaning mallard roost.

The rest of his family was not reported as living there until the census of 1769. Like many planters of the time, the Cantrelles split their time between their city and country homes. There were a few plantations prior to that, but the area was slower to develop than nearby St. John and Ascension Parishes because of hostile tribes like the Chitimacha and Houma. Raids on settlements occurred up until 1748. Flooding was also a constant concern on the Acadian Coast.[302]

Jacques Cantrelle was named commandant during the French possession. As commandant, Jacques Cantrelle established relations with the nearby Native American tribes. Jacques knew all too well the importance of peacefully coexisting with the local Native Americans. Jacques was also charged with welcoming the first Acadian refugees to Louisiana. The first four Acadian families arrived from New York shortly after Jacques and his sons-in-law settled at Cabahanoce. Many more Acadians arrived in 1765 from Halifax via Saint-Domingue and in 1766 from Maryland. It was then that the area began to be known as the Acadian Coast. So many settlers came to Cabahanoce that the French administration divided the district into sub-districts and named co-commandants, Jacques Cantrelle's sons-in-law, Louis Judice for the upper and Nicolas Verret for the lower.[303]

All was not copacetic for Jacques and his fellow French Creoles during the transition from French to Spanish possession. Louisianans were in limbo between the two imperial powers. Speculation about which empire actually ruled the colony led the local powerbrokers to take matters into their own hands. The secret Treaty of Fontainebleau of 1762 was intended to entice Spain to ally with the French against England in the Seven Years War. The treaty ceded the Louisiana Territory and the Isle of Orleans from France to Spain but was kept under wraps for nearly a year and a half. Initially, Spain was reluctant to accept the burden of a colony they knew little about and did not want to spend the money on military resources to occupy Louisiana. It was not until April 21, 1764, that the treaty was made public in Paris. Finally, in October 1764, Louisiana's director general, Jacques Blaise D'Abbadie, published excerpts from King Louis XV's letter that informed Louisianans that they were about to be under the rule of His Catholic Majesty Carlos III of Spain. The colonists were vehemently opposed to losing their French status. They immediately took action to reverse the course of events. A meeting was held in New Orleans with representatives from each parish attending. They passed a resolution begging the French Crown not to sever ties with Louisiana. Jacques Cantrelle attended the meeting and signed the petition. Jean Milhet, a wealthy New Orleans merchant, was selected to present the memorial to the king. Once in Paris, Milhet, with the help of retired Governor Bienville, delivered the resolution to Prime Minister De Choiseul and asked him to present it to the king. De Choiseul declined because he had advised the king on the cession of Louisiana and his judgement would be called into question.

    A year passed and Milhet did not return home, nor did Spain send anyone to take possession of the territory. These circumstances gave the colonists hope that the official transfer would not come to pass. However, in July of 1765, hope gave way to despair and anger when a letter arrived addressed to the Superior Council informing them of the imminent arrival of Don Antonio de Ulloa from Havana. But Ulloa did not step foot in Louisiana until March 5, 1766.[304] The new Spanish governor arrived with three civil officers, three capuchin monks, and a paltry eighty to ninety troops.[305] Ulloa fully expected that the existing French troops would enlist under his command and pledge allegiance to Spain; however, they refused to serve. Due to lack of military backing, the attitude of the populace, and the economic chaos of the colony, Ulloa decided to postpone the colony's official transfer. Ulloa retreated to La Balize and raised the French flag there. La Balize was a French fort and settlement near the mouth of the Mississippi River. Ulloa's stated reasons for going to the inhospitable delta formation was to oversee the construction of a new fort and ship channel.[306] To the confusion of the colonists, the French flag continued to fly over the Place d'Armes in New Orleans, and existing French officers were kept in place under the administration of Ulloa with the tepid support of the Spanish treasury. Former French governor Aubry was ordered by the French government to support Ulloa and the transfer. Ulloa asked Aubry to stay on as head of the French military and kept the Superior Council in place. Despite his tenuous authority, Ulloa imposed Spain's stiff trade restrictions on the colony to begin to rectify the territory's fiscal state. The Commercial Decree issued in September of 1766 drew immediate reaction from the merchants and planters. The most powerful among them met and drafted a petition to the Superior Council and voiced their concerns about trade restraint. Jacques Cantrelle was among the leaders and signers. Because Cantrelle was the commandant in charge of the militia in St. James Parish, his resistance was of concern to Ulloa. Tensions rose to an untenable level with the issuance of the Commercial Edict of 1768 that prohibited trade with the French Caribbean and limited trade to only a few Spanish forts.[307] Planters and merchants were in a frenzy and desperate to protect their financial positions. They lost all hope of returning to French rule when Milhet returned to Louisiana and reported that France had rejected the colonists' plea to rescind the cession of Louisiana to Spain.[308] Local meetings were held around the colony. Impassioned speeches whipped up even more animus toward Spain. Another meeting was called in New Orleans. An address to the Superior Council was drafted in which Ulloa was declared a usurper and oppressor. The document listed his numerous infractions, the most egregious of which was his failure to exhibit and register his credentials with the Superior Council or the citizenry.[309]

    A plot was devised to oust the governor and the formation of a new republic was considered. French Creoles with ties to the Superior Council set out to sow seeds of fear and resentment toward the Spanish among the German and Acadian settlers northwest of New Orleans. The newly arrived Acadians were told that Ulloa had no intention of helping them but planned to sell them into slavery. The Germans were led to believe that Ulloa would not pay them for the grain that had been purchased by his administration. Ulloa and Aubry learned of the rumors and sent Gilbert St. Maxent, a French officer who had aligned himself with Ulloa, to the German Coast to pay off the debts and calm the settlers' fears. The conspirators knew their plan would fall apart if St. Maxent fulfilled his mission. Nicolas Lafrénière, the attorney general and one of the principal leaders of the conspiracy, instructed Joseph Villeré of the German Coast and André Verret of the Acadian Coast to arrest St. Maxent.[310] They captured St. Maxent and held him at Jacques Cantrelle's plantation. According to Ulloa's account of the incident, the treatment of St. Maxent during his capture was cruel and inhumane. He wrote, "They tied him hand and foot. They walked over him with their horses. They made him row a boat for an entire day without giving him anything to eat or drink, calling him the most insulting of names, such as dog, rabble, and traitor to the fatherland of his sovereign. They locked him up later in a small, narrow pigeon with two men guarding him, pointing their drawn swords at his chest, threatening to kill him, and giving the same treatment to the slave who had come with him."[311]

On the morning of October 28, 1768, the Acadians and Germans marched to New Orleans and entered the city to join forces with the rebels there. Commerce in the city shut down and everyone anxiously waited to see what the insurgents might do. Ulloa feared for his own safety as well as that of his pregnant wife. Aubry spirited the Ulloas onto the Spanish frigate, *El Volante*. The ship was not seaworthy, so they sailed for Havana after boarding the French merchant vessel, *César*, at La Balize. They departed for Havana on November 16, 1768, and arrived in early December.[312] Ulloa immediately reported his version of the coup d'état to the Spanish Crown and identified the ring leaders: Denis-Nicolas Foucault, the financial officer of the colony, and Nicolas Chauvin de Lafrénière, the attorney general. King Carlos III sent General Alejandro O'Reilly along with 2,600 Spanish troops to quell the insurrection. Upon his arrival, O'Reilly hoisted the Spanish flag over New Orleans. He rounded up twelve of the leaders of the conspiracy and put them on trial. All were found guilty, and their property was confiscated. Lafrénière and three others were executed, and the rest were imprisoned for many years. O'Reilly gave amnesty to those who signed the petition to expel Ulloa. Even though Maxent was held captive at Jacques Cantrelle's home, he was not considered an instigator of the revolt.[313]

In the 1750s, Jacques Cantrelle donated land and money to establish the church parish of St. Jacques de Cabahannocer. The Mississippi River has long since claimed the original church. It was replaced with a new church in 1841. Jacques Cantrelle died on January 18, 1778, and was buried under the church altar. St. James is one of the original nineteen parishes created on March 31, 1807, by an act of the Orleans Territorial Legislature. Previously, it was referred to as the First Acadian Coast. It took its name from the church parish St. Jacques or St. James.

Michel Bernard Cantrelle
1750-1814

Michel Bernard Cantrelle was born in New Orleans on March 24, 1750. He was the son of Jacques Cantrelle and Marie Larmusiau. Like his father, Michel was a dedicated public servant as well as a planter. Michel moved to St. James Parish to his father's indigo plantation sometime after 1766. His brother-in-law, Nicolas Verret, had been running the family's plantations and was commandant of the First Acadian Coast. The Acadian Coast was a settlement above New Orleans on the east bank of the Mississippi River which is now St. James and Ascension Parishes. At age twenty, Michel was a lieutenant in the militia under Verret's command. When Nicolas Verret died in 1775, Michel took over as commandant. A short time later, Michel married Magdelaine Croiset, daughter of François Croiset and Marie Anne Trepagnier. Sadly, Magdelaine died in childbirth the next year in September 1778. She was buried in the cemetery near St. James church. A year later, on November 20, 1779, Michel married Madeleine Celeste Andry, daughter of Louis Antoine Andry and Marie Jeanne Lapierre. The marriage was witnessed by several dignitaries including Governor Gálvez.[314] Michel and his bride continued to live at his parent's home. Michel's brother, Jacques II, along with his sister Marie (the widow of Nicolas Verret), and her children also lived in the home.

Michel and his younger brother, Jacques II, served under Governor Bernardo de Gálvez during the American Revolutionary War. By 1779, war between Spain and Great Britain was imminent.

The Americans had already cultivated a relationship with Gálvez who had secret orders from King Carlos to admit, duty-free, 300 muskets with bayonets, 100 barrels of gunpowder, cloth, and medicine.[315] The supplies were shipped up the Mississippi River to Fort Pitt to help the American rebels. Gálvez was careful to keep his sanction of this and future shipments confidential as to maintain the illusion that Spain was neutral in the war between the American colonies and their mother country. When Spain declared war on England in May of that year, Gálvez was given permission by King Carlos to attack the British. Gálvez knew timing was critical to successfully defeat the British. Fort Bute, the British post at Manchac, had been reinforced with hundreds of German mercenaries. Rumors swirled of a British plan to capture important Gulf Coast posts via attacks from Canada down the Mississippi as well as from Pensacola. Just as Gálvez was getting ready to march toward Manchac, a ferocious hurricane struck dead center at New Orleans during the night of August 17. Nearly all Gálvez's ships were destroyed or grounded. The storm was so intense that some of his ships were found in the woods. Buildings, homes, crops, and livestock were destroyed. In addition, most of the provisions and arms for the attack were lost.[316] Gálvez called a meeting of the citizenry to inform them of the British threat to New Orleans and with great dramatic flair, asked for their assistance in defending their city. Despite their personal losses due to the hurricane, the men of New Orleans joined Gálvez's fighting force. Finally, on August 27, after his ships had been raised and repaired, Gálvez marched toward Manchac with five hundred Spanish regulars, sixty white Creole militiamen, eighty free blacks and mulattoes, and nine American volunteers from New Orleans.[317] Along the way, they stopped to gather more troops at the German and Acadian coasts. Seven-hundred sixty men, of whom one-hundred sixty were Native Americans, joined Gálvez. Michel Cantrelle and Jacques Cantrelle II, along with Nicolas Verret, their nephew, lead La Premiere Compagnie des Milices de la Côte des Acadiens, know by the locals as Cabahannocer Company. The Acadian Coast Militia fought under Gálvez at Baton Rouge, Manchac, and Mobile. The brutal heat and humidity of the Gulf Coast in August proved too much for many of the soldiers. Gálvez lost nearly a third of his troops along the 115-mile trek to Manchac. Once they reached Fort Bute, Gálvez was informed that most of the British soldiers had gone to Baton Rouge. Gálvez and his men quickly defeated the small garrison at Fort Bute and made their way to Baton Rouge after a six-day rest. Gálvez devised a plan to take the fort at Baton Rouge with as little bloodshed as possible. He instructed the militia to create a diversion in the woods surrounding the fort while he and his regular troops positioned munitions aimed at the other side of the structure. Michel Cantrelle was given command of four militia companies.[318] After several hours of bombardment, British Lieutenant Dickinson asked for terms of surrender. Gálvez demanded the submission of all forts along the Mississippi. Dickinson complied and the forts were ceded to Spain, even the strategically important Fort Panmure at Natchez.[319] Gálvez returned to New Orleans victorious and set about planning his attacks on Mobile and Pensacola. In March of 1780, Gálvez and his multi-ethnic forces successfully captured Mobile. Michel Cantrelle's leadership and valor during the battle earned him the rank and salary of lieutenant in the Spanish Royal Army. The following spring, Gálvez's Gulf Coast campaign was complete with the capture of Pensacola, the seat of government of British West Florida. Michel returned to the Acadian Coast after the Gálvez Expedition and remained commandant during the rest of the Spanish period.

In 1799, General Napoleon Bonaparte orchestrated a coup in France and established the governing body called the Consulate and named himself as First Consul. Napoleon had a grand scheme to expand the colonial empire in the West Indies and the Mississippi Valley. The islands of Guadalupe, Martinique, and Saint-Domingue would produce sugar, molasses, rum, coffee, and cotton for France. Louisiana and the Floridas were needed to supply French Caribbean troops with flour, timber, and salted meat. Furthermore, French goods would be marketed at New Orleans and sold from there along the Mississippi Valley.[320] Despite the relatively primitive conditions in the city, New Orleanians ate and dressed as if they were in Paris. Their desire for European finery was insatiable, so merchants had a ready market.[321] Napoleon immediately began negotiations with Spain to acquire Louisiana and the Floridas. He understood that Spain's control over Louisiana was weakened by the Pickney Treaty/Treaty of San Lorenzo between Spain and the United States in 1795. Spain pledged friendship toward the United States and relinquished control over what became the Mississippi Territory and recognized the 31st parallel as the United States southern boundary. King Carlos IV agreed to give Louisiana to France but refused to cede the Floridas. In exchange for Louisiana, the king received a throne for his son-in-law, the Duke of Parma in Italy. The Third

Treaty of San Ildefonso was signed on October 1, 1800, by French minister Louis Alexandre Berthier and Spanish secretary of state Don Mariano Luis de Urquijo. The final agreement of retrocession was not signed by Carlos IV until October 15, 1802.

On August 20, 1802, Napoleon Bonaparte appointed Pierre Clément de Laussat colonial prefect of Louisiana, but Laussat did not leave France for Louisiana until January of 1803; he arrived in March. Laussat was a member of the French legislature and helped write France's new constitution under Napoleon. Without the knowledge of Laussat or the people of Louisiana, the Louisiana Purchase treaty transferred the territory to the United States just one month later. Laussat's assignment changed, and his new position was commissioner of the French government for the retrocession of Louisiana from Spain to France and from France to the United States. Laussat was not given official notice of the impending transfer of Louisiana to the United States until August 18, 1803; however, speculation about the cession was rampant much earlier.

Even though his assignment changed, Laussat remained committed to getting to know the land and people of Louisiana to ensure a smooth transition. In November of 1803, Laussat began traveling along the Mississippi River's left bank. With the help of Jean Baptiste Charpin, he looked over the land and properties and traveled on horseback to notable plantations as well as the homes of some Acadian settlers. They stopped at the plantations of the Destréhans, Andrys, Trépagniers, LeBourgeois, and Bringiers to examine their operations and get to know the planters.[322] After spending two nights at the home of Marius Pons Bringier, Laussat and Charpin set off in a boat and traveled three hours upriver to Michel Cantrelle's plantation. Laussat commented in his account of the trip that he already knew Michel as he had given him some wood ducks, prized for their taste and beautiful markings. Laussat told of clouds of ducks overhead and on the water near Michel's plantation. Pierre Laussat described Michel as a "worthy and distinguished gentleman" and his sugar mill as "the finest and best arranged in Louisiana."[323] Michel's plantation also had a lumber mill that was among the largest in the area. Other smaller planters used his mills to process their sugar and lumber.

The Cantrelle plantation was located on land formerly inhabited by the Houma tribe. Ninety members of the Houma tribe remained in the area and lived in the backlands of the Cantrelle, Verret, and Judice lands.[324] Four families, about fifteen people, lived on the Cantrelle land. This group was led by Mico-Houma or Chac-Chouma.[325] Commandants were often liaisons between the government and local tribes.[326] The Cantrelles had a close relationship with the tribe members. Michel's children hunted with them and spoke their language, which was similar to Choctaw.[327] The Native Americans moved freely among the plantations and hunted and raised crops on the land.[328] The Houmas also spoke French, and some of the women took European names and wore European clothes.[329] Planters often relied on Native American hunters to add to their meat supply. They also helped to recapture runaway enslaved people.

In 1804, after the transfer of the Louisiana Territory to the United States, Michel Cantrelle was reappointed as Commandant of the First Acadian Coast by the American governor, William C. C. Claiborne. Claiborne was familiar with Michel Cantrelle's stature in the community as a Revolutionary War hero, a humble and trustworthy commandant, and a wealthy, well respected member of an esteemed old French family. Claiborne realized that Cantrelle could help the new government garner the citizens' support along the Acadian Coast. President Jefferson was impressed with Michel Cantrelle's credentials and reputation and directed Governor Claiborne to appoint him to the Legislative Council for the Territory of Orleans. Jefferson and Claiborne were somewhat concerned about Cantrelle's inability to speak English but thought that his appointment was important to gain the support of the Francophile population. Michel Cantrelle respectfully declined to serve on the legislative council and gave as his reason his lack of qualifications for so high a trust.[330] He was careful not to insult Claiborne and Jefferson, unlike Evan Jones, Étienne de Boré, and Daniel Clark who declined as a form of protest against the territory's governmental structure.[331] Cantrelle might have had some trepidation about not speaking English and being unfamiliar with American law. Michel Cantrelle's reticence to serve on the legislative council could have been financial as well. Spanish military officer, Sebastian Nicolas de Bari Calvo de la Puerta, known as Marqués de Casa Calvo, was His Majesty's commissioner for establishing the western border and limits of the province of Louisiana. Casa Calvo remained in Louisiana after the transfer from Spain to France and from France to the United States. He was thought to be the source of rumors that Spain might eventually take back Louisiana.[332] Casa Calvo also let it be known that he would revoke the pension of any militiaman who helped establish the American government. If this was true,

Michel Cantrelle had a lot to lose. He had served in the Spanish military for thirty years.[333] He also feared the loss of his position and property if Louisiana was retroceded to Spain yet again. Michel, no doubt, understood what citizens went through a generation before at the hands of Governor O'Reilly when they resisted the transfer of Louisiana from France to Spain.

Governor Claiborne did not hold Michel Cantrelle's decision not to serve against him. He remained Commandant of the First Acadian Coast until parish governments were reorganized in 1805. The position of commandant was eliminated, but Michel was named Parish Judge of the Parish of Acadia. This was the highest position at the parish level. Cantrelle managed to carry out his duties as a parish official and please American authorities while maintaining the respect of the citizens he served. Governor Claiborne was so impressed with Michel's integrity and adherence to the law that he used him as an example to President Jefferson that Louisianians were coming around to the American way of government. In a letter to Jefferson, Claiborne described Cantrelle, "The County Judge (a Mr. Cantrelle) supports a most excellent Character; he is a native of the Province, and has for forty years been a favorite of the people; he is a just, and human man; in his Character as Judge of the County, he gives universal satisfaction."[334] Claiborne told the president of a particular case in which Cantrelle showed that justice was meted out with impartiality. In Spanish Louisiana, favoritism based on social position, family ties, and wealth was the rule rather than the exception. Claiborne recounted the story when Judge Cantrelle upheld the petit jury's judgement against his son-in-law, Anselm Roman, and sentenced him to one month in prison and a $500 fine for assault.[335] Interestingly, although Claiborne lauded Cantrelle for his adherence to the laws of his new country, he ultimately pardoned Roman after hearing the circumstances of the case from Cantrelle.[336] In 1807, the Parish of Acadia was divided into St. James and Ascension Parishes, and Michel was named Judge of St. James Parish. Judge Cantrelle was concerned about his lack of knowledge of the American system of justice and worked tirelessly to conduct proceedings in a fair and judicious manner. He held his seat until 1812 when the new state constitution was ratified. Michel Cantrelle represented St. James Parish at the 1811 state constitutional convention and was one of five chosen to write the constitution's final draft.[337] Michel died on October 24, 1814, at the age of sixty-four. He was buried in St. James Catholic Church Cemetery.

Verret Family

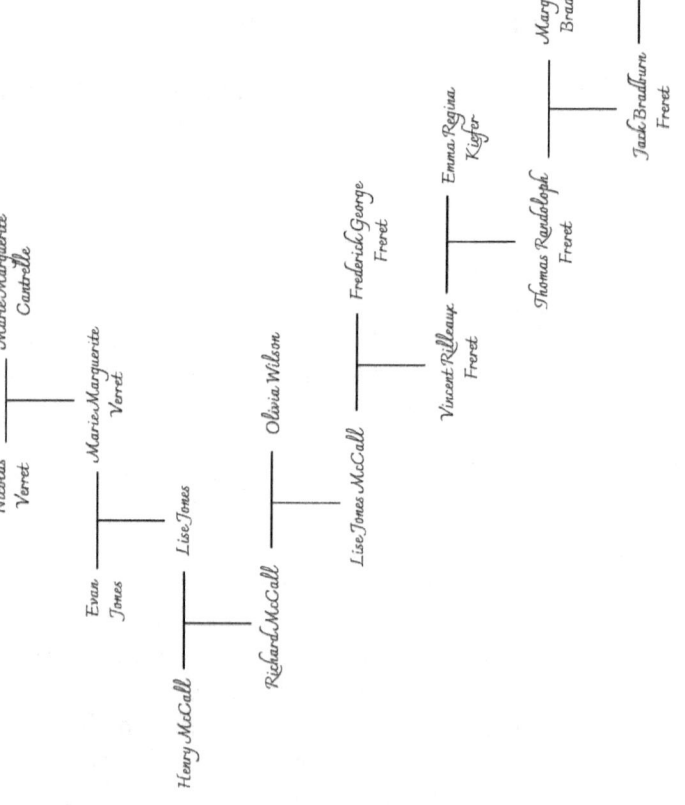

The Verret Family

Nicolas Pierre Verret

1725-1775

Nicolas Pierre Verret was born in New Orleans in 1725. He was the only child of Michel Joseph Verret and Marie Marguerite Bailliff. Nicolas's mother died when he was only four years old. His father married Marguerite LaBranche in 1732. The couple had six sons and raised them along with Nicolas in New Orleans. Michel Joseph died in 1747 when Nicolas was 22 years old and still a minor according to 18th century French law. After his father's death, his stepmother married Alexandre Bauré III. Bauré was named Nicolas' tutor and gave his permission for him to marry Marie Marguerite Cantrelle, daughter of Jacques Cantrelle and Marie Larmusiau. Nicolas was twenty-three years old, and Marie was sixteen. The couple had seven children and lived on Bourbon Street until 1763; they remained solely in New Orleans until 1769. After 1769, the couple divided their time between New Orleans and St. James Parish.

In 1762, Nicolas Verret obtained a land grant of ten arpents from French Governor Kerlerec and Nicholas Denis Foucault, the ordonnateur or chief financial officer of the Louisiana Territory. This was among the first land grants at Cabahonoce. The parcel was next to the land grants of his father-in-law Jacques Cantrelle and Louis Judice, who was married to Marie Jeanne Cantrelle, the sister of Marie Marguerite. Then, in 1765, Nicolas obtained a second land grant of twenty arpents front from Governor Aubry and Foucalt. Nicolas Verret's Cabahonoce Plantation was between the Mississippi River near

St. James and Bayou Lafourche near Plattenville. That same year, the French governor appointed Verret and his brother-in-law Louis Judice co-commandants of the district of the First Acadian Coast.[338] The two oversaw the settlement of the Acadian refugees that arrived from Halifax, Nova Scotia. Governor Aubry wanted them to watch over the settlement's progress and distribute food and supplies to those in need.

In addition to his duties as commandant, Nicolas managed his father-in-law's adjacent indigo plantation and finally moved his family to Cabahonoce in 1769. This move followed a particularly tumultuous time in Louisiana. France ceded Louisiana to Spain in 1762 in the secret Treaty of Fontainebleau at the end of the French and Indian War/Seven Years War. The transfer was kept secret for over a year so Spain could prepare to protect its new territory from British encroachment. However, Spanish governor, Antonio Ulloa, did not arrive in Louisiana until March 1766. A quasi-government was set up and French Governor Aubry remained in Louisiana until December of 1766. To add to the administrative confusion, Governor Aubry was involved in advising Ulloa and other Spanish officials until his departure. Before he left Louisiana, Aubry wrote to Ulloa and lauded the work of Nicolas Verret and Louis Judice and recommended that they retain their positions as co-commandants. He told of the heroic effort and sacrifice put forth by Verret and Louis Judice and his wife Marie Jeanne.

During Nicolas Verret's tenure as commandant, there was great distress among the Acadian settlers. Many of them suffered from disease and malnutrition. Their only nourishment was rice and corn which was allotted to them by the Spanish Crown. In June of 1766, Verret wrote to Governor Ulloa on behalf of the sick and suffering Acadian refugees and detailed their plight. He told of a pregnant woman who was so malnourished that she was unable to produce enough milk for her baby. Verret praised the king's generosity and humbly pleaded for relief for those in his district. Verret asked for aid, flour, and that a hospital be built to care for the sick settlers.[339] Eventually, Ulloa responded with aid; however, some Creole leaders convinced the Acadians that Ulloa was not to be trusted and that he would betray them. Uncertainty about the permanence of the cession, economic chaos, and the imposition of Spanish trade restrictions alarmed and angered the wealthy planters and merchants in Louisiana. Many Acadians joined the Creole rebels in the insurrection of 1768 in which Ulloa was ousted from Louisiana.[340]

Spain sent Governor Alejandro O'Reilly to bring order to the colony and punish those responsible for the insurrection. He formally appointed Nicolas Verret as commandant and Judge of the First Acadian Coast under his Catholic Majesty. Nicolas was retained as commandant despite the fact that his brother, André, was involved in the detaining and torture of Gilbert Antoine de St. Maxent, one of Ulloa's emissaries sent to the Acadian Coast prior to the insurrection of 1768.

As commandant, Nicolas' duties included preserving peace, examining travelers' passports, assisting settlers in obtaining land grants, preventing smuggling, registering the sale of land and enslaved people, acting as judge in minor cases, and serving as a notary public.[341] O'Reilly created a militia for each district and ordered that all males between the ages of sixteen and fifty serve in the militia. Land grants were contingent on military service. The commandant of each district was also the head of the militia. Nicolas Verret led the Verret Company of the First Acadian Coast. His brothers-in-law, Jacques Cantrelle II and Michel Cantrelle, as well as his sons, Jacques and Augustine, served under him.[342] Nicolas Verret served as commandant until his death on November 5, 1775.

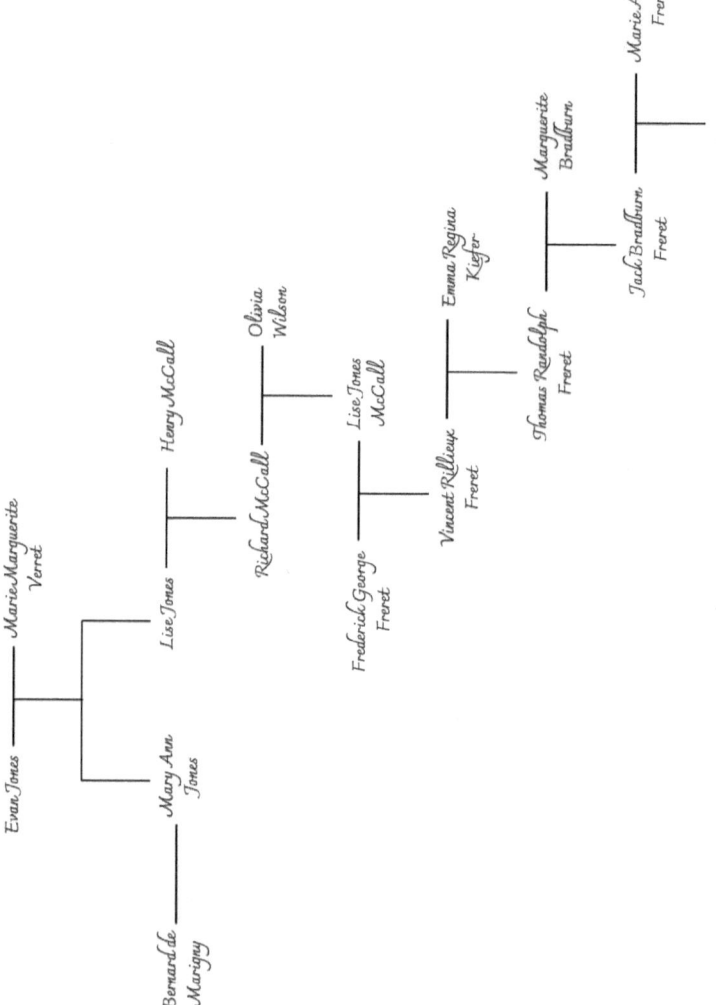

The Jones Family

Evan Jones
1739-1813

Evan Jones was an enigmatic leader in Louisiana. He was the son of devout Quakers, yet he was a Roman Catholic and a founding member of the Protestant Episcopal church in New Orleans. He was an American, a Spanish citizen, and an Englishman who was married to a French-Creole woman. He was a philanthropist as well as a slave holder and trader.

Evan Jones was the son of Dr. Evan Jones and Mary Stevenson. He was born in New York on August 17, 1739. In his early thirties, Evan worked for New York and Philadelphia mercantile houses that regularly did business along the Amite River in Spanish Louisiana and in Pensacola during the British Possession. In the mid-1760s, Evan and his brother, James, moved to British West Florida. Around 1765, the Jones brothers arrived in New Orleans from Mobile and expanded their enterprise into Spanish Louisiana with the help of George Johnstone, the Governor of British West Florida. Johnstone wrote a letter of introduction to Governor Antonio de Ulloa of Louisiana that described Evan Jones as "the most reputable man among us to make my compliments."[343] The Spanish welcomed Evan and James Jones and gave them land on the Amite River and Thompson Creek. The Joneses began producing indigo in addition to their trade business. The two brothers' land holdings spanned the Gulf Coast, which at the time was divided between Spain and Great Britain because of the Treaty of Paris that ended the French and Indian/Seven Years' War.

They supplied the Spanish and British colonists with flour, indigo, fur, and enslaved people. In addition to land in Louisiana, the Jones brothers also had large landholdings in British West Florida. In 1766, Evan Jones acquired patents to a commercial lot fronting on Pensacola Harbor and four hundred acres bordering East Lagoon.[344] The next year, Evan and James received title to some islands in Middle River and 50 acres of land on the mainland at Pensacola. They went into partnership with Jacob Blackwell, collector of customs at Mobile and member of the West Florida Council, and bought 500 acres of land on the East River above Pensacola. By the late 1760s, the Jones Brothers were well known throughout the Gulf South, were instrumental in the financial development of West Florida, and helped draw settlers to the area. Evan Jones was such an influential member of the community in West Florida that Lieutenant Governor Elias Durnford recommended him for a seat on the legislative council.[345] James Jones was already a member of the governing body.

The Jones brothers were honored to have leadership roles in the community and were tireless in their pursuit of integrity. In February 1770, Evan was involved in a duel with former lieutenant governor, Montfort Browne. The pervious August, West Florida Council member David Hodge, along with James and Evan Jones, accused the Lieutenant Governor of fraud. It is possible that the reason for the duel was that the Jones brothers questioned Browne's ethics. When Montfort Browne and Evan Jones faced off, Evan's gun misfired, and Browne got off a devastating shot. The bullet went straight through Jones but did not hit any vital organs. Even so, he was close to death for several days but eventually recovered.[346] The Provincial Council ultimately proved the allegations against Browne and sent him back to England.[347]

In 1769, Governor Alejandro O'Reilly was appointed by the Spanish Crown as Governor of Louisiana. During that time, James Jones remained in West Florida and Evan represented their interests in Louisiana.[348] O'Reilly was appalled to find that the trade restrictions put in place by the Spanish were all but ignored by British traders. He ordered British traders to leave the colony, but many simply moved to nearby British Manchac or Pensacola. O'Reilly managed to curtail the business of unlawful traders; however, many continued to supply the colony with flour, other food products, and enslaved people.[349] O'Reilly refused to admit that the British traders were thumbing their noses at his authority. Ultimately, necessity dictated that O'Reilly ease the restrictions on trade as supplies got low and people were desperate for the food and other goods that the outlaws could provide.[350]

Oliver Pollock, an enterprising Irishman who was reared in Philadelphia, was granted almost exclusive trade rights by O'Reilly. Pollock met O'Reilly years earlier when they were both in Havana. Because of their prior relationship, O'Reilly granted Pollock trading rights in the city to provide needed goods to the people of Louisiana. Pollock then persuaded O'Reilly to permit the Jones brothers to continue trading as well.[351] O'Reilly and the Joneses had a reciprocal agreement. The Joneses helped O'Reilly supply the colony, and in turn, he helped them and other English merchants collect debts owed to them by suppliers trading in the Spanish Port of New Orleans.[352]

O'Reilly was detested by the Creole population because of the execution and imprisonment of the rebels who ousted previous Governor Antonio de Ulloa. In 1768, there was a group of Creole planters who were opposed to becoming part of the Spanish Empire and resisted the restrictions placed on slave trading. They organized a rebellion and drove Ulloa from the colony. Shortly after O'Reilly arrived in Louisiana, he exacted justice and was dubbed "Bloody O'Reilly" by the Creoles. Interestingly, Evan Jones's future in-laws, the Verrets and Cantrelles, were intimately involved in the rebellion but were not among those who were imprisoned or executed.[353]

Having business in both West Florida, a British stronghold, and Spanish Louisiana forced Evan Jones to choose allegiances. In 1779, Spain declared war on Great Britain and secretly funded and supplied the American rebels. The Jones brothers were forced to become Spanish citizens after the fall of Mobile and Pensacola to Spain. Evan settled in Louisiana and became a Roman Catholic. Conversion to Catholicism was not mandatory, but those of other faiths could not openly practice their religion, nor could they marry another Protestant or Catholic without the presence of Catholic clergy. Evan Jones was pragmatic and ambitious. He knew that allegiance to Spain and the Catholic Church were essential to maintain and grow his business and political clout.

That same year, Evan Jones became a member of the Spanish

Company of the Distinguished Caribiniers Militia.[354] Governor Gálvez of Louisiana created this elite militia for the sons of large slave holders. It followed that Jones was a part of this unit as he supplied many enslaved people and products to wealthy planters. Jones joined the cavalry unit after the capture of Baton Rouge. He then served with the Iberville Militia and German Coast Disciplined Militia. It does not appear that he ever saw action.

The Jones brothers fared well as Spanish citizens. They, along with other Louisiana based Anglo-Americans, used their East Coast trading connections to facilitate shipments of ammunition for the American Continental Congress during the War for Independence.[355] Evan Jones became further entrenched in Louisiana and in 1780 purchased more land and a home in the Lafourche District. The next year, he married Creole Marie Marguerite "Pomponne" Verret, daughter of Nicolas Verret.[356] The couple maintained homes in New Orleans and Lafourche and had four daughters and three sons. The eldest and youngest sons died in childhood, and one of their daughters, Mary Ann, who was married to Bernard de Marigny, died when she was 26 years old.

Evan Jones entered the Creole world by marrying into an old French family. He wanted to further connections with Spanish authorities, so he began networking. Jones asked his nephew, Philemon Dickinson, to write to General George Washington on his behalf. In his letter to Washington, Dickinson asked him to facilitate an introduction for Jones to Louisiana governor General Bernado de Gálvez.[357] Washington noted his affection and respect for Dickinson, but politely declined on the basis that he had had very little contact with Gálvez and would not feel comfortable intervening. Even without Washington's help, Evan and James Jones continued to amass a great fortune. By 1782, the relaxed trade limitations became permanent, and the Jones brothers expanded their trade business. Two years later, Evan Jones operated a sanctioned slave trading firm and merchant business in New Orleans, and his influence grew.[358] Jones became an asset to the Spanish as he had close ties to the elite French Creole population through his father-in-law. He also spoke French, Spanish, and English so he could communicate and do business with all the citizens of Louisiana. The Jones brothers suffered a significant financial setback when they lost their New Orleans homes and their warehouse full of merchandise in the Good Friday fire of 1788. They were able to weather the loss but dissolved their partnership in about 1891 before James left for an extended trip to Europe.

In 1797, Governor Manuel Gayoso named Evan Jones Commandant of the Lafourche District. His tenure as commandant was short and began with controversy. Early in 1798, Jones antagonized the Isleños, the Canary Island settlers in the district. He threatened to confiscate their land if they did not keep the levees in good repair. The Islanders reported Jones's actions to Spanish authorities. They claimed that Evan Jones demanded that they work to repair levees owned by the Crown. The Isleños refused to do the work because they would have been required to work without pay, and that was not the way things were supposed to be done. To make matters worse, Jones then assessed the Isleños people to pay for the levee repairs. Although Governor Gayoso and Evan Jones had a good personal relationship, the governor decided to send a representative to meet with the Isleños and hear their grievances. Governor Gayoso knew that the Crown could not afford to have colonists upset with Spanish authority because that could impact their ability to draw new settlers to the area. Gayoso sent Captain Francisco Rivas to meet with a group at the home of one of the Isleños leaders. Before Rivas could submit his report to Gayoso, Jones resigned, citing personal reasons.[359]

Shortly after his term as commandant was over, Evan Jones took an extended trip back to the East Coast and reconnected with family and friends there. His brother, James, had returned to the United States and was killed in a duel in New Jersey in May of that year. Evan was the executor of James's estate, and he probably had to tend to the probate and business affairs of his brother. He was also named tutor of James's son, James, whose mother was his former slave, Aggy. James Jones met his fate at the hands of Henry Brockholst Livingston, an attorney and son of the former Governor of New Jersey. Livingston, a Republican, penned an editorial that poked fun at James Jones, a Federalist. Jones took offense at the jab and reportedly confronted Livingston when he happened upon him strolling with his wife and children on the streets of New York. Jones struck him with his cane and tried to tweak his nose. Livingston was incensed by the gesture that publicly humiliated him, and he challenged James Jones to a duel. On May 9, 1798, the two met across the river in New Jersey at the Weehawken Cliffs.[360] This was a frequent choice of duelers as New Jersey had more lenient laws concerning duels, and the venue was hidden from sight.[361] Livingston fired a single shot and killed Jones. The Federalist newspapers clamored for justice, but public sentiment was with Livingston for having been accosted in front of his wife and children. Livingston was never prosecuted for James Jones's death, although the incident is said to have caused him great angst throughout the rest of his life. Henry Broadhurst Livingston's career was not impacted by Jones's killing. He became a justice on the Supreme Court of New York and was appointed as Associate Justice of the United States Supreme Court by Thomas Jefferson.

While on the East Coast, Evan Jones began a quiet campaign to be named American Consul from the United States to Spanish New Orleans. Secretary of State Timothy Pickering wrote to President John Adams on Jones's behalf. Pickering said that he met Evan Jones through General Philemon Dickinson while he was visiting from New Orleans. Pickering asked President Adams to consider appointing Jones as consul to New Orleans. He enclosed a letter from General Dickinson attesting to Jones's character. Pickering lauded Jones's accomplishments and stated, "Mr. Jones's intimate knowledge of the Spanish government and weight of character there [New Orleans] would be highly advantageous."[362] President Adams agreed to Pickering's request and approved the commission. Pickering was unaware that General Dickinson had introduced Evan Jones to the president while Jones was visiting. Adams was complimentary about his meeting with Jones and said that he would expect nothing less from the brother of such a family.[363]

When Evan Jones returned to New Orleans from the East Coast, he learned that his friend and ally, Governor Gayoso, had died. Upon his arrival, he presented himself as United States Consul to acting governor for military affairs, Colonel Francisco Bouligny. Jones was dressed in his full American Navy uniform.[364] Bouligny recommended that Jones not be recognized as consul because he had accepted the position while still a Spanish subject.[365] Bouligny said that Jones's acceptance as consul would have to come from the Captain General of Cuba, Marqués de Someruelos. The Captain General was furious about the appointment because he too considered Jones a Spanish subject. He went so far as to call the acceptance of the appointment treasonous and ordered Evan Jones's arrest. Governor Casa Calvo intervened on Jones's behalf and told Somerielos that Jones was an important person in the community and was very wealthy and well thought of in New Orleans. Casa Calvo cautioned against creating a problem with the United States. He feared that, in retaliation, the United States might make it difficult for the Spanish officials at Natchez.[366] Somerielos did not enforce the arrest order but refused to recognize Jones as consul. Jones, however, continued to act as consul.[367] Casa Calvo's pragmatism only went so far. Later that year, the governor revoked the standing of vice-consul Hulings and refused to accept Jones as consul. Jones felt so strongly about his commitment to serve in his position as consul, despite opposition from Spanish officials, that he continued to serve for a year and a half without pay.[368] He even risked his livelihood as a trader. The Intendant-general, Ramon Lopez de Angulo, filed a petition in Saint-Domingue to revoke Evan Jones's international trading privileges. The case ended when Spain ceded Louisiana back to France in October of 1800 and the action was dropped.[369]

Non-recognition of Jones as U.S. consul not only affected Jones personally but had implications for the United States concerning trade in Louisiana. Evan Jones wrote several letters to Secretary of State Timothy Pickering outlining the problems, but the secretary was unresponsive.[370] After Thomas Jefferson was elected, Evan Jones reiterated the plight of American traders in New Orleans to the new Secretary of State, James Madison. Jones explained that he believed that Spanish practices in New Orleans were in violation of the Pickney Treaty that provided for free navigation of the Mississippi River by American ships. In the letter to Madison, Evan Jones defended his right to be U.S. consul regardless of the claims of the Spanish. Jones said that it was ridiculous that he was assumed to be a Spanish citizen when he accepted the appointment. He explained that he was living in West Florida and became a de facto Spanish citizen when Mobile fell. An emotional Jones wrote, "You will observe Sir that the Marquis [Casa Calvo] now affects to regard me as an officer in the Spanish Militia. It is true that I was formerly ordered to act as such, and did obey; but it is equally true that the Marquis has for near two years past had in his possession the original letter of his predecessor in office, Don Francisco Bouligny, accepting in a most formal manner my resignation, and thanking me for my services.

"It is also certain, that ever since the Marquis' arrival in New Orleans, now near two years, he has seen me publickly (sic) wear the Uniform of the American Navy, (which has now become so offensive to him) without making the smallest objection to it; and moreover, he knows, that I did not put that Uniform on, but by the express permission of his Predecessor, signified to me in writing, by the then, and present Secretary of Government!

"It is of little consequence to my Country, (however it may affect me) whether I wear a brown coat or a blue one; but the Marquis, not content with cavilling (sic) at my dress, has in his letter of the 30th of April, ordered me in the most positive terms, to refrain from every Consular function; and, having no power to resist, I must obey."

Ultimately, Thomas Jefferson and James Madison relieved Evan Jones of his position as U.S. Consul. They understood that Jones's contentious relationship with the Spanish made him ineffective. He was replaced by Daniel Clark, a wealthy NewOrleans merchant.

Unbeknownst to Jones, the people of Louisiana, President Jefferson, and Secretary Madison, Louisiana no longer belonged to Spain as of October 1, 1800. Once again, the people of Louisiana had little agency over their citizenship. President Jefferson was unaware of the secret Treaty of San Ildefonso that retroceded New Orleans from Spain to France until the fall of 1801. In August of 1802, Napoleon appointed Pierre Clément Laussat to serve as Colonial Prefect of Louisiana to handle the transition of Louisiana from Spain to France. Laussat arrived in New Orleans in March of 1803. The Jefferson administration was concerned about the development and worried that navigation of the Mississippi would be affected, so they decided to offer to buy New Orleans. A month after Laussat's arrival, Napoleon agreed to sell not only New Orleans, but the entire Louisiana Territory to The United States. Laussat, however, did not receive official notice of the sale until August of that year. In June of 1803, Laussat was appointed as commissioner of the French government for the retrocession of Louisiana from France to Spain and then from France to the United States.

The official retrocession to France took place on November 30, 1803. The ceremony was a formality to placate the Franco-centric population. Spanish governor Juan Manuel Salcedo turned over the keys to Laussat. The Marqués de Casa Calvo, the previous governor, then released all Louisiana residents from their oaths of allegiance to Spain. This declaration officially ended the question of Spanish citizenship for Evan Jones.

The transfer of the Louisiana Territory to the United States would take place just one month later. In the interim, Laussat dismantled the Cabildo and set up his own municipal government and planned for a smooth transition to the United States. He appointed Étienne de Boré as mayor and formed a city council, *conseil de ville*, made up mostly of influential French businessmen and merchants. Laussat felt this gesture was important to honor the memory of those Frenchmen who had been killed under the O'Reilly administration. Laussat wisely included three Americans on the council: Jones, Donaldson, and Watkins.[372] Evan Jones was an astute choice. He was an experienced businessman, had a working relationship with Spanish merchants, had served as the American Consul to Louisiana, and was married to a member of the influential French Verret family. Jones's appointment on the council could help integrate political and cultural factions. He spoke fluent French and Spanish and had intimate ties to both, yet he was an American.

On December 20, 1803, Louisiana changed hands for the tenth and final time. Laussat presided over the formal transfer of the Louisiana Territory to appointed governor-general and intendant William Charles Cole Claiborne and General James Wilkinson. In his address, Laussat assured the residents of Louisiana that they would be endowed with all the rights of American citizens as he quoted from the treaty. He absolved all Louisianians of their allegiance to France. At that moment, the clash of cultures began. The young Anglo-Saxon Protestant, William C. C. Claiborne, did not know how to relate to the mostly Catholic population. Frenchmen, Spaniards, Germans, Americans, Native Americans, and people of African descent made up the culturally diverse community. Claiborne did not speak French, nor was he familiar with Louisiana culture or customs. In addition,

Louisianians saw Claiborne's far-reaching power as unprecedented and regarded him with suspicion. Evan Jones, because of his ties to all parts of the community, could have been a valuable ally to Claiborne, but the two were at odds from the beginning.

Early in 1804, Congress passed an act for the organization of the Orleans Territory and the Louisiana District. The act divided the Louisiana Territory into the two sections, the Territory of Orleans (most of present-day Louisiana) and the Louisiana District (land above the 33rd parallel). The merchants and planters were opposed to many of the act's provisions. Of particular concern was the lack of representation of the people and the stipulation that enslaved people could not be imported from other countries or other parts of the United States. This restriction on slave trade was seen by many as unfair as this was not the case in other parts of the Union such as Charleston, South Carolina. Also, the division into two sections made population requirements for statehood more difficult to meet.

Governor Claiborne became the lightning rod for the Jefferson administration's policies. Although it was customary for the United States to require a learning period for citizens of territories that were formerly part of countries with non-republican forms of government, Louisianians felt that they were being treated unfairly. It didn't help that Claiborne had given a less than positive assessment of the Louisiana citizenry to Secretary of State Madison, and his opinions were made public. In his letter to Madison, Claiborne described the inhabitants as mostly honest but stated, "The Merchants as well as the Planters in the country appear to be wealthy: their habits of living are luxurious and expensive: but, by far the greater part of them are deplorably uninformed... Frivolous diversions seem to be among their primary pleasures: and the display of wealth and the parade of power constitute their highest objects of admiration ... But the principles of a popular government are illy (sic) suited to the present state of society in this province."[373] Thomas Jefferson heeded Claiborne's advice and signed the bill that granted only quasi-citizenship to Louisianians despite national debate and opposition from some in Congress like John Quincy Adams. Under the act, the president had total control over the governor and would appoint the legislative council.

Claiborne understood that the rich and powerful of the Orleans Territory were quite unhappy with the act and their perceived ill treatment by their new government. Discontentment grew, and on May 16, 1804, Mayor Étienne de Boré resigned after the New Orleans Municipal Council refused to file a formal protest against the act. A short time later, Colonel Bellechasse, commander of the New Orleans Militia, and Pierre Derbigny, secretary register of the council, also resigned.[374] Claiborne knew he had to act quickly to quell the unrest amongst the powerbrokers. The once vibrant economy of New Orleans was stymied by the prohibition of slave importation and the devaluation of paper money used under Spain.[375] Claiborne attempted to placate the merchants and planters and keep the New Orleans economy viable by granting their request to establish the Louisiana Bank. He did so without the approval of President Jefferson or the Treasury Department. Governor Claiborne named Evan Jones, Pierre Sauvé, and Beverly Chew to distribute the shares.[376] Ultimately, Jefferson ordered the bank charter revoked because the establishment of the bank violated federal banking laws.

After the notice of revocation of the bank charter, Claiborne recognized that he had to rededicate himself to his goal of successfully integrating the French and Spanish Creoles into the United States. This would prove more difficult than the American governor anticipated. On May 31, 1804, a public meeting of planters and merchants was held to discuss grievances concerning the act. The leaders were Evan Jones, Daniel Clark, Étienne de Boré, and Edward Livingston. Edward Livingston was a recent arrival to New Orleans, but quickly became part of the city's political and social elite. Edward Livingston's connection to Evan Jones helped him enter the tight-knit society of New Orleans. Edward Livingston's cousin Philip had close ties to Evan Jones from his days in Pensacola where he was secretary to the governor of British West Florida. Also, Philip's cousin, Margaret Livingston, was married to Evan Jones's brother, Thomas.[377] Interestingly, Henry Broadhurst Livingston, who killed Evan's brother James, was Edward Livingston's cousin.

Previously, Edward Livingston had been the mayor and district attorney of New York. He was appointed by Thomas Jefferson as recompense for helping him with his election campaign in New York.[378] Also, Edward's brother, Robert Livingston, negotiated the Louisiana Purchase for the Jefferson administration. Edward Livingston resigned his position in New York under intense pressure from the Jefferson administration after financial irregularities were discovered in the New York District Attorney's office. Although it was ultimately proven to be a clerk who embezzled the funds, Livingston's reputation was tarnished by the affair. Livingston vowed to make restitution but knew he had to leave New York to resurrect his career.[379]

At the meeting in New Orleans, which was held with Governor Claiborne's cautious blessing, the assembly chose Evan Jones, Edward Livingston, James Pitot, and Pierre Petit to write a remonstrance to Congress regarding the Governance Act.[380] Edward Livingston wrote the actual document. The memorial began by assuring the members of Congress that the undersigned merchants of the City of New Orleans were loyal to the United States and would abide by the Constitution which "holds out to them the enjoyment of the equal Rights and Privileges of Citizens."[381] The Memorial laid out the dire consequences of the Governance Act for both commercial and agricultural interests. It closed with, ". . . such arrangements will put us on equal footing of citizens of the United States from the Moment their Flag was hoisted in the City."[382] These words echoed Article III of the cession treaty with France. The Memorial was presented at a second public meeting on July 1, 1804. Pierre Derbigny, Jean Noël Destréhan, and Pierre Sauvé were selected to present the Memorial to Congress. All three men served on the City Council under Laussat.

Governor Claiborne was concerned about the letter to Congress and knew he had to inform his superiors in case they heard rumors and assumed he did not have the situation under control. Even though he was suffering from yellow fever, he wrote to James Madison and President Jefferson and told them what he knew about the yet unseen Memorial. While nearly sixty merchants signed the Memorial, Claiborne specifically named Edward Livingston as the writer, supported by Daniel Clark and Evan Jones.

In the meantime, General James Wilkinson, governor of the Louisiana District, supplied the Jefferson administration with intelligence on prominent men from the Orleans Territory that might make suitable leaders and legislative representatives. Evan Jones and a Mr. LaBigarre were the sources of the information. Jefferson's notes indicated that the opinions of LaBigarre were suspect, but said of Evan Jones, "his manners stiff, but his integrity irreprocable (sic), has decent talents and a better kndege (sic) of the province than any other American."[383] These notes were based on information that the president got from Secretary of the Treasury, Albert Gallatin, who knew Jones from New York.[384] As expected, the character sketch of Evan Jones that was provided to Jefferson was complimentary. He was described as "a man of education, an American by birth and by attachment. He is talented, proud, high spirited, rich, ardent, and decisive at sixty-five years of age."[385] Jefferson also asked Claiborne to provide a list of prospective candidates for the legislative council. Claiborne's deliberations and answer took longer than Jefferson was willing to wait. Claiborne sent his list to Jefferson on August 17, but by August 16, Jefferson had already sent his tentative list to James Madison.[386]

In a letter dated August 30, 1804, President Jefferson informed Claiborne that he was to be governor of the territory and listed other leadership appointments. The Frenchmen Jefferson named were Boré, Poydras, and Bellechasse. Jefferson directed Claiborne to select three others from a list of Frenchmen. The Americans listed were Benjamin Morgan, Daniel Clark, Dr. Watkins, Evan Jones, Roman, and Wikoff. Claiborne was to choose between George Pollock and Dr. Dow for the seventh American seat.[387]

Claiborne responded to Jefferson on October 5. He lauded the president's choices of judges and secretary. He explained that Derbigny, Sauvé, and Destréhan were not selected because they would be the bearers of the Memorial to Congress and would not be able to attend council meetings. Claiborne respectfully took issue with Jefferson's selection of Evan Jones. He wrote, "I have communicated to the Secretary of State [Madison], the conduct of Mr. Evan Jones (one of the counsellors) will not appear in favorable Light." Jones was not on Claiborne's list of recommendations, but Jefferson undoubtably knew of Jones's power, intellect, linguistic ability, and connections to both the Creole and American communities. Claiborne followed Jefferson's instructions and sent each man, including Evan Jones, a letter informing him of his appointment. By October 8, Dr. Watkins had accepted, but Evan Jones had declined his appointment. In a letter to Governor Claiborne, Jones thanked President Jefferson for such an honor but stated ". . . but in my present situation I do not feel myself at liberty to accept the appointment. Conjointly with almost all the Inhabitants of Lower Louisiana I have signed a Memorial to Congress."[388] The next week Jones published his letter in the local papers and the story was picked up in newspapers around the country.[389]

Critics viewed Jones's public refusal as political maneuvering and a grab for political power in a developing political party.[390] Jones was publicly skewered in an opinion piece in the *Union*. The writer alluded to Jones's love of money and questioned the veracity of his self-sacrificing statement, "– but I cannot consent, for the consideration to do an act which I think subversive of the rights and liberties of my fellow citizens."[391] Another, even more blistering condemnation of Jones's character was penned a short time later and published in the *Union*. Flagellus, the writer, doubted Jones's claim, "I was born an American – I glory in the name." Flagellus pointed out that Jones was born a British citizen in New York and was a Spanish subject in Pensacola. He went on to say that Jones's new-found patriotism was a product of political animus. Flagellus accused Jones of having a vendetta against the United States due to his removal as American Consul. The writer contended that Daniel Clark, his replacement as Consul and one-time political rival, was now an ally in Jones's anti-administration scheme.[392]

William Claiborne continued to be wary of Jones's political influence over the other appointees. He wrote to James Madison that he suspected that Jones's goals were to embarrass the local government and to force Congress to acquiesce to the wishes of the memorialists.[393] Claiborne sent another letter to Madison a few days later and personally attacked Evan Jones and questioned his ability to sustain his influence over other appointees. He wrote, "There are some persons who believe him dishonest, and there are but few whose Esteem and Confidence he processes."[394] However, Claiborne underestimated the resolve of some of the other appointees. Later, he regretfully informed Secretary Madison that Mr. [Michel] Cantrelle and Mr. [Daniel] Clark had also declined to accept positions as members of the legislative council. He expressed relief that Julien Poydras had accepted his commission, but worried that if others followed Jones, there would not be enough members to form a quorum.[395] A follow-up report was sent to President Jefferson. Governor Claiborne listed those who declined their commissions: Stephen de Boré, Evan Jones, Michael Cantrelle [Michel Cantrelle], Jack Romain [Roman], Gaspar Dubus, Bellechasse, and Robert Dow. Those who accepted were Julien Poidras [Poydras], William Wikoff, Benjamin Morgan, John Watkins, and William Kenner. In addition, recently named members who were serving on the council were George Pollock and Eugene Dorcier.[396] Claiborne was finally able to get a quorum by December but by the barest of margins. There were times between December 1804 and March 1805 that a quorum could not be obtained. Even so, Claiborne did not appoint new members. He could not afford to set himself up for further public rejection and humiliation.[397]

In December of 1804, Derbigny, Destréhan, and Sauvé, arrived in Washington D.C. and delivered the Memorial signed by 2,000 heads of families. The letter was introduced to the House of Representatives by Maryland Republican Joseph Nichols. Nichols summarized the requests of the memorialists and said, "Louisianans prayed for an alteration of the law so far as to allow them to be their own legislators, not dividing the Territory into two governments, and not prohibiting the importation of enslaved people."[398] Finally, a new bill for the Government of the Orleans Territory was crafted and passed on March 2, 1805. The new act gave the Territory of Orleans ordinary territorial rights, an elected legislature, and a delegate to Congress. The Memorialists saw this as a failure. They were not granted statehood, and little had changed, since under the new act, the federal government could restrict the operations of the laws made by the Territorial Legislature.[399]

Louisiana was in a state of turmoil. Louisianans were unsure of their place in the Union. Would they remain Americans? After all, Louisiana had changed hands ten times since it was claimed by René Robert Cavelier, Sieur de La Salle for the King of France. There were rumors that Spain would recapture the territory if mounting tensions escalated into war over the border between Louisiana and Texas. Moreover, the new Governance Act provided little solace to those who wanted full rights as United States citizens. Former Vice President, Arron Burr, saw the unrest in Louisiana as an opportunity to resurrect his flagging political career. Thomas Jefferson replaced

Burr on the ticket for the election in 1804. Burr then decided to run for governor of New York but lost in a devastating defeat. Burr was outraged at the things Alexander Hamilton said about his character during the campaign and partially blamed him for his defeat. Burr challenged Hamilton to a duel. Historians disagree about exactly what happened during the duel, but Alexander Hamilton was mortally wounded and died thirty-six hours later on July 12, 1804.

Smarting from political defeat and negative public reaction to the killing of Hamilton, Aaron Burr headed south and stopped at Blennerhassett Island near Parkesburg, West Virginia, in mid-1805. In early June, he met with General Wilkinson, governor of the Louisiana Territory at Fort Massac. Wilkinson provided Burr with a barge and supplies. He also wrote letters of introduction for Burr to his wealthy and powerful friends and former Spanish officials in New Orleans. Burr arrived in New Orleans on June 25, 1806. Rumor and speculation were that Burr was planning some sort of plot to regain political power. Exactly what Burr intended to do is unclear. The scuttlebutt around Washington D.C. was that Burr endeavored to separate the western states and territories from the United States and set up a new country. However, Burr told British officials that his objective was to capture New Orleans and West Florida. A third scenario shared by Burr to General Wilkinson and Daniel Clark was the invasion of Mexico. Publicly, Aaron Burr was simply surveying and settling the land he bought on the Ouachita River.[400]

Aaron Burr remained in New Orleans for three weeks. While he was there, Burr stayed at the home of Edward Livingston and was often in the company of Daniel Clark and Evan Jones.[401] Interestingly, General Wilkinson, who was an officer in the United States Army, put Burr in contact with those who opposed Governor Claiborne and were leaders of the Mexican Association. The Mexican Association was a group of about 300 New Orleans businessmen who supported the liberation of Mexico and other Gulf Coast Spanish holdings to form a new country.[402] General Wilkinson was not new to intrigue. From 1797 until 1811, he was known as Agent 13 in the Spanish Secret Service.[403] Evidence suggests that four U.S. presidents: Washington, Adams, Jefferson, and Madison, as well as members of their Cabinets and Congress knew about Wilkinson's duplicity, yet they continued to turn a blind eye to his double life. They needed his military leadership and didn't want the country to think that the military had run amok. This would be counter to the principles of the young nation. Wilkinson denied any impropriety and fiercely guarded against proof of his acting as an agent for Spain.[404]

Burr left New Orleans in July and traveled to Tennessee, Kentucky, and Missouri gathering support for his plans. In July of 1806, Aaron Burr sent a coded letter to General Wilkinson telling him that he had "commenced the exercise." He later told Wilkinson that he estimated that the capture of New Orleans would take about three weeks.[405] Up until September of that year, Burr was convinced that the people of New Orleans would support his venture.[406] On September 8, Burr wrote to Daniel Clark and wanted to meet. Clark did not meet him and responded that he would not be involved in Burr's plan and had to leave for Washington D.C.[407] Remarkably, Clark left for Congress without informing Governor Claiborne of the threat to New Orleans, and neither did any other officials who knew of the plot. Eventually, General Wilkinson had a change of heart and informed President Jefferson of Burr's plan; however, not until Burr had started his trek toward New Orleans. Wilkinson probably betrayed Burr because he became concerned that his double-agent activity would be found out. General Wilkinson arrived in New Orleans in November of 1806 and requested that Governor Claiborne declare martial law to protect against the city's capture. Claiborne refused because he felt that was the province of the legislature. President Jefferson had already gotten intelligence reports about Burr's actions and sent additional troops to protect New Orleans. Burr was unaware of the developments and continued to press toward the city. His operatives contacted General Wilkinson to enlist his support but were told that he would fight the traitors.

Wilkinson proceeded to make arrests of the most conspicuous of Burr's supporters, despite Claiborne's refusal to institute martial law. Curiously, neither Daniel Clark, Edward Livingston, nor Evan Jones was among those arrested. It is possible that the three powerful men had too much knowledge of General Wilkinson's involvement, so he did not want to be at odds with them.[408] Aaron Burr was arrested several times and released due to lack of evidence. He was finally brought before Chief Justice John Marshall on March 26, 1807. Marshall ruled that there was insufficient evidence for treason but scheduled Burr for trial on high misdemeanor charges. President Jefferson was furious about Marshall's decision and did everything he could to see that Aaron Burr was convicted. Even though President Jefferson took a personal interest in the trial and appealed to his countrymen to come forward with information, Burr was acquitted.

General Wilkinson was court martialed and investigated for treason, but he was never indicted. Daniel Clark was closely associated with Aaron Burr, and many assumed that he was intimately involved in the conspiracy. He blamed Wilkinson for furthering this idea to the public. Clark was so distraught about his marred reputation that he wrote a book that defended his name and pointed a finger at Wilkinson, branding him a Spanish spy. In his book, Clark included a letter from Evan Jones as proof of General Wilkinson's corruption. In the letter, Jones recounted a time in 1789 that General Wilkinson stopped at his plantation on his way to Kentucky. During the visit, General Wilkinson told Jones that he [Wilkinson] had left a large sum of money in the care of someone who was so strong that he could take $2,000 with one hand from off a mule or horse. Clark used this retelling in his book as evidence of Wilkinson's ill-gotten gains. It's unclear if Evan Jones had any involvement in the Burr conspiracy, but it seems likely since he kept company with Burr while he was in New Orleans and had a personal relationship with some of the other major players: Wilkinson, Clark, and Livingston. After Clark's death, Wilkinson published his side of the story and defended his honor while attacking Clark's integrity.[409]

During the aftermath of the Burr trial, in December 1807, General Wilkinson's wife Nancy was dying of tuberculosis. She was still in Natchez at the time but was brought downriver to New Orleans to be with her husband. Mrs. Wilkinson was taken to the home of Evan Jones's daughter and son-in-law, Mary Ann and Bernard de Marigny. She remained there until her death on February 23, 1808. Bernard de Marigny served as the aide-de-camp to General Wilkinson until 1808. Given the intimate nature of such a position, it seems unfathomable that de Marigny was unaware of General Wilkinson's role in the Burr conspiracy or his clandestine activity. Ironically, Evan Jones served as foreman of the grand jury that indicted Judge James Workman and Lewis Kerr for being leaders of the Mexican Association and making a military expedition against a foreign state with whom the United States was at peace.

After the Burr conspiracy, Claiborne's detractors fell out of political favor in New Orleans, and the Creoles, who had been supportive during the call to arms to defend the city against Burr, rose in power. Evan Jones did not hold political office after his refusal to serve on the Territorial Council, but he continued to expand his business interests. In 1806, he was nominated as a territorial delegate for the U.S. House of Representatives but was narrowly beaten by Daniel Clark. He was on the board of regents for the University of Orleans that was established in 1805 and was on the board of directors of the United States Bank at New Orleans from 1810 to 1811.[410] Evan Jones was involved in the early years of granular sugar production in Louisiana. During the late eighteenth century, Étienne de Boré successfully produced granular sugar on a large enough scale to turn an incredible profit. He realized a $5,000 profit from his 1796 harvest and processing.[411] Ever the astute businessman, Evan Jones saw the potential for sugar cultivation and refining. In 1807, he began planting and processing sugarcane on his land in Lafourche. Jones used horse-powered mills and open kettles to refine his sugar.[412] Evan and his wife, Marie Verret, lived between their homes in New Orleans and at their large farm in Lafourche.

Evan Jones's service to his community went beyond civic and business interests. In 1806, he was one of the incorporators of Christ Church, the first Protestant Episcopal Church in Louisiana. Evan converted to the Roman Catholic faith during the Spanish possession of Louisiana so he could marry Marie Verret and remain in favorable standing with Spanish officials. Evan had deep Quaker roots from his parents and grandparents and might have felt called to go back to his Protestant faith toward the end of his life. An appeal to the Protestants of New Orleans was published in the *Louisiana Gazette* on April 30, 1805. The writer lamented the fact that the English population had found it important to be immersed in political dissension but had not taken any steps to provide for ministry. The author urged Protestants to execute a plan for providing for a church and clergy. Evan Jones was among the fifty-three Protestants who met to form a new religious association. They planned to raise money to build a church, secure an act of incorporation, and voted to elect the Protestant denomination among Episcopalian, Presbyterian, and Methodist. Episcopalian received the most votes, possibly due to its similarity to Roman Catholicism in the predominantly Catholic city. The founders selected Philander Chase as the church's first clergyman. He preached his first sermon on November 17, 1805, at the Cabildo. Services were held at various buildings around the city until 1816 when the church was built.[413]

Evan Jones was a devoted father. That he married off his daughter Mary Ann to the immature gadabout Bernard de Marigny seems inconsistent with that idea. However, it was the practice of the day among the elite to cement and grow political and economic dynasties through marriage. In May of 1804 Mary Ann Jones married Bernard de Marigny. Bernard was an eighteen-year-old French Creole who stood to inherit his father's large estate when he reached the age of majority. He was under the guardianship of Solomon Prevost. Prevost was married to Evan Jones's sister-in-law, Marguerite Verret. Bernard de Marigny was politically connected and very wealthy. During the retrocession period, Pierre Laussat and his family lived on the top floor of the Marigny home while Laussat was Prefect of Louisiana.[414] The marriage of his daughter strengthened Jones's ties to the Creole elite and allowed him to create strong political and social alliances with other powerful planters and merchants.

Bernard de Marigny was a controversial figure to be sure, but historians disagree as to the depths of his depravity and irresponsibility. Bernard de Marigny's family was among the *Ancient Régime* of prerevolutionary France which elevated his social status and power. His father died when Bernard was fifteen or sixteen years old. His mother, Jeanne Marie Destréhan, died two years before her husband. As the oldest son, Bernard inherited most of his family's considerable fortune. He was sent away to Pensacola, Florida, and London for mercantile training, but he was called back to New Orleans because tales of his wild behavior were reported to his guardian.[415] Local lore painted the young Marigny as reckless with money, a gambler, and a philanderer. Some in the Anglo-American community looked down on Bernard because of his decadent lifestyle. In a letter to Thomas Jefferson, Elizabeth Trist referred to him as a "very rich but dissipated creole."[416]

According to the marriage contract, Bernard de Marigny was worth $100,000 which included landholdings, enslaved people, and debts owed to him.[417] Shortly after the marriage, Bernard became even wealthier by speculating in land deals. As Bernard was only eighteen at the time, his affairs were still under the care of his guardian, Solomon Prevost. Under Prevost's guidance and through an act by the Legislative Council, Bernard subdivided his plantation near the city and offered the lots for sale. He held the mortgage on many of the properties and made money on the notes' interest. Bernard employed engineer Barthelemy Lafon to layout the streets. The Conseil de Ville passed an ordinance on May 18, 1805, that authorized Marigny to establish Faubourg Marigny, the first subdivision outside of the city.[418] A story repeated in many accounts of his life claims that Bernard de Marigny had to sell his plantation land to pay off gambling debts. This seems to be myth instead of fact as the Marigny fortune grew considerably after the establishment of the Faubourg.[419]

Mary Ann Jones and Bernard de Marigny had three children together. Clement, their first son, was born in 1805 and died in infancy. The next two sons, Prosper and Gustave, were born in the following two years and survived until adulthood. The next year, Mary Ann became gravely ill. It is unclear what the illness was or whether she contracted tuberculosis from Nancy Wilkinson, who died in her home two months earlier. Evan Jones knew he had to do something to try and save his daughter's life. He and one of Mary Ann's sisters took her to the East Coast to some warm springs. Elizabeth Trist, a New Orleans transplant, wrote to her friend Thomas Jefferson to ask if the Joneses might stay with him at Monticello on their way to the Springs. Trist acknowledged in her letter that Evan Jones's politics didn't align with theirs, but that he was a gentleman.[420] The Joneses might have been headed to Warm Springs in Bath County, Virginia, as that is where Thomas Jefferson later went to get relief from his rheumatism. It was a frequent practice for the well-to-do and elite to drink and bathe in the mineral waters of warm springs in hopes of curing illness. Evan Jones and his daughters never made it to Monticello. Instead, they went directly to Philadelphia. It is possible that their plans changed because Mary Ann became desperately ill, and Evan decided to take her to Philadelphia for medical care. Before their deaths, Evan's brothers, John and Thomas, were physicians in New York and later in Philadelphia. His cousin, Thomas Cadwalader, had also been a physician in Philadelphia. It is likely that Evan sought help from some of their colleagues. The doctors in Philadelphia were unable to save Mary Ann. She died there on June 15, 1808. Evan and his daughter took Mary Ann's body home to New Orleans. She was buried in the corner of the garden on her plantation in a sepulcher that her husband had made for her. Father Antonio de Sedella blessed the land and the tomb before her burial.[421]

Evan Jones died on May 11, 1813, and was buried in the cemetery in Donaldsonville. His remains were eventually moved to New Orleans and reinterred in the McCall tomb in St. Louis Cemetery No. 1. In his will, Evan Jones stated that he wanted to be buried on the right-hand side of his beloved children, James and Thomas, in an enclosure that he had made in the Protestant burial grounds of New Orleans. At one time there was a Protestant section of St. Louis No.1. Part of it was in the way of an extension of Tremé Street. In 1822, the city offered Christ Church a tract of land in the Faubourg St. Mary for a new Protestant cemetery, which later became known as the Girod Street Cemetery. By the 1830s, all Protestants were moved to Girod Street or elsewhere in St. Louis No.1. Thomas and John Jones are not listed on the McCall tomb, so it is unclear where they were finally buried or if Evan's wishes had been followed and he had initially been buried next to them. It is possible that Thomas and John's remains were placed in the Girod Street Cemetery, but it was closed and repurposed in the 1950s.

Evan Jones's will was a tribute to those he loved. He carefully selected personal items to be bequeathed to specific family members and loved ones. He left his wife, Marie (Pomponne), his repeating watch as a sign of his affection and friendship and his mourning ring with the hair of his deceased brother James. Mathilde, his eldest daughter, received her brother John's watch and Evan's silver pencil case. Thomas's gold watch was left to his youngest daughter Lise. Evan left his seal ring with his crest on it to his middle daughter,

Celeste. Evan seemed to mourn the deaths of his children years after they died. He referred to them as "beloved" and "never to be forgotten." Thomas died in 1796 from yellow fever. That was the year of the first epidemic in New Orleans when 695 people died. It is not known how or when John died.

Evan Jones named his daughter Mathilde as one of the executrixes of his estate and praised her for her industry, care, and good conduct. He made it clear in his will how much he trusted his wife's judgement and that she was to be given the authority to make all decisions regarding their two minor daughters, Lise and Celeste. Although Evan Jr. was the eldest and a male, he was not named executor. Evan Sr. stated that his son had made imprudent business deals and engaged in misconduct. Even so, he directed that one half of his estate go to Marie, while the other half should be divided among his children and grandchildren with Evan getting an equal share to his sisters. However, advances that were given to him would be counted against his inheritance from his Uncle James Jones. Evan took great care to see that his brother James's child was cared for. In 1810, when Evan's will was written, Jim was twenty years old. He was to receive the five hundred dollars left to him by his father as well as the interest earned on the money while he was under Evan's guardianship. Evan provided for the young boy's education and well-being after his father's death.

Marie Verret lived eight years after her husband's death and died in 1821. The year of Evan's death was brutal for the Jones family. Evan, Marie's only surviving son, died just two months after his father. Mathilde died three months after her father's death. There is no information about the causes of the deaths; however, it is plausible that they were a result of disease since they died close together and were young. Celeste was married for a short time to Henry McCall and died in 1815 without any children. Lise, Marie's only surviving child, married her sister's widower in 1817 and had six children.

Bringier Family

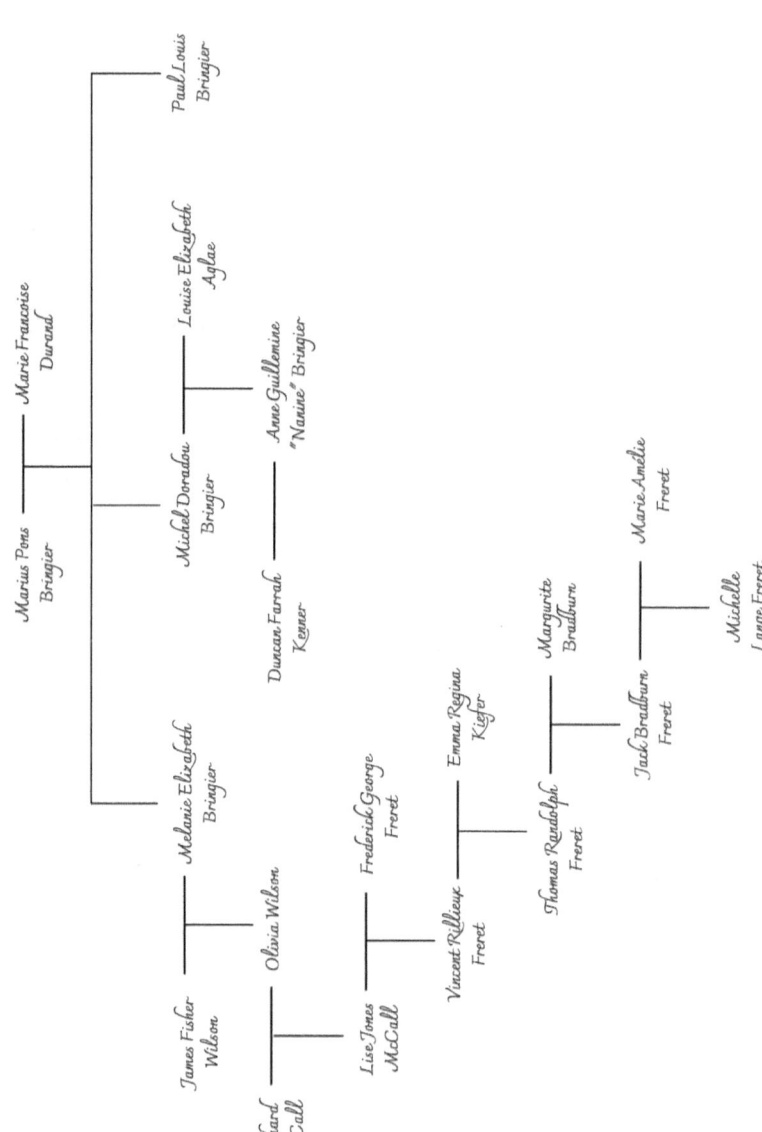

The Bringier Family

Emmanuel "Marius Pons" Bringier
1752-1820

Marius Pons Bringier was born in Provence and was the youngest of twenty sons born to Pierre Bringier De Lacadiere and Louise Agnes Arnoux.[422] In 1781, Marius Pons left France with his wife Marie François Durand to avoid the political tensions that were brewing and to seek his fortune in the Caribbean. The couple sailed for Martinique where Marius Pons and his brother Vincent became partners in a plantation.[423] Life on the island was not easy for the young Bringier couple. Marie gave birth to two babies, each of whom lived only a few days.[424] Marius and his brother's business failed and the two had a falling out. Marius decided to head for the Spanish colony of Louisiana to begin again. The Bringiers set sail with their belongings and the enslaved people who worked their land and arrived in New Orleans in 1783. They acquired land in the Tchoupitoulas district above New Orleans and set to work establishing a plantation. Marius Pons Bringer also established himself as a merchant and supplied planters of the Acadian and German Coasts with necessities and enslaved people.[425] Marie gave birth to the couple's first son, Paul "Louis," in 1784. Marius worked diligently at planting and caring for his crops, but the location proved to be a poor choice due to frequent flooding from crevasses in the levee.[426] Living and working conditions were so difficult that many of the enslaved people who worked the land became ill or died.[427]

In 1785, the Bringiers decided to abandon the plantation and move to present-day St. James Parish. The rich soil of the First Acadian

Coast and cooperative weather conditions allowed Bringier's indigo and tobacco crops to flourish. Soon he invested in an adjacent plantation and finally three more. By 1789, Marius Pons Bringier owned a string of properties that he consolidated into one massive plantation he named Maison Blanche. Despite their French heritage, the Bringiers chose to call the plantation by its English name, White Hall.[428] Marius Bringier was an innovator and leader in the community. He was the first planter in the Mississippi Valley to import cotton seed. He experimented with the crop at his own plantation and offered seeds to planters up and down the Mississippi River from his home near present-day Donaldsonville to Baton Rouge and Pointe Coupee. After the first growing season, Marius sent his son Louis and a work crew of enslaved men to collect the cotton from other planters. The planters received proceeds based on shares. The cotton was then ginned and bagged at White Hall. Marius Bringier contracted with Daniel Clark to export the cotton.[429]

The Bringiers' family and fortune grew. Another son and four daughters were born at White Hall.[430] The home was an enormous French Gothic château appointed with marble covered exterior walls and marble walkways.[431] The magnificent exterior hinted at the luxurious interior that included tapestries, elaborately carved mahogany furniture, ornate silverware, and oil paintings.[432] The family spent their winters in their city home, a townhouse on Canal Street.

Marius Pons Bringier's unmatched hospitality was legendary. All travelers along River Road were graciously welcomed at White Hall and provided with private visitors' quarters, a personal servant, and meals. The plantation was one of the centers of social activity in St. James Parish. The Bringiers were known for throwing elaborate dinner parties and entertaining dignitaries such as the Spanish governor and Pierre Laussat, the French Colonial Prefect in charge of Louisiana's transition during the Louisiana Purchase. In 1798, the exiled Duc d'Orléans, the future Louis-Philippe King of France, and his brothers visited White Hall. The Bringiers hosted a dinner in their honor. Marius Bringier spared no expense in entertaining his royal guests. They dined on local delicacies like snipe, shrimp, and fish and drank rare wines. The extravagant party was talked about among Louisiana's elite for years. There were exaggerated accounts that included stories of the china plates being smashed against the marble fireplace at the end of the meal because they never again would have such royal guests.[433]

As the patriarch of the Bringier family, Marius Pons generously provided lives of privilege for his children. Like most young French Creole men of means, sons Louis and Doradou Bringer were educated in France. His daughters and their husbands were given plantations and business opportunities; however, the young women had little control over their own lives. Their father chose their husbands and gave them no choice but to abide by his wishes. Françoise "Fanny," the eldest daughter, was the first to marry. In 1801, Fanny's brother, Louis, arrived home at White Hall with Christophe Colomb, a Frenchman and Saint-Domingue refugee whom he met in New Orleans. Louis enlisted the help of his charming friend to explain to his father how he had lost such a large amount of money gambling in New Orleans when he was supposed to be there representing his father's business interests. Colomb entertained the family with his worldly knowledge and colorful stories. Marius Pons was so taken by Christophe that he forgave Louis and invited the visitor to stay at White Hall. The thirty-one-year-old Frenchman was offered Fanny's hand, and he married the sixteen-year-old on January 26, 1801, in St. James Church. Marius gave the couple a piece of land and had a house built for them. Bocage was beautiful, and the couple, despite their age difference, seemed well suited to each other. It soon became apparent, however, that Christophe was interested in art and music, not managing a plantation. Fortunately, Fanny had her father's drive and business acumen. Wealthy Southern women of the era were often educated by tutors, and their study usually focused on reading and writing. They studied grammar and composition with an emphasis on letter writing and scripture. The daughters of planters were often schooled in basic mathematics so they could understand the plantation accounting.[434] Fanny would have received such an education but was not expected to manage a plantation on her own. However, she realized that if Bocage was going to succeed, she would have to take the almost unprecedented step and run the plantation's affairs. She consulted books and sought advice from friends and family members.[435] The unconventional couple was married for twenty-five years until Fanny's death in 1827.

Elizabeth Louise "Betzy" was the next to marry. Two years later, she followed in her sister's footsteps and was betrothed to a French refugee from Saint-Domingue who was also a much older man. Augustine Tureaud was the son of a wealthy aristocrat in LaRochelle France. He was sent to Saint-Domingue to manage a plantation owned by his father after his behavior with women and vices had embarrassed the family. He was forced to flee Saint-Domingue for New Orleans during the revolution there. He established himself as a merchant and cotton factor and was invited to White Hall to assess some of the Bringer cotton that was to be part of a business deal between the two men.[436] Inclement weather forced Augustine to extend his visit for two weeks. During that time, he and Marius Pons grew close as they reminisced about life in France and the Caribbean. Marius Pons enjoyed the affable A.D.Tureaud's company so much that he offered to establish a business partnership with him with the caveat that he must marry his fourteen-year-old daughter Betzy.[437] Tureaud's account maintained that Marius Pons stipulated that Betzy had to agree to the marriage. Most accounts claim that Betzy was horrified at the thought of marrying the grey-haired, thirty-eight-year-old man but finally acquiesced. When Betzy was fifteen, the couple was married on May 24, 1803, at White Hall. Marius Pons gave the couple a plantation home and land he named Union. A.D. shed his reckless lifestyle and had an illustrious business career and life as a public servant. Augustine Tureaud managed Bringier's stores in New Orleans. Marius Pons Bringier established the first general country store in Louisiana. Family ties ensured that Marius Pons's interests were carefully looked after by someone with keen business skills. In 1803, A.D. was appointed to the Municipal Council by French Colonial Prefect Pierre Laussat. In his notes, Laussat referred to Tureaud as son-in-law of M. Bringier and one of the best businessmen in New Orleans. After the Louisiana Purchase, Governor William C.C. Claiborne appointed Tureaud captain of the cavalry and commander of the militia under Commandant Michel Cantrelle. A.D. remained in St. James Parish and served as treasurer of the Acadia District, justice of the peace, and finally as judge in St. James Parish from 1812 until his death in 1826.[438]

The youngest daughter of Marius Pons and Maire Durand, Melanie

Elizabeth, married William Simpson of Savannah in January of 1809, when she was fifteen years old. Melanie's dowry was considerable. Her father gave William Simpson $4,000 in Louisiana Bank stock and $8,000 in cash. Simpson was a partner in the Indian trading house of John Forbes and Company based in Mobile and Pensacola. Simpson handled operations in their New Orleans location. The company held enormous tracts of land in Florida that they obtained from the Choctaw Nation as repayment of debt, the most famous of which was 1.3 million acres of land in West Florida along the Apalachicola River known as the Forbes Purchase.[439] Additionally, William Simpson was a land speculator. One of his biggest purchases was 20,000 arpents along the Amite River in the St. Helena section of the Baton Rouge District.[440] Sadly, Simpson died in 1813. The couple had no children, so he left the bulk of his estate to Melanie. The young, wealthy widow moved back to White Hall to live with her parents.[441] Melanie was involved in managing her assets and worked closely with her husband's former business associates. She grew particularly close to James Fisher Wilson and married the Scotsman in 1816. They quickly established a family; a son and a daughter were born by 1820. Tragically, James died in 1821 while Melanie was pregnant with their third daughter.

White Hall was once again the venue for a grand wedding when Françoise "Laure" Bringier married Noel Auguste Baron Jr. on May 12, 1810. Baron was French like two of the other sons-in-law and was a successful commission merchant or factor. The year he and Laure were married, Baron went into business with P. F. (Pierre François) DuBourg, a close friend and business associate of Marius Pons Bringer. The firm of DuBourg and Baron represented many of the wealthy planters of southern Louisiana.[442] Noel and Laure lived on St. Charles Avenue in New Orleans and raised their seven children. They did not have a residence in St. James like the rest of the Bringier family. Noel died in 1833 and left an insolvent estate, and Laure was unable to provide for herself and her young children.[443] Ultimately, her brother Doradou and her son Jules provided her with a house.[444]

MICHEL "DORADOU" BRINGIER 1789-1847

Michel "Doradou" Bringier, the son of Marius Pons, was the quintessential Creole planter and owner of L'Hermitage Plantation, given to him by his father.[445] He was an aide-de-camp to General Andrew Jackson during the Battle of New Orleans. Doradou was educated in Paris and was deeply connected to his French heritage. Doradou named his plantation L'Hermitage after the home of his commander, General Jackson. Doradou's was also an arranged marriage to young fourteen-year-old Louise Elizabeth "Aglae" DuBourg de Ste. Colombe. Aglae's father, Pierre DuBourg, was a successful commercial agent who often represented the business interests of Marius Pons Bringier. The marriage cemented the business alliance between the two families. After the death of his father in 1820, Doradou bought White Hall from the estate. His reputation for honesty and his head for business were unmatched among his peers. He amassed a great fortune and was one of the wealthiest people in Louisiana.[446] Aglae and Doradou split their time between L'Hermitage and Melpomene, their New Orleans mansion. They had a large family, three sons and six daughters, and lived a socially active but quietly respectable life. In following with the customs of the elite, Doradou made sure his daughters married well and enlarged the Bringier dynasty. Marie Elizabeth "Rosella," the oldest of the daughters, married Hore Browze Trist, the ward of Thomas Jefferson. Louise Marie "Myrthe" married Richard "Dick" Taylor, son of President Zachary Taylor. The youngest of the Bringier daughters, Anne "Octavie," married General Allen Thomas who became the United States Minister to Venezuela.[447] The marriage of Anne Guillemine "Nanine" Bringier to Duncan Farrar Kenner was perhaps the most beneficial to ensuring the continuation of the Bringier legacy in terms of maintaining and expanding their plantation holdings.

Duncan Farrar Kenner
1813-1887

Old-line Creoles like the Bringiers and influential Anglo-Americans intermarried; however, this scenario typically required that the Americans who married Creoles spoke French and honored and took on many of their Franco-centric customs. This was the case with the marriage of Duncan Kenner and Nanine Bringier. Duncan Kenner was born in Louisiana and was the son of Virginian William Kenner and Natchez-born Mary Minor. Shortly after they were married in 1801, the William Kenners emigrated from the American Natchez Territory to Spanish New Orleans. William Kenner was successful in real estate, commercial trade, and commission enterprises and served on the Legislative Council under Governor Claiborne. His biggest financial venture was as a commercial agent or factor for planters.[448] Factors extended credit to planters until their crops were sold. They also served as middlemen between planters and buyers in Northern or English houses or sent crops directly to New York or Liverpool.[449] It was advantageous for factors to form relationships with successful planters. William Kenner often represented the Bringer family.[450] It is through his father's business and social connections that Duncan Kenner met and married the Creole heiress.[451] Kenner was an acceptable match because he spoke fluent French, had traveled extensively in Europe, and was schooled by this father in Creole culture. Although Duncan Kenner was an American by birth, he clearly understood and was accepted in Creole society.

During the Civil War, Duncan Kenner was a representative in the Confederate legislature. Toward the end of the war, Kenner convinced New Orleanian Judah Benjamin, who was the Secretary of War for the Confederacy, and Jefferson Davis, the President of the Confederacy, that he should be part of the delegation to persuade Britain and France to officially recognize the Confederacy as a sovereign country. Kenner was chairman of the Ways and Means Committee and realized the Confederacy's dire financial straits. As part of this last-ditch effort for European support, the Confederacy pledged to abolish slavery. With Jefferson Davis's approval, Duncan Kenner, under the alias A.B. Kingslake, snuck across union lines to New York. On February 11, 1863, he sailed from New York to Britain. By the time Kenner reached London with the petition, it was too late. The Confederacy had all but lost the war after General Sherman's string of victories.[452]

Kenner's sugar plantations in Ascension Parish, Ashland and Bowden, were among the most successful in the South before and after the Civil War. Kenner was a forward-thinking planter and employed innovative equipment and methods for cultivating sugar. Ashland was raided by Union forces in July of 1862, shortly after New Orleans fell to the Union Army in March of that year. The Union army sent 300 men to raid the plantation and arrest Kenner for his role as a representative in the Confederate Congress. Kenner evaded capture and escaped to Europe with his family, but his prized thoroughbreds were confiscated, the house was sacked, and his assets were seized.[453] Duncan Kenner and his family remained in Europe after the war ended while he considered his options. Kenner knew that many of the South's political leaders like Jefferson Davis were in prison, while others like Judah Benjamin had also escaped to Europe.

With great apprehension, Kenner decided to return to Louisiana and rebuild his fortune. General amnesty was granted to Southerners in an attempt to put the nation back together. However, President Johnson's plan for amnesty included particularly harsh conditions for those in the planter class and who were leaders of the Confederacy. Confederates who owned property valued at more than $20,000 had to personally apply for amnesty and ask for forgiveness.[454] Kenner went to the United States embassy in Paris to take an oath of allegiance to the United States and was interviewed about his role in the

Confederacy. Kenner denied having a leadership role and omitted his mission to Europe on behalf of the Confederacy. His pardon was eventually granted, and his property was returned to him. Upon his return to Ascension Parish, he found that Ashland and Bowden were in better shape than many other plantations because they had remained operational during the war through the federal government's leasing program.[455] Kenner once again turned his attention to sugar as well as cotton and other investments. He used the proceeds from his real estate investments to finance rebuilding his plantations. As was the case before the war, Kenner used modern technology like the Rillieux apparatus on his sugar plantations to rebuild his wealth.[456] He is credited by many as having been one of the driving forces behind the post-war recovery of the sugar industry in Louisiana. Kenner was the president of the Louisiana Sugar Planters' Association, an organization formed in 1877 to lobby to maintain the sugar tariffs currently in place and to investigate and report on the latest technological advances in the sugar industry. He remained the president for ten years until his death in 1887.

In an often-repeated story in the slim information about Norbert Rillieux, Duncan Kenner found his old collaborator and acquaintance in the Bibliothèque Nationale in Paris deciphering hieroglyphics. In addition to his business relationship with Norbert Rillieux, Kenner had close ties to Rillieux's relatives, the Musson/Degas family. In 1880, while visiting Rillieux, Kenner asked him about his new work on perfecting his process for evaporation. Kenner's visit to see Norbert Rillieux was likely intended to get Rillieux to bring his knowledge and expertise to Louisiana sugar planters to energize the industry and give it a competitive edge in the world market.[457] Duncan Kenner remained a vocal advocate for the sugar planters of Louisiana until his death.[458]

Paul "Louis" Bringier "Don Louis" 1784-1860

Paul "Don Louis" Bringier was an engineer, surveyor, planter, explorer, cartographer, geographer, miner, geologist, naturalist, secret agent, and filibuster. He was the firstborn son of Marius Pons Bringier and Marie Durand. Don Louis was the black sheep of the Bringier family. From most accounts, he didn't even look or behave like the rest of his relatives, and some in the family would have preferred not to be associated with him.[459] He had dark hair, grey eyes, olive skin, and a muscular build but was only five-foot four and somewhat unattractive. He was brilliant and inquisitive like others in the family, but he was also wily, impetuous, flashy, and temperamental.[460] Don Louis's moniker probably came from an encounter with the Spanish Governor Francisco Luis Héctor, Baron de Carondelet.[461] In 1796, Governor Carondelet visited Louis's father at White Hall. Marius Pons, true to his reputation, was the consummate host and spared no expense when he entertained the governor. Governor Carondelet was so appreciative of his host's extraordinary generosity that he wanted to compensate him, but Bringier would not hear of accepting payment of any kind. Governor Carondelet decided that he must show his gratitude, so he gave twelve-year-old Louis a land grant of 40,000 acres where the Black and the Ouachita Rivers merge.[462] His nickname, Don, was a Spanish honorific title given to gentlemen of distinction and wealth. It was probably a sardonic statement about Louis's land ownership at such a young age.

Like most elite Creole young men, Louis was sent to Paris for his education and probably studied engineering given that he worked on machinery and flood gates on his father's estate. Once he returned to Louisiana, he assisted his father in running the plantation. Marius Pons was impressed with his son's abilities and sent him to New Orleans to conduct business transactions and collect payments. Family lore alleges that Don Louis was just sixteen years old at the time.[463] The wiles of the city proved too much for the exuberant youth. While in New Orleans, he was seduced by women, spirits, and gambling and squandered his father's money. Don Louis knew his father would be angry and disappointed, so he enlisted the help of his new friend, Christophe Colomb, whom he met while in New Orleans.[464] The pair set off for White Hall, and Colomb succeeded in charming Marius Pons into forgiving Louis, but it would take time for him to earn back his father's trust.

In the meantime, Louis joined the Mexican/South American scientific expedition of the world-famous naturalist Alexander von Humboldt.[465] Humboldt's work was revered by the scientific community. Charles Darwin credited Humboldt's narrative of his journey with inspiring his longing to travel to distant lands and emulate the way he studied.[466] Humboldt was born in Prussia in 1769. He was trained at the School of Mines in Saxony, and in 1792, he was appointed to the mining department of the Prussian government. He rose to a supervisory position and traveled around Germany. He established his own mining school and invented mining technology. His work in the mines afforded Humboldt the opportunity to observe geological formations and collect samples. He honed and broadened his knowledge and skills by reading works by the great scientists, philosophers, and economists of the time. Humboldt conducted his own experiments and published articles about his findings.[467]

After five years in the mines, Humboldt longed to explore further.[468] He used his considerable inherited fortune to fund an expedition to the Spanish colonies in Central and South America. He was granted a royal permit to do so by the Spanish prime minister and set sail with French botanist Aimé Bonpland. They spent five years, 1799 – 1803, collecting samples, exploring, mapping, and observing natural phenomena and the cultures of the aboriginal people in New Spain.[469]

Humboldt took meticulous care to produce accurate maps. He used newly calibrated instruments and compared his findings to those of earlier explores.[470] During the final year of the expedition, he drew a new map of Mexico while at the Royal School of Mines. It was the most extensive and complete map of the region to date.[471] During the final leg of his journey, Humboldt spent time studying Mexican mines. At that time, New Spain was the world's number one producer of silver, yielding two-thirds of the world's output.[472]

In 1804, after his time in Mexico and South America, Humboldt visited the United States. He longed to return to Paris where he worked and studied for many years but stated in a letter to President Jefferson, "I could not resist the moral interest of seeing the United States and benefiting from the consoling nature of a people who know how to appreciate the precious gift of liberty. I hope I can have the good fortune of paying my respects to you in person and admiring at close range a philosopher-magistrate who is admired on two continents."[473]

Humboldt saw Jefferson as a kindred spirit in both science and politics, humbly requesting a visit with him and wondering if the president had heard of him. President Jefferson responded and assured Humboldt that he was familiar with his work. Jefferson conveyed his utmost respect for the renowned scientist and welcomed his visit.[474] The president understood that Humboldt's maps of Mexico could provide him with much needed information about the United States' disputed border with Mexico.

After his trek through Mexico and South America with Humboldt and Bonpland, Louis returned to New Orleans and served in the Orleans Militia with his father. Over the next two years, he worked for his father and proved himself to be a valuable asset to his business operations in New Orleans. When Louis was twenty-three, Marius Pons gave him a piece of property and a house on Charters Street in the French Quarter as an advance on his inheritance. Louis sold the property less than a week later to Joseph Tricou, but two days after that, Marius Pons bought the property back from Tricou.[475] It is possible that Louis sold the property given to him by his father to pay off gambling debts. At first, Don Louis resisted the lures of the city, but again he gambled away his father's money as well as his own.[476] He was embarrassed and dreaded his father's disappointment. Don

Louis's pride and unconventional spirit propelled him to embark on a quest to prove himself worthy of the Bringier family. He took off on adventures and gained and lost fortunes while he was away from home. Louis did not return home to White Hall for several years, probably not until sometime between 1813 and 1814.

Family members claimed they did not know where Louis was when he disappeared, and they were grief stricken. His mother was distraught and prayed for his safe return.[477] The Bringers later found out that Louis was exploring the Arkansas and Missouri territories.[478] Most accounts of Louis's life put him in Arkansas in 1810 but do not tell his whereabouts from 1807 to 1810. The Bexar Archives, the official Spanish documents of Texas under Spanish and Mexican rule, have orders for the arrest of Louis Bringier and a description of his physical appearance which were disseminated throughout the Interior Provinces. It is unclear why there was a warrant for Louis's arrest, but authorities apprehended him, and he was in the royal prison in January of 1810.[479] While there, Louis divulged to his captors that Napoleon Bonaparte would invade New Spain in May of that year.

It is possible that Louis returned to Mexico during that period to search for gold and silver and seek his fortune. While traveling with Humboldt, Louis learned about Mexican mines and developed the skills needed to prospect for the precious metals. While there, he might have been branded an illegal immigrant and/or an agent for Napoleon Bonaparte. Prior to 1808, settlers from Louisiana were welcomed in New Spain. That changed in 1807 when Napoleon's army occupied Spain and forced the abdication of King Carlos IV and his son Ferdinand. The following year, Napoleon named his brother Joseph King of Spain, which included New Spain. Napoleon decided to use agents to garner support for his brother's authority. In the initial stages of the operation, Napoleon used freelance operatives to promote support of his brother's reign. Ultimately, Napoleon realized that maintaining control of the Spanish American colonies would take valuable resources away from his efforts in Europe. Rather than cede the territory to another country, he hoped that Latin Americans would rebel and gain their independence. He instructed his agents to work to foment revolution and promote liberation. In 1808, there was pushback against immigrants living in Latin America. The Mexican viceroy ordered the arrest of all aliens and the confiscation of the property of every Spaniard who supported Napoleon's brother as king. It is possible that Louis Bringier was arrested because he was a freelance agent and illegal immigrant. His supposed knowledge of an invasion indicates that he was in a position to know the plans of the French.[480]

After his release from prison, Louis headed for Arkansas in the upper portion of Louisiana where gold had recently been discovered. The first evidence of Don Louis at the Arkansas Post is a deed that was posted for twenty acres of land he purchased at the mouth of the Arkansas River in December of 1810.[481] According to early settler William Pope, in 1809, a hunter and trapper named Trammel discovered what appeared to be gold on a high bluff on the Arkansas River some fifteen miles above present-day Little Rock. The hunter took his find to the Arkansas Post and sold it to a man who then sent it to New Orleans to have it evaluated. Experts proclaimed it to be pure gold, and the news spread quickly throughout the city. It is likely that Don Louis got wind of this and decided to use his mining and geology skills that he learned while in Mexico with Alexander von Humboldt.

Pope claims that shortly after gold was discovered near the Arkansas Post, an expedition was launched out of New Orleans led by a Captain Hillare, who was in fact Jean Lafitte, the infamous privateer.[482] It is likely that Don Louis prospected with Lafitte in Arkansas. Some historians suggest that Judge Pope was mistaken about the year and that Lafitte's expedition took place years later. In fact, Lafitte did visit Arkansas in 1816 and used the alias, Captain Hillare. It is possible that Louis knew Jean and Pierre Lafitte before he left New Orleans for Arkansas through their mutual associate, Daniel Clark.[483] Daniel Clark was a wealthy merchant and a close friend and business associate of Marius Bringier. Louis worked for him when he was young and maintained a relationship with Clark until he died. The Lafitte brothers had been involved in commercial ventures with Clark since their early time in New Orleans.[484] Jean and his brother, Pierre, were deeply involved in the smuggling and trading of enslaved people even after the prohibition of foreign slave trade in 1807. It is unclear if Jean was involved in the actual capturing of Spanish ships or if he just brokered deals between other privateers and his brother Pierre, who then sold the enslaved people in New Orleans.[485]

In 1811, Louis left the Arkansas Post and traveled throughout Arkansas and as far west as Missouri. He explored up the Arkansas River to present-day Oklahoma and lived among the Native Americans. As Humboldt and Bonpland did, Louis collected samples, made observations about mineral formations, discovered dinosaur fossils, and documented Native American life. Years later, his observations and scientific notes about the region were published in *The American Journal of Science and Arts*.[486] Some scholars of the day, including Professor Stillman who published Bringier's report were somewhat dismissive of Bringier's writing as it was sometimes rambling and to a certain degree, "immethodical."[487] However, some present-day researchers such as Conevery Bolton Valencius, contend that his documentation of Native American people of the region is detailed and valuable.[488] It should be noted that in the article, Bringier apologized for writing in English as it was a language that was not his most familiar, which could account for some of the deficiencies in his writing.[489]

Louis Bringier wrote extensively about the Osage and Cherokee tribes who lived in the upper Louisiana Territory. He immersed himself in their worlds and understood their medicine, religion, farming, hunting practices, and mores. He lauded the traditions and morals of the Osage people but had harsh words for the Cherokee tribe. This could have been a natural bias toward the Cherokee as they were British allies. Louis understood their languages and noted similarities between the Cherokee language and the language of the Otomi people in the Mexican Province of Michoacán. Louis might have encountered the Otomi people while with Humboldt when he traveled to that province in 1803.[490] Don Louis lived among the Cherokee along the St. Francis River and learned the mining techniques that they developed long before Europeans arrived.[491]

While exploring the region in January of 1812, Louis witnessed and documented the first aftershock of the cataclysmic New Madrid earthquakes in present-day Missouri. He described two minutes of violent shaking that caused thousands of trees to blow up, split, and fall down. He recounted that the earth exploded and spewed carbonized wood that rained back down in a black dust shower. At the same time, Louis saw parts of the earth sink and black liquid rise to the belly of his horse. In his article, he went into detail about the earthquake's geological ramifications.[492] Geologists theorize that what Louis experienced was the first principle after-shock of 7.3 magnitude following the initial earthquake in December of 1811 that would have registered 7.5 magnitude.[493]

After the earthquake, Don Louis headed east, and at some point, between January and June of 1812, he was in Philadelphia.[494] This is significant because at the time, Philadelphia was a base for those who supported Mexican independence, many of whom would make their way to New Orleans. A major figure in support of revolution in Mexico, General Joseph Amable Humbert was also in Philadelphia at the same time. Humbert was a former French General who served in Napoleon's army but was stripped of his rank and dismissed for expressing opposition to Napoleon's imperialism as well as conduct unbecoming an officer. It was rumored that Humbert had affairs with Napoleon's sister and his commanding officer's wife.[495] By 1813, Humbert was in New Orleans recruiting an army to invade Texas even though the United States was at war with Great Britain and would need all necessary soldiers. The conflict with Britain seemed remote and was not seen as an imminent danger to many in New Orleans. Humbert remained in New Orleans, and a year later, he was named general-in-chief of the Republican armies in Mexico. Colonel José Bernardo de Gutiérrez de Lara, a Mexican revolutionary leader and emissary to the United States, was also in Philadelphia prior to coming to New Orleans and possibly at the same time as Humbert and Bringier. Gutiérrez later sailed to New Orleans in February of 1812 using U. S. State Department funds. Jose Alvarez de Toledo y Dubois fled Spain and was also among the anti-royalist group living in Philadelphia, and he too later landed in New Orleans. Another expansionist and supporter of Mexican insurgency, Dr. John Hamilton Robinson, was in Philadelphia. John Robinson had at one time lived in New Orleans, was the United States envoy to the Interior Provinces of New Spain, and traveled as a naturalist and surgeon with Zebulon Pike during his Southwest expedition. When Robinson's tenure ended as envoy, he remained in Philadelphia and hired soldiers for a Mexican invasion scheme and helped Gutiérrez prepare to recruit in New Orleans.[496] Robinson also ended up back in New Orleans and volunteered as a physician during the Battle of New Orleans. Dr.

Robinson and Louis Bringier probably knew each other from New Orleans through their mutual friend, Daniel Clark.[497] The two men almost certainly planned together while they were in Philadelphia, and it is possible that Bringier acted as a liaison for Gutiérrez once they were in New Orleans.

Gutiérrez succeeded in putting together a coalition of local business leaders to support his cause. In 1814, he led a governing junta or council for Revolutionary Mexico that was based in New Orleans. Don Louis was among the inner circle of this coalition and a member of the junta.[498] Juan M. Picornelle was named president of the provisional government. Picornelle had been part of previous failed campaigns in Mexico and took refuge in New Orleans. Humbert was in command of military planning. The group planned to send an army to the Bay of Matagorda on ships owned by the Lafittes. They would then launch their attack from Matagorda on Tampico and Altamira.[499] The scheme was never actually plausible and lacked sufficient financial backing. Other members of the junta included Edward Livingston and Pierre and Jean Lafitte. Edward Livingston was the personal council for the Lafittes and had previously been a leading member of the defunct Mexican Association that supported the goals of Aaron Burr.[500] In addition, a loose coalition of financiers formed called the New Orleans Association. The group was made up of New Orleans businessmen who aimed to finance revolution in Mexico so they could be first to snap up land and capitalize on new trade opportunities and smuggling when the royalist government fell. The enterprising entrepreneurs saw an opportunity for great wealth.[501]

The activities of those in support of Mexican revolution did not go unnoticed by the Spanish government. Father Antonio de Sedella, or Père Antoine as he was known to New Orleanians, was the pastor of St. Louis Cathedral and is thought to have provided information on the goings-on of the group to Luis de Onis, the Spanish minister in Washington D.C. Sedella had been pastor under the Spanish period in New Orleans and secretly remained loyal to the Spanish monarchy after the Louisiana Purchase. He was believed to be the head of a Spanish spy ring in New Orleans.[502] Sedella was able to turn a member of the council and learn the details of their plan.[503] The friar informed Spanish Consul Diego Murphy, who passed on the information to

Luis de Onis. Onis immediately contacted Secretary of State James Monroe and protested the acts of aggression by United States citizens. The plan disintegrated due to lack of funding and the public outing of the plot.[504]

In the waning days of 1814, New Orleanians could not ignore the war with the British any longer. The Redcoats were bearing down on the city under the leadership of General Edward Pakenham. There was a call to arms and most able-bodied men: Creoles, Anglo-Americans, free people of color, Native Americans, — enslaved people, citizens, and noncitizens — heeded the call. General Humbert offered his services to Andrew Jackson. He was eager to ingratiate himself to the people of New Orleans and undoubtedly relished the opportunity to settle the score with his old nemesis, General Pakenham.[505] Louis Bringier joined the force as well as the other leaders of the junta, including Jean and Pierre Lafitte. Prior to the battle, the Lafittes were under arrest for smuggling . They were granted full pardons for their efforts in defeating the British at the Battle of New Orleans.

After the war, Louis headed to Philadelphia as did Jean Lafitte, ostensibly for different reasons. Lafitte sought compensation for supplies and money he used during the Battle of New Orleans, while Louis pursued publishing the maps he made during his western travels in upper Louisiana. The exact timing of Louis's visit is unclear, but it was before 1816 and after the Battle of New Orleans in January of 1815. Louis established a reputation for himself as an explorer and cartographer and collaborated with William Darby and John Melish.[506] William Darby was a surveyor who meticulously mapped the state of Louisiana. In 1815, a New York publishing house printed an announcement of a forthcoming collection of Darby and Bringier's maps.[507] According to W.D. Williams, the book never came to fruition.[508] While in Philadelphia, Darby and Bringier met with John Melish, one of the first American cartographers. Melish traveled the United States from 1806 to 1811 and mapped much of his travels. He also pulled together the work of other explorers into the first map of the United States with contiguous British and Spanish possessions that extended to the Pacific Ocean. In the introduction to his book, Melish stated that just before publication, he was visited by Lewis [sic] Bringier and William Darby. They presented him with maps: Bringier's was of the whole of that part of the Missouri Territory, known by the name of Upper Louisiana, from the northern boundary of the state of Louisiana to above St. Louis and from the Mississippi to the 23rd degree of west longitude, and Darby's was the state of Louisiana. Melish thought their findings were so significant that he altered his final map even after all the plan work was finished and the plates were made. Melish noted that Darby's map had been published and that he was in possession of Bringier's map along with his observations of mountains and minerology. Melish stated that Bringier's map would probably be published soon. There is no evidence that Bringier's maps and notes were ever published by Melish.[509]

Post-war Upper Louisiana was flooded with Americans seeking opportunity. The Spanish feared the influx of people would buoy the expansionist goals of the United States and endanger their hold on Mexico. In order to find out how much of a threat this was, Father Sedella devised a fact-finding spy expedition. He recruited Jean Lafitte as an agent for Spain even though the Lafitte brothers had previously waylaid Spanish galleons and stolen their goods. French immigrant and local New Orleanian, Arséne Lacarrriére Latour, was also tapped to lead the mission. Latour was a highly respected engineer, architect, and cartographer and served under Jackson at the Battle of New Orleans. Latour's skills were needed because the Spanish knew little about the Arkansas and Missouri territories and wanted to find possible routes that the Americans might take to gain access to adjacent Spanish possessions. In addition, he was to observe the population and assess their loyalty to America. Louis Bringier joined the elite group as well.[510] His extensive knowledge of the area and expertise as a miner were important as the cover story for the mission was that the group was going to mine for silver and gold in Arkansas. Jean Lafitte traveled under the pseudonym, Captain Hillare, and Latour used the alias, John Williams.[511] Versions of the story vary as to whether Louis Bringier left from New Orleans with Lafitte and Latour or if the pair met him in Arkansas on Louis's land at Crystal Hills. It is also unclear whether Louis returned to New Orleans with them or stayed in Arkansas.

It is probable that Louis's interest in the whole affair was two-fold. He wanted to assist his cronies, Jean Lafitte and Arséne Latour, and seek his fortune in gold and silver. Louis Bringier bought more land in Arkansas and petitioned Congress to permit United States citizens to open and work mines of precious metal discovered on public lands.[512] Historian Rafe Blaufarb claims that Louis Bringier disappeared in 1818, and upon his return, said that he had been involved in a plot to take over Mexican silver mines.[513] Having no luck in Arkansas, Louis might have moved to Mexico to seek his fortune. Mexican authorities would not have wanted a non-native to gain power and financial success, especially in the lucrative silver market. Historian Craig Bauer tells the story that Don Louis made a fortune mining for silver in Mexico. He even visited friends and family in Lower Louisiana and flaunted his newfound riches during his stay. He returned to Mexico to continue his lavish lifestyle and intended to give a ring to a woman he met there.[514] As was typical for Louis, his luck ran out. He was imprisoned and his property and land were confiscated. More alarming was the fact that he was condemned to death. In a desperate effort to save his life, Louis informed the priest sent to minister to him that he was a relative of Bishop DuBourg in Louisiana. He implored the priest to contact the bishop. Louis also conveyed to the priest that his brother was very wealthy and would pay handsomely for his return. Bishop DuBourg was the uncle of Doradou's wife and did intercede on Louis's behalf. Doradou secured the ransom and headed to Mexico to rescue his wayward brother.[515]

Louis returned to Louisiana and spent time living between his brother Doradau's plantation, L'Hermitage, and White Hall. Marius Pons died in 1820 and his two sons inherited his mansion and land. Louis sold his interest in the plantation to Doradou, and the Bringier brothers worked together and engaged in land speculation. Their largest investment was Houmas Plantation in Ascension Parish.[516] Louis settled down after his father's death and became a surveyor. He moved his primary residence to New Orleans, although he is listed as living in Ascension Parish in the 1840 census. He was named Surveyor for the City of New Orleans and Surveyor General for the State of Louisiana about 1825. In 1835, as Surveyor General, in consultation with Bernard de Marigny, Louis drew the plans for the town of Mandeville on the north shore of Lake Pontchartrain. The plans included governance and operations, as well as civic structures, streets, markets, churches, and wharves.[517] He also laid out the neighborhood of Esplanade Ridge in New Orleans and built a house there.

Even though Don Louis gave up his wondering ways, he remained unconventional and was seen as eccentric and somewhat embarrassing to his family. A great divide in the family came when Louis decided to marry for the first time when he was nearly fifty years old. On October 22, 1831, Louis married the much younger Herminie Guignard. Not only did his family object to the age difference, but they were extremely disappointed that he married someone below his social rank.[518] The couple had three children: Letitia, Louisa, and Charles. Although Louis and his brother continued to do business together until Doradou's death in 1847, the rest of the Bringier family had little to do with him or his wife and children. Herminie was mentally unstable, and an interdiction was sought by some of her family members after Louis's death in 1860.[519] Don Louis died intestate and his estate was nearly insolvent, so his children did not inherit any Bringier money. Many years after Louis's death, a young Mexican man called on some members of the Bringier family and claimed to be Don Louis's son. After giving them the details of his mother and Louis, the family believed him and gave him a small stipend to open a barbershop in New Orleans.[520] He was a gracious, kind man and ran a successful business. When he heard that his half-sisters were financially destitute, he gave them money to help them live. They invited him to live in their home. This stunned the extended Bringier family and created an even greater rift within the family.[521] Don Louis's accomplishments were overshadowed by his family's shame over his nonconformist lifestyle. When asked about their peculiar relative, members of the family often emphasized his eccentric nature and dismissed some of his achievements and anecdotes as exaggerations or as behavior unbecoming a gentleman.

Freret Family

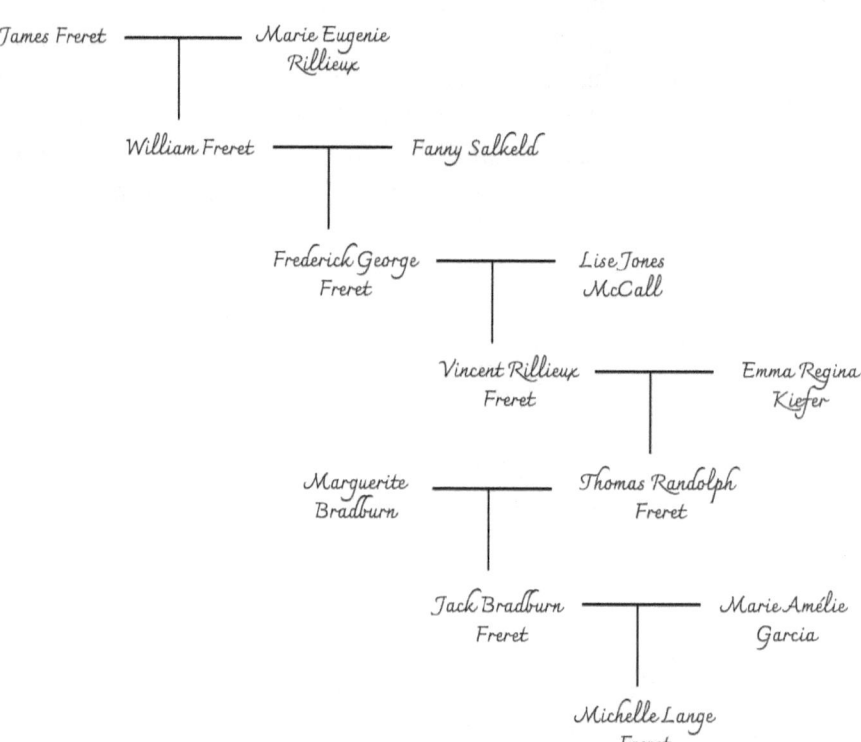

The Freret Family

JAMES FRERET SR.
1773-1834

James Freret was born in London on March 25, 1773. He was the son of a silk weaver, Jean Freret, and Marie Magdelaine Herubel. James's father was born in France in the Normandy region. Jean and Marie left France for London around 1769. In August of that year, after his father died, Jean Freret was formally released from his apprenticeship to his father. They settled in Spitalfields, a district in the East End of London in Middlesex County and within the London Borough of Tower Hamlets, where other French weavers were already established. Many families fled religious persecution in the late 1600s when King Louis XIV revoked the Edict of Nantes that allowed French Protestants to worship openly. James was the youngest of five children. His three oldest siblings were born in France: Susannah Magdelaine, Jean Baptiste, and Marie Jeanne. Elizabeth and James were born in Spitalfields. James was baptized in April of 1773 at L'Église de l'Artillerie or the Artillery Church, a Huguenot/French Protestant church. James's sisters, Susannah and Elizabeth, married silk weavers and remained in London. Susannah married James Stewart and their son James moved to New Orleans and married his cousin Eugenie Freret, daughter of James Freret and Eugenie Rillieux. Marie Jean married Michel Dupray and remained in Middlesex County. Marie Magdaline, James's mother, died in 1790 and was buried at Christ Church in Spitalfields. Jean and his son, Jean Baptiste, returned to France to continue weaving. Before James's father left London, he drafted his will. He divided his English assets among his three married daughters and James. His British estate was worth over £2,000.[522] Jean Freret must have been a master silk weaver rather than a simple weaver or journeyman who toiled six hours a day for little pay. Jean Baptiste inherited the entirety of his father's French estate. James left London and settled in Spanish New Orleans in January of 1793 when he was twenty years old.[523] His father died in 1802, at which time he inherited his share of the estate.

Within a few years of his arrival in New Orleans, James was a successful cotton factor. Cotton factors acted as commission merchants and bankers to planters. They advanced money and purchased supplies, including enslaved people. They also acted as agents and sold the cotton. Cotton factors undertook large risks as agricultural products were somewhat unpredictable. The planter's note, backed by his contract with the factor who warehoused and insured the cotton, afforded the planter credit. In addition, the factor had control over his client's total yield, even if it exceeded the value of the loan and cleared the planter's debt. Large sums of money were advanced by cotton factors upon the word of a planter, often with no formal collateral.[524] Because of this, the character of the prospective client was carefully considered. The factor and the planter frequently developed close life-long business and social ties.[525] Cotton factors wielded enormous power and had tremendous opportunity for profit. By the late 1790s, many planters in the lower Mississippi Valley switched from growing indigo to cotton, at which point the cultivation of cotton increased at breakneck speed. Julian Poydras from Pointe Coupee was one of James Freret's biggest clients. In just two years, Poydras went from exporting twenty tons of indigo per year to exporting fifteen thousand tons of cotton per year. By August of 1800, Poydras had a contract with James Freret to export 100,000 250-pound bales of cotton.[526]

Four years after his arrival, James married New Orleanian Marie "Eugenie" Rillieux when he was twenty-five years old. Fr. Antonio de Sedella married the couple at St. Louis Cathedral on July 20, 1797, when Eugenie was eighteen years old. She was the daughter of wealthy merchant Vincent Rillieux and Marie Tronquet and the sister of wealthy cotton factor Vincent Rillieux Jr. Eugenie's father was so wealthy and had so many assets that the inventory of his estate was over 400 pages long.[527] Vincent Rillieux died in February of 1800 and named James Freret as executor.

Before his marriage, as was required, James petitioned the church to marry Eugenie. Although James was baptized in the French Protestant church, in his petition, he swore that he was of the Roman Catholic faith. Because New Orleans was part of the Catholic Spanish Empire, all marriages had to be performed in the Catholic Church and both parties had to be Catholic. As was customary, witnesses were presented to attest to the sworn testimony of the betrothed. Robert Doss stated before the priest and Vicar General Thomas Hassett and Notary Francisco Moutin that he had known James Freret for twelve years in London and averred that James was of the Roman Catholic faith, single, and not betrothed to anyone other than Marie Eugenie Rillieux. Another witness for James was James Carrick, who had also known James for twelve years and declared the same facts. A marriage license was granted by the Vicar General and was extended to the priest of the Cathedral, Fr. Sedella, or Père Antoine, as he was known to locals, to proceed with the banns.

The legitimacy of James and Eugenie's marriage was called into question and an inquiry was opened by Fr. Sedella in October of 1799. It came to Fr. Sedella's attention that when James testified as a witness in a court case, he swore on the Holy Bible in the manner of a Protestant. A public interpreter, Pedro Darwin, was assigned to the case as James spoke English and French, but not Spanish. During the inquiry, James was asked what religion he professed. He responded that since his marriage, he professed the Roman Catholic religion. James was then asked if he remembered giving testimony in a suit filed by Mayor Gabriel Fonsberry against Tore Gillard. James answered that he did remember the testimony. Sedella probed further and asked if in his declaration he swore to tell the truth on the Bible, a custom practiced by Protestants. James did not answer directly but stated that he did not know if the Catholics took their oath only by God and the Cross, or if they did so on the Bible and the Holy Gospel as was done by Protestants.[528] Prior to his oath in the Fonsberry case, the interpreter for the court recorded that he asked James what religion he was. James responded that he was Protestant. When asked why he had claimed to be a Protestant, he said that there was no special reason. The proceedings of 1799 were suspended for several unspecified reasons.

New citations were issued, and the inquiry was reconvened on August 6, 1801. In the interim, Eugenie's father died, and she gave birth to her first son, James Peter, the year before. The couple was expecting their second child, John, during the inquiry. If the marriage were to be declared illegitimate, it would have scandalous consequences for Eugenie and her children. At the start of the new proceeding, James was asked if he made his vow before God and the Cross, by the Holy Gospel or by the Creator of the Heavens and Earth. Understanding full well the consequences of his answer, he said, "by the Holy Gospel." James testified that a few days before his marriage, he professed abjuration of his errors from the sect of Calvinism to Fr. Juan Brady. He stated that he then made his confession with the same priest. The questioning continued: Had he ever received Communion; In what religion was he educated; Had he continued to act as a Catholic after his abjuration; and Why had he stated that he was a Protestant in the Fonsberry matter? James told the inquiry court that he had received Communion about a month before his marriage but did not receive on the day of his nuptials because he had inadvertently broken his fast. He stated that his parents were French and that he was educated in the Roman Catholic faith. He added that at age twelve, he passed to Calvinism in London, but when he came to New Orleans, there was no church of Calvinism, so he sometimes went to the Catholic church.[529] He claimed that after his rejection of Calvinism, he acted as a Catholic. James contended that Pedro Derbigny, the interpreter in the Fonsberry case, asked him if he took the oath by the cross or the Bible.[530] He replied that he took the oath on the Bible and the Holy Gospel as he had done in London. Finally, James was asked why, in these proceedings, had he taken his oath by the Holy Gospel as the Protestants do. He declared that if he told the truth, it was the same to swear by the Holy Gospel as by the Cross or any other manner.[531]

The church leaders must have been satisfied with James's testimony, as his infant son, John, who was born in March of 1802, was baptized by Fr. Sedella on January 29, 1803. It was usual for babies to be baptized within six weeks of birth. There is no explanation in the record as to why John's baptism was delayed for almost a year.

It could be that the ruling from the inquisition had not been decided until 1803. It is also possible that James was not in New Orleans near the time of John's birth. During that year, James was arrested and convicted of violating slave trading laws and was held in Spain. However, his sentence of imprisonment was vacated on January 15, 1803, because of ambiguity in the law.[532]

    William, the couple's third son, who was born on November 21, 1803, was baptized, but not until March of 1806. Marie Eugenie, James and Eugenie's only daughter, was born in February of that year and was baptized on the same day as William. William's baptism was delayed for more than two years. James's business required that he travel abroad for prolonged periods of time. He traveled to Cuba, England, and Europe to visit business contacts and friends. He was probably out of the country for an extended time when William was a young baby. It is also possible that the delay in his baptism was because of the Louisiana Purchase. People in Louisiana now had a choice regarding baptizing their children in the Roman Catholic faith. James had undergone intense scrutiny by Fr. Sedella, and he was raised in a Protestant tradition. He might have been ambivalent about baptizing the children in the Catholic church. There was enormous upheaval in the local church triggered by Louisiana's retrocession to France and its transfer to the United States. At the time of William's birth, there was no official Bishop of Louisiana. Bishop Peñalver was transferred to Guatemala in 1801, and a replacement was not sent. The King of Spain knew that the secret treaty that retroceded Louisiana from Spain to France had been signed in October of 1800, so he did not name a bishop. Although Louisiana had at one time been a French colony, it had been under a king. By November of 1803, when Louisiana was transferred back to France, the First Republic was in place, and church and state were separate. One month later, Louisiana was then officially transferred to the United States. Local church jurisdiction and authority were even murkier, and power struggles ensued among the clergy. Louisianians had never experienced living without a monarch and neither had the local clergy.[533] To make matters even more complicated, Spain continued to pay the clergy in New Orleans, and Casa Calvo, the former Spanish governor, remained in the city. Vicar General Patrick Walsh, who had been appointed by the previous bishop, assumed authority. Fr. Sedella refused to accept this and resigned in protest, but later rescinded his resignation. A rowdy meeting was held at the cathedral on March 14, 1805, and the parishioners asked Père Antoine to remain as pastor, rejecting Fr. Walsh.[534]

James continued to develop a successful business in the cotton industry, and he and Eugenie raised their children in New Orleans until tragedy struck. Eugenie Rillieux Freret died on March 12, 1808, and left behind four young children. James eventually remarried but maintained a close relationship with the Rillieux family. In 1815, he married Heloise Marguerite St. Marc, a native of Saint-Domingue. They had three sons: George, Eugene, and Edmond. James was elected alderman in 1816, continued in the cotton business, and built one of the first cotton presses in the city. A cotton press was a low warehouse in which cotton was compressed into bales so it could be shipped more efficiently. The Freret Press was established about 1819 on Royal Street and employed a baling machine that James invented.[535]

Like many successful businessmen of early New Orleans, James did his civic duty and was a member of the city council during the Macarty administration from 1816 to 1820. His brother-in-law from his first marriage, Vincent Rillieux, was on the council at the same time. During James's time on the council, the city experienced an outbreak of "American typhus," later to be recognized as yellow fever. The mayor and the council passed ordinances to stop the spread of the disease and created the Board of Health in 1817. The Board of Health outlined sanitary measures and included the following provisions: the streets had to be kept clean, oysters were not to be sold between May and September, slaughterhouses had to be licensed and inspected, public markets had to close at noon so they could be cleaned, meat had to be covered when in transit through the streets, refuse could not collect in drains or gutters, and burials had to take place in public cemeteries.[536]

The Freret Press flourished and grew, and James moved his operation to Faubourg St. Mary on the square bounded by Carondelet, Union, Baronne, and Perdido.[537] James, his second wife, and their three sons lived next door to the press on the corner of Baronne and Gravier. In August of 1830, the Freret Press burned along with 2,100 bales of cotton and supplies.[538] *The Natchez Democrat* reported, "There can be no doubt that the fire was occasioned by design."[539] The press was insured, but the payout did not cover the extensive losses. James Freret died a few years later on April 16, 1834. The press was not rebuilt before his death, and the land was eventually bought by the city.[540] Most of James's money was tied up in landed property and enslaved people. He had many debts when he died, and it was necessary to sell all the enslaved people and some of the property to satisfy his obligations. James's oldest three sons, James, John, and William, owned and operated the Freret Brothers Cotton Press and bought many of the enslaved people who belonged to their father's estate.

WILLIAM FRERET SR.
1803-1864

William Freret was born on November 21, 1803, days before the transfer of Louisiana to the United States from France. He had two older brothers, James and John, and a younger sister, Eugenie. Sadly, William's mother, Eugenie, died in 1808, when he was just five years old. William, James, and John attended the College of Orleans when they were young. It is not clear at what age the boys started their formal education, but boys as young as seven boarded at the school. The day students were indigent boys who could not afford the boarding fees, so it is likely that the Frerets lived at the school. The college was established in 1811 and was on the corner of Hospital Street (now Governor Nicholls) and St. Claude in the old mansion house of the Tremé Plantation where St. Augustine Church is today. The students studied Greek, Latin, Spanish, mathematics, history, science, philosophy, and literature; all instruction was in French.[541] The children remained close to their mother's family. Their uncle, Vincent Rillieux Jr., acted on their behalf in legal matters. James often wrote letters to his aunt and uncle, Marie Heloise Rillieux, his mother's sister, and her husband, Jean Louis Melchior Reynaud. He complained about the food at school and wished they would come for a visit. Eugenie probably lived with the Reynauds because in his letters, James asked them to give her a kiss.[542]

In 1815, James Freret Sr. married Marguerite Heloise St. Marc. In September of that year, the Freret brothers were sent to Formby, a town twelve miles north of Liverpool, to study engineering, and Eugenie, it seems, remained with her aunt and uncle. The boys studied in England for at least four years.

While the brothers were in England at school, George Salkeld, a cotton factor who lived in Liverpool, took the boys under his wing. Salkeld was a partner in Salkeld, Barclay & Co., one of Liverpool's largest importers of American cotton between 1806 and 1815.[543] The partners also owned a large cotton plantation near Pensacola.[544] The company's major supply source for cotton was New Orleans.[545] George Salkeld was a business associate and friend of James Freret Sr. The young Frerets grew close to the Salkelds and spent school vacations and holidays with them at their home.[546] The Salkelds eventually moved to New Orleans, and George was appointed British Consul in 1826. When they returned from England, James, William, and John joined their father in the cotton business but eventually opened their own press. William Freret married Fanny Salkeld, George's daughter, a few years later. Fanny and William had four children: William Alfred, Fanny, James (died young), and Frederick George.

The Freret brothers were engaged in politics, entrepreneurial ventures, and philanthropic causes. They established a large cotton press in Faubourg St. Mary on St. Charles Avenue between Perdido and Poydras extending back to Baronne Street There were small houses between the warehouses for the workers.[547] The Freret Brothers Press was a landmark in the city and the brothers were considered "industrial pioneers of the American Quarter."[548] William served in the Louisiana Legislature from 1835 to 1837 and was elected Mayor of New Orleans twice, from 1840 to 1842 and 1843 to 1844. James was an alderman in the administrations of six mayors, beginning in 1828, and was elected Sheriff over Bernard de Marigny in 1853. He was a charter member of the Chamber of Commerce and served on the board of directors of the City Bank, Union Bank, and the New Orleans Drainage Company. James and William invested in the Exchange Hotel Company, the brainchild of Samuel J. Peters, and built the Merchants' Exchange on Royal Street.[549] Exchanges were especially popular in port cities. They provided traveling businessmen with lodging but were also meeting places for local entrepreneurs. Most exchanges, including the Merchants' Exchange, offered other amenities such as banking and legal services, reading rooms, food, and drink.[550] The Merchants' Exchange, designed by James Galliard Sr. and Charles Dakin, boasted auction rooms, meeting areas, and trading floors as well as a soaring atrium. In the years just before the Civil War, the trading center was leased by a firm that conducted slave auctions. The Exchange was also a social center for foreign and local powerbrokers who met at the bar where the cocktail was invented or in the Billiard Club on the third floor.[551]

William and James actively worked to help those in need. In 1840, the two brothers, along with several other prominent citizens, founded the Samaritan Society of New Orleans. The purpose of the privately funded organization was to provide relief to indigent people at all times but particularly during epidemics.[552] William was also active in the Episcopal church and served on the Vestry of Christ Church Cathedral in 1841. After the secession of Louisiana, James helped found the Association for Relief of Sick and Wounded Soldiers and served as its president.

James and William aligned themselves with the nascent Whig party which formed in 1834 in opposition to Jacksonian policies. It was a loose coalition that brought together fiscal conservatives and states' rights advocates. Former Secretary of State Henry Clay was one of the party's leaders and ran for president under its banner three times. William was an ardent supporter and close friend of Clay, the Great Compromiser. In the late 1830s, a splinter wing of the party emerged and temporarily developed into the Native American Party, a quasi-third party.[553] The Frerets briefly affiliated themselves with the new party, but eventually were brought back into the Whig fold.

Immigration dramatically increased in the 1830s, and a majority of immigrants supported Democrats. Whigs feared a loss of power and the inability of "foreigners" to understand America as a democratic republic. The goals of Nativists were to repeal the naturalization laws and restore the Alien and Sedition Acts.[554] The Louisiana chapter's manifesto stated, "We feel constrained to warn our countrymen, that unless some steps be speedily taken to protect our institutions from these accumulated inroads upon our national character, from the indiscriminate immigration, and naturalization of foreigners, in vain have our predecessors whether native or naturalized, toiled and suffered, and fought and bled and died, to achieve our liberties, and establish our hallowed institutions."[555] The National Nativist Movement was decidedly anti-Roman Catholic; however, the Louisiana affiliate was based in predominantly Roman Catholic New Orleans, so these sentiments were either not present or not voiced in the local chapter.

William Freret's first city-wide political race was for Mayor of New Orleans in 1840. The Native American Party drafted him to run against incumbent Charles Genois. William Freret did not have the support of naturalized Whigs because of his stance on immigration laws, but despite intense opposition to his repeal stance, he narrowly defeated Mayor Genois. On election night, a large celebration was held at the Freret home. Enormous crowds gathered outside on the street where guns were fired, and bands played.[556] Freret managed to convince those who were opposed to his Nativist views that he would carry on his duties as mayor and represent all the people of New Orleans. The Whig party coalesced around the Freret administration, and despite difficult financial circumstances in the city due to the crash of 1837 and the flood of 1840, Mayor Freret managed to stabilize the city's fiscal health. Although the city was able to meet its financial obligations, Mayor Freret failed to foment economic growth. Freret was viewed as an honest, capable mayor, devoted to the betterment of the city and its citizens.

In 1841, a year into his first administration, William Freret, along with American businessmen Samuel J. Peters, Joshua Baldwin, Dr. J. M. Picton, J. A. Maybin, Robert McNair, and Thomas Sloo, was responsible for pushing through the act signed by Governor Roman that authorized the City of New Orleans to establish public schools. Every white child within the three municipalities was eligible to attend school in their respective municipality. Local taxes were collected to support the schools and the state treasurer was also required to pay an annual sum.[557] Each municipality had its own board of directors and executive officer. The schools had a difficult start with few students at first. Some citizens were opposed to public education, and the large Catholic population often chose to educate their children in Roman Catholic institutions. The community soon came around to the idea of public schools, and attendance in the Second Municipality increased from thirteen students in 1841 to 950 the next year.[558]

It was said of Mayor Freret that he was not concerned about his popularity but took his responsibilities seriously and with personal attention not typical of an executive. He often took it upon himself to visit and assess public works in progress and to drop in on public institutions. There is an often-repeated story that exemplifies why William Freret was considered an efficient and reliable servant of the people. One particularly frigid winter night, Mayor Freret conducted an impromptu inspection of the prison to make sure that the inmates were properly cared for and sufficiently warm.[559] Acts like this garnered him the support of a wide cross section of the citizenry.

Freret ran for reelection against Democrat Denis Prieur on the Native American ticket with the tepid support of the Whigs. The issue of naturalization proved divisive and ultimately cost Freret the election, as the Creole population was adamantly opposed to his views on repealing and replacing the laws that regulated citizenship. Prieur took no stance on the topic and claimed that the issue had no bearing on his ability to act as mayor. His avoidance of the issue was effective, and he defeated Freret. Denis Prieur took office in 1842 but only stayed for eight months. He resigned to take a statewide position as recorder of mortgages. A special election was held to fill the remainder of Prieur's term. The Whigs, stung by Prieur's victory in the 1842 election, realized that they needed to adopt some of the Democrat methods in order to be successful in electing his replacement. Party leaders knew that a fractured party and lackluster endorsement would not produce a Whig winner. The Whig convention, or Clay Club as Whig local chapters were called, backed William Freret to run against Democrat Charles Genois. William Freret won with one of the largest margins ever given a Whig for the office of mayor.[560] Freret's election was significant to the Whig party on a state level as the newly elected Democrat, Governor Mouton, threw his political weight behind the loser, Genois.

William Freret's second term was somewhat uneventful, but he continued to work tirelessly for the city. Fire was of constant concern in nineteenth century New Orleans. Freret understood its danger for the city as a whole and the havoc it could wreak on individuals since his father's business had been destroyed by arson. Mayor Freret created a contest that became a tradition in the city. Each fire company in the city competed to see which one could throw a water stream the highest and knock off a stuffed eagle perched on top of a pole erected on a lot on Peters Street.[561] Throughout his second administration, William Freret continued his commitment to public education in New Orleans. The first public high school in the city opened in December of 1843. Freret was intimately involved in the school system and was president of the Board of Directors during his time as mayor.[562] School applicants applied directly to the mayor, and he personally evaluated the merits of each prospective high school student.

William Freret ran again in 1844 for the top municipal post against Democrat Edgar Montegut. Montegut was endorsed by the *Louisiana American* but was not officially nominated by his party. Montegut's Creole roots worked to his advantage. There was minimal interest in the election, and voter turnout was light. Montegut eked out a win with 557 votes to Freret's 465 votes. As usual, there were accusations of fraud; however, in this case, there seems to have been some facts to support the contention. There was considerable evidence that many of the voters were illegally naturalized and granted the right to vote. Naturalized citizens typically aligned themselves with the Democrats. At the time, local and state court judges could grant naturalization on behalf of the United States government. Lafayette City judge Benjamin Elliott was impeached and removed from office in 1844 for unlawfully naturalizing almost 2,000 people, many of whom voted in the election.[563] Election officials at various wards were accused of shutting down the polls when men of questionable citizenry were turned away. The claim was also made by some that lawful citizens were prevented from voting and that the election was not conducted properly. William Freret presided over a mass meeting of New Orleans citizens that was called immediately after the election. A committee was formed to draft a set of resolutions that condemned the process of the recent election although the results were not overturned.[564]

In 1850, President Millard Fillmore nominated William Freret to be the Collector of Customs for the district of Mississippi in the state of Louisiana. Freret's job entailed protecting against smuggling, but also required monitoring the legal comings and goings of ships. He was approved by the Senate and took office. His tenure was short due to a controversial filibuster ship that launched from New Orleans and headed toward Cuba to support a reported rebellion and encourage support for Cuba's annexation to the United States.

Cuba became a major power in the international sugar industry after the revolution in Saint-Domingue in 1789 caused the collapse of the sugar industry there. Planters escaped the Revolution and relocated to Cuba and Louisiana, bringing with them a wealth of knowledge about sugar. Spain recognized the opportunity to capitalize on the situation and quickly moved to fill the void in sugar production. Spain removed all export taxes on Cuban sugar and shipped it to Europe. Within twenty years, sugar production had doubled in Cuba, and by 1840, it was the richest colony in the Spanish Empire.[565] Cuba turned out an astounding one-third of the world's sugar by 1860.[566]

The late 1840s and 1850s were tumultuous years on the Spanish colonial island of Cuba. There was a fiscal crisis in Cuba due to an oversupply of sugar on the world market, stiff competition from European beet sugar manufacturers, and the push by the British to end slavery worldwide. These circumstances created factions among Cuban sugar growers and lead to political and economic instability.[567] Some favored continued reliance on slave labor, while others who did not rely on slave labor championed independence from Spain. A small minority of wealthy sugar producers advocated the use of wage workers instead of enslaved people. Those who wanted to continue using slave labor saw the annexation of Cuba to the United States as a way to maintain the slavery model.[568]

American leaders were eager to expand democracy and increase the United States' holdings. They believed that Cuba's proximity and shared business interests made the annexation of Cuba inevitable.[569] In 1848, President Polk offered Spain $100 million for Cuba.[570] Spain refused the offer to the disappointment of the United States government as well as many Cubans. These conditions inspired expeditions by filibusters to Cuba. Filibusters were groups of men, who without the consent of the U.S. government, raised capital and soldiers to instigate insurrections. In the late 1840s, some in the United States favored Cuba's forcible annexation. This movement was fueled by newspapers whose purpose was to criticize the Spanish government in Cuba. *La Verdad* in New York and *La Patria* in New Orleans played an important part in garnering support for filibuster expeditions aimed at Cuban annexation to the United States.[571]

At first, the primary goal of the Cuban filibuster was to free the Cuban people from the Spanish monarchy and spread freedom. This objective eventually mingled with the Southern goal of bringing more slave states into the United States, and ultimately morphed into a Southern cause altogether.[572] Venezuelan-born Narciso Lopez was a filibuster, also known as a freebooter or soldier of fortune, who was determined to liberate Cuba from Spain. At one time, he was a Cuban soldier and served in the Cuban Colonial government.[573] In 1848, Lopez attempted to incite an insurrection and overthrow the new regime in Cuba because he was angered about losing his position in the government. The rebellion was unsuccessful, and Lopez was forced to flee to the United States.[574] Lopez was determined to achieve his goal and organized filibuster expeditions from the United States. Even though neutrality laws in the United States prohibited private American citizens from participating in wars with foreign powers, Lopez tried three time to invade Cuba with hired forces and money raised from U.S. businesspeople. His first attempt in New York was stopped by the federal government. Lopez then decided to move his operation to New Orleans.[575] The initial filibuster from New Orleans in the fall of 1848 ended with the defeat of Lopez and his return to New Orleans. In the summer of 1851, New Orleans newspapers reported that there had been some uprisings in Cuba, but Cuban officials denied the stories.[576] Lopez took this opportunity to solicit soldiers and raise money in the form of bonds contingent upon a successful mission.

Earlier that year, President Fillmore issued a proclamation condemning filibustering and warned that those who engaged in filibustering would be subject to stiff fines and would not have the protection of the United States.[577] Despite the proclamation, Lopez raised $50,000 and recruited more men than he could use, including William Crittenden, nephew of the United States Attorney General, John Crittenden.[578] At dawn on August 3, 1851, Lopez and his men set sail. The *Pampero* left the dock at the foot of Lafayette Street and headed for Cuba. Crowds of well-wishers lined the levee waving and cheering as the ship departed. There were so many men aboard the ship that it was not seaworthy, so nearly one hundred had to be left behind before the ship could continue its journey.[579] Lopez and his crew arrived in Cuba to find lackluster support among would-be rebels. The mission was a complete failure. Over one hundred men were captured and sent to Spain, and more than fifty in the party were executed, including Lopez and Crittenden.[580] The *New Orleans Bee* of August 22, 1851, gave gruesome details of the deaths and expressed outrage at the Spanish soldiers and officials who carried out the heinous acts.[581] New Orleanians, fuming over the Cubans' actions, stormed the Spanish consulate in New Orleans and vandalized the portraits of Queen Isabella and the Captain General of Cuba.[582] The attack on Cuba, although not sanctioned by the government, and the sacking of the Consulate at New Orleans put the United States in a precarious diplomatic position with Spain. President Fillmore steadfastly refused to negotiate on behalf of the captured filibusters. Eventually the president gave into pressure from constituents from the North and South and sent Secretary of State Daniel Webster to negotiate the release of the prisoners in Spain.[583] Reparations were made for damages to the consulate, and federal officials in New Orleans were dismissed.

One high profile official who lost his job because of the Cuban affair was William Freret, Collector of the Port of New Orleans. The Fillmore Administration accused Freret of neglect of duty. Some national newspapers, sympathetic to Fillmore, accused Freret of being complicit in the filibuster and willingly allowing the *Pampero* to leave the port.[584] William Freret was seen nationally as sympathetic to the annexation cause as he owned enslaved people himself. Even though many local newspapers defended Freret, he was devastated by the public humiliation on a national level. In and around New Orleans, William Freret was regarded as a well-liked, efficient mayor who worked tirelessly to make sure scandal did not mar his administration.[585] Freret published his correspondence with the Treasury Department during the *Pampero* incident along with his version of the events in hopes of repairing his reputation. Freret accused the administration of using him as a scapegoat to appease the Spanish Crown. He claimed that he was unaware of the impending departure of the *Pampero* and that it was his impression that she was not seaworthy and needed repairs. He further claimed that if he had known of the departure, he would have been powerless to stop it, as the nearest federal troops were 110 miles away, and it took at least three days for correspondence to reach them. Freret went on to note that the United States Marshal, the United States District Attorney, the acting District Attorney, and the United States Judge were all away from the city for the summer. He questioned how he, a lone civil servant, was supposed to stop an entire ship full of men and a mob set on seeing them depart.[586]

Many New Orleans newspapers defended Freret's actions and reputation. *The Daily Delta* stated, "Mr. Freret has nothing of the Filibuster about him. . . The departure of the *Pampero* could not have been prevented by all the vigilance in the world."[587] *The New Orleans Courier* condemned the president and asked for sympathy for James P. Freret, Sheriff of New Orleans, because his brother had been removed from office.[588]

The Captain General of Cuba hoped that the actions of the United States would put an end to filibustering and to any plans for annexing Cuba. This was not to be. The acquisition of Cuba continued to play a role in American politics. It became a partisan issue, with the Democrats favoring annexation. This threatened to compromise the island's already fragile stability. In 1852, Democrat Franklin Pierce was elected president. Pierce fulfilled a campaign promise, and in 1854, directed the American minister in Madrid, Pierre Soulé, to offer Spain $130 million for Cuba. Pierre Soulé was a former Louisiana attorney, state senator, and United States senator. Even though he was a diplomat, Soulé was not known for his tact or discretion and often offended Spanish ambassadors and court officials. Soulé, along with the American ministers to Britain and France, wrote and signed what became known as the Ostend Manifesto. The declaration stated that if Spain would not sell Cuba to the United States, that taking the island by force would be considered. It further stated that the refusal of Spain to sell Cuba would be considered hostile. The manifesto created a furor in the United States and precipitated disastrous national election results for the Democrats. In order to regain its political footing, the Pierce administration quietly stepped away from its goal of taking Cuba.[589]

After his dismissal, William Freret went back to private life and focused on running the Freret Brothers Press as his brother James was sheriff and had many public responsibilities. After the secession of Louisiana from the Union and the beginning of the Civil War, hundreds of militiamen drilled and prepared for a Union attack at the Freret Brothers Press yard. Confederate leaders and New Orleanians realized that General Winfield Scott, commander of the Union Army, saw the occupation of New Orleans as key to strangling the economy of the Confederate States. As the Union Navy made its way toward New Orleans and the capture of the city was in its sights, Confederate General Mansfield Lovell declared martial law in New Orleans on March 15, 1862. The citizens readily gave up some rights in hopes of protecting the city from those who sympathized with the Union and sought to work toward the city's capture. All adult white males, except unnaturalized foreigners, were required to take an Oath of Allegiance to the Confederate States of America. *The Daily Delta* praised the decision and declared, "The demon of discord, at this moment, is twin brother to the demon of treason…Here in New Orleans, since the proclamation of Marshal Law, it is hoped that malcontents and Yankee sympathizers will find that the atmosphere is unhealthy for persons of their temperament."[590] General Lovell appointed William Freret, Cyprian Dufour, Pierre Soulé, and Henry Ogden as Provost Marshals. By the end of March, William Freret resigned his post because of a serious illness. *The Picayune* lamented, "The resignation of Mr. Freret on account of ill health, deprives the city of the public services of one of our best and most respected citizens."[591]

On April 29, Admiral Farragut's cadre of thirteen ships equipped with two hundred guns arrived at New Orleans. Surrender was inevitable and Union representatives Captain Bailey and Lieutenant Perkins disembarked and made their way through the streets of New Orleans toward city hall. An angry mob began to follow the pair and tried to stop them from reaching their destination, desperately hoping that they could somehow stop the impending surrender. Some men who understood the consequences of resistance tried to reason with the crowd but were unsuccessful. Finally, William Freret and L. H. Forstall made their way through the throng and escorted the two officers to their destination and most assuredly avoided bloodshed.[592] City officials signed the surrender papers, and the occupation of New Orleans began. Union troops were quartered at Freret's Cotton Press, and Major General Benjamin Butler took charge of the city.[593]

William Freret's other properties, including his home on the corner of Baronne and Second Streets, were also seized by Union officials. The Confiscation Act of 1862 stipulated that Southern rebels in Union occupied areas had sixty days to take an oath of allegiance to the United States. President Lincoln cautioned against the seizing of property because he feared that such a practice would be detrimental to his ultimate goal of reuniting the nation. Lincoln reluctantly signed the bill into law but declared that the property would be returned when the war was over and the nation was one again. Approximately 68,000 people in New Orleans took the oath of allegiance. William Freret did not live long after his beloved city fell. It's unclear where he and Fanny lived after his home was taken. William Freret died on June 14, 1864, after a lengthy battle with a heart condition. He was buried in the Girod Street Cemetery in the Salkeld tomb where his father-in-law, George Salkeld, was interred. His wife later moved his remains to Cypress Grove Cemetery. His son, William Freret Jr., fought for and gained the return of his father's property after his death.

A

Acadians, 77, 79-80, 91-92
American School of Ethnology, 43
Andry, Bernard Noel "Manuel", 17-21
Andry, Gilbert Thomassin, 18
Andry, Madeline, Celeste, 80
Arkansas Post, 74-76, 136-137
Arkansas Territory, 135-136
Ascension Parish, 36, 77, 82, 87, 130-131, 142
Ashland Plantation, 130-131
Aubry, Charles Philippe, 79-80, 90-91

B

Bailliff, Marie Marguerite, 90
Baron, Noel Auguste Jr., 126
Battle of Baton Rouge, 83-84
Battle of Liberty Place, 66
Battle of New Orleans, 10-11, 127, 138, 140
Bayou Bonfouca, 2, 6
Bayou Lafourche, 32, 91
Bayou Manchac, 4, 5
Bayou St. John, 5, 6, 11
Bayou Terre aux Boeufs, 15
Beauregard, P.G.T., 58-59, 62, 64
Bellechasse Plantation, 34-36
Benjamin, Judah P., 34-36, 140
Bocage Plantation, 124
Bonaparte, Napoleon, 25, 42, 84-85, 103, 135-136
Bonpland, Aimé, 133-134, 137
Boré, Étienne de, 2, 86, 104, 106, 108, 114
Bouligny, Francisco, 101, 103
Bourbourg, Charles Étienne Brasseur de, 42-43
Bowden Plantation, 130-131
Brennan's Restaurant, 4
Bringer, Michel "Doradou", 127-128, 142-143
Bringier, Anne Guillemine "Nanine", 128-129
Bringier, Elizabeth Louise "Betzy", 128
Bringier, Françoise "Fanny", 124
Bringier, Françoise "Laure", 126
Bringier, Marius Pons, 85, 122-126, 132-135
Bringier, Melanie Elizabeth, 125-126
Bringier, Paul "Louis" (Don Louis), 132-143
British West Florida, 96-98, 102, 111, 126
Brown, James, 18
Brown, Montfort, 97
Burr, Arron, 110-114

C

Cabahonoce, 90-91
Cantrelle, Jacques, 89-98, 105
Cantrelle, Jacques II, 81-83
Cantrelle, Marie Marguerite (Verret, Marie Marguerite Cantrelle) 90
Cantrelle, Michel Bernard , 82-87
Carondelet, Francisco Luis Hector, baron de, 132
Casa Calvo, Marqués de, 86, 102, 104, 150
Champollion, Jean Jacques, 42, 47

Chauveau, Jean, 15
Chenet, Marie Marguerite, 2
Cherokee, 137
Cheval, Louison, 12
Christ Church, 114, 117, 155
Claiborne, William C. C., 14-20, 86-87, 104-112, 125
Clark, Daniel, 86, 103, 160-109, 111-114, 123, 136, 139
Clay, Henry, 155, 157
College of Orleans, 153
Colomb, Christophe, 124, 133
Committee of One Hundred, 58-64
Company of the First Acadian Coast, 92
Company of the Indies, 17, 74
Confiscation Act of 1862, 164
cotton factor, 147, 154
cotton industry, 8-9, 68-69, 123, 147, 151, 154
creole, 2, 11, 13, 33, 36, 39, 55, 66, 79, 91-92, 98-99, 108, 114-115, 129, 140, 157-158
Crescent City White League, 64-65
Cuban filibuster, 159-162
Cuckow, Emily, (Rillieux, Emily Cuckow), 46, 49, 51

D

Daniel Clark, 86, 103, 106-114, 123, 136, 139
Darby, William, 140-141
DeBow, J.D.B., 41, 48
Degas, Edgar, i, iv, 67-70
Deslondes, Charles, 18-20
Dickinson, Philemon, 99, 101
drainage - New Orleans, 47
Dred Scott v Sanford, 46
DuBourg, Louise Elizabeth "Aglae", 127
Duff, Mary Ann Dyke, 45-46
Durnford, Andrew, 32

F

Faubourg Marigny, 116
Faubourg St. Marie, See Faubourg St. Mary, 6, 8, 151, 154
filibusters, 159-161
Fillmore, Millard, 160-161
First Acadian Coast, 82, 86, 91-92
First Battalion of Free Men of Color, 10
Forstall, Edmond, 30, 35-37, 52-53
Fort Bute, 83
Fort Rosalie, 75-76
free people of color, 14, 16, 23, 39-40, 43, 46, 54-56, 58, 140
free women of color, 12-16
Freret Brothers Cotton Press, 154, 162-163
Freret Cotton Press, 8
Freret William Sr., i, 30-31, 153-164
Freret, James P., 37, 149, 153-155, 162
Freret, James Sr., 8, 11, 146-154
Freret, John, 149, 150, 152-154
Freret, Marie "Eugenie", 146, 150, 153-154

Freret, William Sr., 164
Friends of Universal Suffrage, 56-58, 63

G

Gálvez, Bernando de, 5, 82-84, 99
Gayoso, Manuel, 100-101
Genois, Charles, 156-157
German Coast Uprising (1811 Slave Revolt), 17-21
Gliddon, George R., 40-43
Grinnan-Henderson-Reily House, 14
Gutiérrez, José Bernardo de Gutiérrez de Lara, 138-139

H

Hampton, Wade, 19-20
Houma Nation, 85-86
Humbert, Joseph Amable, 138-140
Humboldt, Alexander von, 133-137

I

Insurrection of 1768, 79-80, 92, 98
Isleños, 100

J

Jackson, Andrew, 10, 32, 127, 140-141, 155
Jefferson, Thomas, 86-87, 101, 103, 105-113, 116, 127, 134
Jones, Evan, 86, 96-18
Jones, James, 96-97, 99-101, 106, 117-118
Jones, John, 117
Jones, Lise, 118
Jones, Mary Ann, 99, 113, 115-117
Jones, Thomas, 117
Judice, Louis, 77, 85, 90-91
July Revolution, 25-28

K

Kenner, Duncan, 45, 47-49, 69, 128-131
Kenner, Harry, 18
Kenner, William, 110-129

L

L'École Centrale, 24, 28, 30
L'Hermitage Plantation, 127, 142
La Balize, 78-80
Lafayette, Marquis de, 26-28
Lafitte, Jean, 136, 190-140
Lafitte, Pierre, 136, 139-140, 153, 156
Lafourche, 99-100, 114
Lafrénière, Nicolas, 80
Landreaux, Honoré, 11
Larmusiau, Marguerite Joseph, (Cantrelle, Marguerite Joseph Larmusiau) 76, 82, 90
Latour, Arséne Lacarrriére, 141

Laussat, Pierre Clémont de, 85, 104, 107, 115, 123, 125
Law, John, 17, 27, 74, 88
Letorey, Jean Baptiste, 32-33
Livingston, Edward, 106-107, 111-112, 139
Livingston, Henry Brockholst, 100-101
Lopez, Narciso, 160-161
Louisiana Bank, 106
Louisiana Militia, 5, 10
Louisiana Purchase, 23, 85, 123, 125, 139
Louisiana Sugar Planters' Association, 47-48, 131

M

Macarty, Augustine (McCarty, Augustin), 11, 151
Madison, James, 102-103, 105, 107, 108-109, 111
Manchac, 4, 5, 83, 97
Marigny, Bernard de, 99, 113, 115-115
Marks, Isaac N., 58, 61-62, 64
McCall, Henry, 1118
Mechanics' Institute massacre, 57
Melish, John, 140-141
Melpomene, 127
Merchants' Exchange, 154-155
Meullion, Jean Baptiste, 14
Mexican Association, 111, 114, 139
Mexican silver mines, 134-135, 142
Mezange, Eulalie, 13, 52
Minor, Mary, 129
Minquetz, Marie Franciennne, 74-76
Missouri Territory, 140-141
Montegut, Edgar, 158
Morton, Samuel, 40
Musson, Germain, 67
Musson, Marie-"Célestine" (Degas,Marie Célestine Musson), 67
Musson, Michel, 58, 62, 64-65, 68

N

Natchez Revolt (Natchez Massacre) 75-76
Native American Party, 155-156
New Madrid earthquakes, 137-138
New Orleans Association, 139
New Orleans public schools, 156, 158
Nicolas Pierre Verret, 77, 82, 90-92
Nott, Josiah, 41-43

O

O'Reilly, Alejandro, 80, 87, 92, 97-98, 104
Onis, Luis de, 139-140
Osage (Native American tribe), 137

P

Packwood, Theodore, 33-34, 36
Pampero, 160-162
Panic of 1837, 32, 56
Pensacola, 84, 96-98, 106, 109, 115, 126, 154
Petit, Pierre, 107
Pickering, Timothy, 101-102
Picornelle, Juan, 139
Pitot, James, 6, 107
plaçage, 12-14
placée, 13
Pollock, Oliver, 98
polygenesis, 40-41
Poydras, Julian, 108-110, 147
Prieur, Denis, 157

R

Reconstruction, 55-58
Republican Party, 55-57
Reynaud, Jean Louis Melchior, 153
Rillieux apparatus, 29-39, 41, 47-49, 51, 131
Rillieux, Edmond Sr., 14, 30-31, 52-66
Rillieux, François, 9
Rillieux, Marie Célestine (Musson, Marie-Célestine Rillieux, 67
Rillieux, Marie "Eugenie"(Freret, Eugenie Rillieux) 11, 31, 146-151, 153
Rillieux, Marie Heloise, 153
Rillieux, Michel Vincent, 6
Rillieux, Norbert, 22-51, 52, 54, 131
Rillieux, Vincent Jr., 8-16, 22-24, 30-31, 37, 52-54, 147, 153
Rillieux, Vincent Sr., 2-7
Robinson, John Hamilton, 138-139

S

Saint-Domingue Slave Rebellion. (Haitian Revolution), 13, 15, 8-19, 159
Salkeld, George, 154
Sedella, Antonio de (Pére Antoine), 117, 139, 141, 147-151
Seven Years War (French and Indian War), 4, 57, 78, 91, 96
Simpson, William, 126
Society of the Friends of the People, 27-28
Somerielos, Marques de, 101-102
Soulé, Pierre, 162-163
Soulié, Jean, 13-14, 52
Soulié, Norbert, 14, 52-53
St. James Parish, 79, 81-82, 87, 90-91, 122-125
St. Louis Cathedral, 16, 28, 139, 147
St. Marc, Heloise Marguerite, 151, 153
St. Maxent, Gilbert, 80, 92
St. Tammany Parish, 2-7
Stewart, Marie Eugenie Freret, 146, 150, 153-154

sugar refining, 29, 32-39, 44, 47-49, 51

T

Thomassin, Marie Anne Marguerite Rillieux, 17
Treaty of Fontainebleau, 3, 78, 91
Treaty of Paris, 3, 7, 96
Treaty of San Ildefonso, 103
Tremé Plantation, 153
Tronquet, Marie Antoinette, 3, 6, 8, 67, 147
Tunica-Biloxi, 2, 7
Tureaud, Augustine, 125

U

Ulloa, Antonio de, 78-81, 91-92, 96, 98
Unification Party, 58-64
United States v. Heirs of Rillieux, 7

V

Van Leer, Matilda Jane Duff.(Rillieux, Matilda), 44-46
Verret, André, 80
Verret, Marie Marguerite "Pomponne", 114, 117-118
Verret, Nicolas, 77, 82-83, 90-92
Villeré, Joseph, 80
Vivant, Charles Sr., 12, 14
Vivant, Constance, 11-16, 22-23, 31

W

War of 1812, 10-11, 127, 138, 140
Washington, George, 26, 27, 99, 111
Whig Party of Louisiana, 155-157
White Hall Plantation, 123-127, 132-133, 142
Wilkinson, James, 104, 107, 111-113
Wilson, James Fisher, 126
Woodland Plantation, 17-21

Y

yellow fever, 9, 11, 17, 19, 22, 107, 118, 151

BIBLIOGRAPHY

(1804, March 31). *Gazeta de Madrid,* p. 677. Retrieved from https://play.google.com/books/reader?id=TpzY5fOufrcC&pg=GBS.PA676

(1811, March 1). *Pittsburgh Weekly Gazette,* p. 2.

(1812, June 3). *Aurora General Advertiser.*

(1851, August 22). *The New Orleans Bee.*

(1852, October 18). *Republican Compiler.*

(1852, May 22). *New Orleans Crescent,* p. 1.

(1857, January 1). *Journal of the Franklin Institute.*

(1857, February 19). *Evening Star.*

(1857, April 21). *New York Daily Times,* p. 5.

(1857, April 21). *New York Daily Times,* p. 5.

(1862, May 18). *Daily Delta.*

(1862, March 28). *Times Picayune.*

(1873, April 1). *New Orleans Times.*

(1873, July 16). *Daily Picayune.*

(1878). *Exposition Universelle de 1878: Les Beaux Arts et Les Arts Decoratifs*. Paris. Retrieved from https://archive.org/stream/ beauxartsdeycor00pari/beauxartsdeycor00pari_djvu.txt

(1881, April 1). *The Sugar Cane: A Monthly Magazine, Devoted to the Interests of the Sugar Cane Industry,* 13.

(1886, March 21). *Times Picayune*.

(1894, October 14). *Le Gaulois. Paris, France: Bibliotheque national de France*. Retrieved from http://catalogue.bnf.fr/ark:/12148/cb32779904b

(1902, July 5). *Louisians Planter and Sugar Manufacturer,* 24(1).

(1911, April 30). *Brooklyn Daily Eagle,* p. 67. Retrieved from http:/bklyn.newspapers.com/image/55358971

(1911, January 1). *Hawaiian Planters' Record,* 5.

(2016). *Appletons' Cyclopedia of American Biography Volume III, III,* 466-467. (I. Ancestry.com Operations, Compiler) Lehi, Utah. Retrieved September 2, 2019, from www.ancestry.com

(2017). Retrieved from St. Tammany Parish Government: http://www.stpgov.org/department_album_view.php?id=140&category=home_gallery2&regpro_minical_month=3&regpro_minical_year=2025

(2017, February 27). Retrieved from Louisiana Landmark Society Pitot House: http://pitothouse.org/

A Greenwood Romance: The Secret of a Great Actress's Death Disclosed After Seventeen Years. (1874, September 6). *Times Picayune,* p. 10.

A Proposition to Erect Not One, but a Hundred Monuments to a Great Inventor. (1886, July 12). The Times Picayune. New Oleans, Louisiana: Newspapers.com. Retrieved January 20, 2017, from https://www.newspapers.com/image/25558097/?terms=Rillieux

A Visior's Guide to New Orleans 1875. (New Orleans). 1875, Louisiana: J. Curtis Waldo, Southern Publishing and Advertising House. Retrieved January 17, 2017, from http://quod.lib.umich.edu/m/moa/AJA2779.0001.001?rgn=main;view=fulltext

Abbott, E. (2011). *Sugar: A Bittersweet History.* New York: The Overlook Press.

Abstracts Of Some Colonial Documents, 1800. (1995, September 15). *Spanish Colonial Documents.* Louisiana State Museum. Retrieved from https://www.crt.state.la.us/dataprojects/museum/spanishcolonial/31_Jan_8_1798_to_Jan_2_1804.pdf

Academie des Inscriptions et Belles-Letters. (1869). *Comptes rendus des seances:de l'anne 1868.* Paris: Boccard.

Acts Passed at the First Session of the Legislative Council of the Territory of Orleans: Begun and Held at the Principal, in the City of New-Orleans, on Monday the Third Day of December, in the Year of Our Lord One Thousand Eight Hundred and Four, and of. (1805). New Orleans: James M. Bradford, Printer to the Territory.

(1835). *Acts Passed at the First Session of the Twelfth Legislature of the State of Louisiana.* New Orleans: J. C. de St. Romes.

(1840). *Acts Passed at the Second Session of the Fourteenth Legislature of Louisiana.* New Orleans: Bullett Magne & Co. State Printers.

Adams, J. (1799, April 22). *From John Adams to Timothy Pickering, 22 April 1799.* Retrieved April 11, 2019, from Founders Online: https://founders.archives.gov/documents/Adams/99-02-02-3452

Adams, P. (2014). *Politics, Faith, and the Making of American Judaism.* Ann Arbor: University of Michigan Press.

(1839). *Address of the Lousiana Native American Association to the Citizens of Louisiana and the Inhabitants of the United States.* New Orleans: D. Felt & Co.

Administrations of the Mayors of New Orleans: William Freret. (2011, November 8). Retrieved Aug 23, 2019, from New Orleans Public Library: http://nutrias.org/~nopl/info/louinfo/admins/freret.htm

Admittance and Seating Policies for the American Theatre in New Olreans in 1820. (2007, September 28). Retrieved March 29, 2018, from Louisiana Digital Library: http://www.louisianadigitallibrary.org/islandora/object/state-lwp%3A3186

Alexander, E. U. (2004). *Notorious Woman: The Celebrated Case of Myra Clark Gaines.* Baton Rouge: LSU Press.

Alfred. (1904, October 8). Alfred Letter to the Editor. *The Louisiana Planter and Sugar Manufacturer, 33*, p. 243.

Allahar, A. L. (1994). Sugar, Slaves, and the Politics of Annexationism: Cuba, 1840-1850. *European Review of Latin American and Caribbean Studies,* 282-304.

Allison, J. M. (1923, January). Paris After the July Days. *The Sewanee Review, 31*(1), 60-72.

American Chemical Society National Historic Chemical Landmarks. Norbert Rillieux and a Revolution in Sugar. (2002). (National Historic Chemical Landmarks program of the American Chemical Society) Retrieved March 16, 2016, from Processing. http://www.acs.org/content/acs/en/education/whatischemistry/landmarks/norbertrillieux.html

American Friends of Lafayette. (n.d.). *Lafayette Timeline - 1757 - present.* (American Friends of Lafayette) Retrieved June 27, 2017, from The American Friends of Lafayettl: https://friendsoflafayette.wildapricot.org/Timeline

Americanists, I. C. (1875). *Proceedings - International Congress of Americanists.* Retrieved from https://archive.org/stream/proceedingsinter1875vol2inte/proceedingsinter1875vol2inte_djvu.txt

(1844). *An Address to the Citizens of Louisiana on the Subject of the Recent Election in New Orleans.* New Orleans: The Bee.

Ancestry.com. (2014). U.S. Newspaper Extractions from the Northeast, 1704-1930. Provo, Utah: Ancestry.com Operations Inc. Retrieved from Ancestry.com: www.ancestry.com

Ancestry.com. (2015). Louisiana, Wills and Probate Records 1756-1984. Provo, Utah: Ancestry.com Operations, Inc. Retrieved from www.ancestry.com

Arthur, S. (1999). *Old Families of Louisiana.* New Orleans: Pelican Publishing.

Austin, P. E. (2016). *Baring Brothers and the Birth of Modern Finance.* Routledge.

Bache, R. S. (1848). *Reports from the Secretary of the Treasury: of scientific investigations in relation to sugar and hydrometers, made under the superintendence of Professor R. S. McCulloh.* Washington D.C.: Wendell and Van Benthuysen.

Bailly, J. S., & Voltaire. (1779). *Lettres sur l'Atlantide de Platon et sur l'ancienne histoire de l'Asie.* Paris: Chez M. Elmesly.

Balcourt, M. (1820). *Polytechnisches Journal,* Band 3, 422-423.

Baptist, E. E. (2016). *The Half Has Never Been Told: Slavery and the Making of American Capitalism.* Basic Books.

Barbados Today. (2017, February 8). *Norbert Rillieux – The Sugar Industry's Engineering Genius.* Retrieved July 28, 2017, from Barbados Today: https://www.barbadostoday.bb/2017/02/08/norbert-rillieux-the-sugar-industrys-engineering-genius/

Bauer, C. A. (1993). *A Leader Among Peers: The Life and Times of Duncan Farrar Kenner.* Lafayette: University of Lousiana at Lafayette Press.

Bauer, C. A. (2011). *Creole Genesis: The Bringier Family and Antebellum Plantation Life in Louisiana.* Lafayette: University at Lafayette Press.

Beauchamp, M. K. (2009). *Instrumbents of Empire: Colonial Elites and U.S. Governance in Early National Louisiana, 1803-1820* (dissertation). College Station: Texas A&M Universtity.

Beckert, S. (2014, December 12). *Empire of Cotton.* Retrieved from The Atlantic: https://www.theatlantic.com/business/archive/2014/12/empire-of-cotton/383660/

Bell, C. C. (1997). *Revolution, Romanticism, and the Afro-Creole Protest Tradition in Louisiana 1718-1868.* Baton Rouge: LSU Press.

Bellazaire Meullion receipt for shares in New Orleans, Opelousas, and Great Western Railroad Co., 1852 October 23. (n.d.). *Meullion Family Papers.* Folder 01-02, 1831-1906. Louisiana Digital Library. Retrieved February 24, 2018, from http://louisianadigitallibrary.org/islandora/object/fpoc-p16313coll51%3A41758

Benfey, C. (1997). *Degas in New Orleans: encounters in the Creole world of Kate Chopin and George Wahsington Cable.* New York : Knopf.

Benfey, C. (1998, Summer). Norbert Rillieux: Chemical Engineer and Free Black Cousin of Edgar Degas. *Chemical Heritage,* pp. 10 & 11; 38-41.

Benjamin, J. P., & Slidell, T. (1834). *Digest of the Reported Decisions of tghe Supreme Court of the Late Territory of Orleans and the Supreme Court of Lousisian.* New Orleans: John F. Carter.

Bennet, R. A. (1909). *A Volunteer with Pike, The True Narrative of One Dr. John Robinson and of His Love for the Fair Señorita Vallois.* Chicago: A. C. McClurg & Company.

Berlin, I. (1974). *Slaves Without Masters: The Free Negro in the Antebellum South.* New York: New York Press.

Bevan, A. K. (2011). *We are the Same People: the Leverich Family of New York.*

Binton, D. G. (1868). The Abbe Brasseur and His Labors. *Lippincott's Magazine of Literature, Science and Education.*

Blaufarb, R. (2016). *Bonapartists in the Borderlands: French Exiles and Refugees on the Gulf Coast, 1815-1835.* University of Alabama Press.

Boggs, J. S. (1999). Catalogue. In G. Feigenbaum, *Degas and New Orleans: A French Impressionist in America.* New Orleans: New Orleans Museum of Art.

Boggs, J. S. (1999). Catalogue. In G. Feigenbaum, *Degas and New Orleans* (pp. 105-264). New Orleans: New Orelans Museum of Art.

Boiling Sugar. (1842, January 29). *Times Picayune.*

Boiling Sugar. (1842, January 29). *The Times Picayune.*

Boiling Sugar. (1842, January 29). *Times Picayune.*

Bourbourg, C. É. (1868). *Quatre lettres sur le Mexique: exposition absolue du système hiéroglyphique mexicain la fin de l'age de pierre. Époque glaciaire temporaire. Commencement de l'age de bronze. Origines de la civilisation et des religions de l'antiquité; d'après le Teo-Amoxt.* Paris: F. Brachet.

Bourgeois, L. C. (1957). *Cabanocey: The History, Customs, and Folklore of St. James Parish.* Pelican Publishing.

Bradley, J. W. (2002). *Interim: W. C. C. Claiborne Letter Book, 1804-1805.* Baton Rouge: Louisiana State University Press.

Bradshaw, J. (2014, October 22). *The Saint-Domingue Revolution.* (D. Johnson, Editor) Retrieved May 10, 2017, from KnowLouisiana.org Encyclopedia of Louisiana: http://www.knowlouisiana.org/entry/the-saint-domingue-revolution

Brasseaux, C. A., & Voorhies, J. K. (1989). *Quest for the Promised Land: Official Correspondence Rliationg to the First Acadian Migration to Louisiana,* 1764-1769. (C. A. Brasseaux, Ed.) Lafayette, Louisiana: The Center for Louisiana Studies - University of Southwestern Louisiana.

Breeden, J. O. (1976, March-April). States-Rights Medicine in the Old South. *Bulletin of New York Academy of Medicine, 52*(3), pp. 348-361.

Bringier, L. (1821). otices of the Geology, Mineralogy, Topography, Productions, and Aboriginal inhabitants of the regions around the Mississippi and its confluent waters. (B. Silliman, Ed.) *The American Journal of Science and Arts.*

Bringier, L., & Darby, W. (New York). *Prospectus of Historical and geographical tracts, with maps, on Louisiana by William Darby and Louis Bringier.* 1815: unknown.

Britannica, T. E. (2009, February 26). *Jean-Sylvain Bailly.* (Encyclopædia Britannica, inc.) Retrieved December 28, 2017, from Encyclopædia Britannica: https://www.britannica.com/biography/Jean-Sylvain-Bailly

Britannica, T. E. (2017, June 20). *Jean-François Champollion.* Retrieved from Encyclopedia Britannica: https://www.britannica.com/biography/Jean-François-Champollion

Britannica, T. E. (2017, May 9). *Lyceum movement.* Retrieved January 20, 2018, from https://www.britannica.com/topic/lyceum-movement

Britannica, T. E. (Ed.). (n.d.). *Ultra French History.* (i. Encyclopædia Britannica, Producer) Retrieved June 17, 2017, from Encyclopædia Britannica: https://www.britannica.com/topic/ultra-French-history

Broglie, A.-L.-V. d. (1887). *Personal recollections of the late Duc de Broglie, 1785-1820.* London: Ward and Downey.

Brown, C. (2009). *The Youngest of the great American Family": The Creation of a Franco-American Culture in Early Louisiana PhD diss.* University of Tennessee. Retrieved from https://trace.tennessee.edu/utk_graddiss/566/

Brown, C. A. (1944, Spring). Alexander von Humboldt as Historian of Science in Latin America. *Isis,* 134-139. Retrieved from https://www.jstor.org/stable/330595

Brown, M. R. (1991). *The DeGas-Musson Family Papers: An Annotated Inventory.* New Orleans: Louisiana Research Collection - Howard Tilton Memorial Library Special Collections. Retrieved from https://specialcollections.tulane.edu/archon/?p=collections/findingaid&id=583&q=&rootcontentid=102489

Brown, M. R. (1999). A Tale of Two Families: The De Gas-Musson Correspondence at Tulane University. In G. Feigenbaum, *Degas and New Orleans: A French Impressionist in America* (pp. 67-98). New Orleans: New Orleans Museum of Art.

Buchanan, B. G. (2016). *Securitization and the Global Economy: History and Prospects for the Future.* Springer.

Buman, N. (2013). Two histories, one future : Louisiana sugar planters, their slaves, and the Anglo-Creole schism, 1815-1865. Baton Rouge, Louisiana. Retrieved from http://digitalcommons.lsu.edu/gradschool_dissertations/1908/

Buman, N. A. (2008). *To Kill Whites: The 1811 Louisiana Slave Insurrection.* Baton Rouge, Louisiana: LSU - Masters Thesis.

Burke, B. (2014). Development of Steady-State Mulitple Effect Evaporator Model and Practicle Application in Sugar Mills. *Proc Aust Soc Sugar Cane Technol,* 36. Retrieved from https://www.assct.com.au/media/pdfs/M%2010%20Burke-2.pdf

Caldwell, R. G. (1915). *The Lopez Expeditions to Cuba 1848-1851.* Princeton: Princeton Universtiy Press.

Campanella, R. (2016, September 1). Gallier and Dankin's Merchants' Exchange. *Preservation in Print.* Retrieved from https://prcno.org/gallier-dankins-merchants-exchange

Cane Sugar. (1907). In F. Freret, & R. M. La Follette (Ed.), *The Making of America: Agricultue Volume 5* (pp. 212-226). Chicago: De Bower, Chapline & Company.

Carter, C. (Ed.). (1940). *The Territorial Papers of the United States Volume 9, The Territory of Orleans, 1803-1812.* Wahsington D. C. : U. S. Government Printing Office.

Chaffin, T. (2011, January 10). Abe Lincoln and Filibuster Fever. *The New York Times.* Retrieved from https://opinionatorblogs.nytimes.com/2011/01/10/abe-lincoln-and-filibuster-fever/

Chambers, D. B. (2010). Slave Trade Merchants of Spanish New Orleans, 1763-1803: Clarifying the Colonial Slave Trade to Louisiana in Atlantic Perspective. In W. Boelhower (Ed.), *New Orleans in the Atlantic World: Between Land and Sea.* New York: Routledge.

Chambon, C. M. (1908). *In and Around the old St. Louis Cathedral fo New Orleans.* New Orleans: Philippe's Printery.

Chandler, R. E. (1986, Autumn). Ulloa's Account of the 1768 Revolt. *Louisiana History: The Journal of the Louisiana Historical Association, 27*(4), pp. 407-437. Retrieved October 9, 2019, from https://www.jstor.org/stable/4232553

Chavez, C. G. (2018, July-September). They Want to Poison the Archbishop-Viceroy! The History of a Conspiracy Investigated by the Inquisition of New Spain (August 1809 - January 1810). *Hist.mex*, 68(1). Retrieved from http://dx.doi.org/10.24201/hm.v68il.3638

Christ Church Cathedral. (n.d.). *Christ Church Cathedral.* New Orleans.

Claiborne, W. C. (1804, October 8). *To James Madison from William C. C. Claiborne.* Retrieved February 5, 2019, from Founders Online: https://founders.archives.gov/documents/Madison/02-08-02-0146

Claiborne, W. C. (1804, October 13). *To James Madison from William C. C. Claiborne 13 October 1804.* Retrieved April 18, 2019, from Founders Online: https://founders.archives.gov/documents/Madison/02-08-02-0168

Claiborne, W. C. (1804, November 5). *To James Madison from William C. C. Claiborne 5 November 1804.* Retrieved February 5, 2019, from Founders Online: https://founders.archives.gov/documents/Madison/02-08-02-0265

Claiborne, W. C. (1804, January 2). *To James Madison from William C. C. Claiborne, 2 January 1804.* Retrieved August 8, 2019, from Founders Online: https://fournders.archives.gov/documents/Madison/02-06-02-0254

Claiborne, W. C. (1804, November 19). *To Thomas Jefferson from William C. C. Claiborne, 19 November 1804.* Retrieved November 1, 2019, from Founders Online: https://founders.archives.gov/documents/Jefferson/99-01-02-0673

Claiborne, W. C. (1804, December 2). *To Thomas Jefferson From William C. C. Claiborne, 2 December 1804.* Retrieved February 5, 2019, from Founders Online: https://founders.archives.gov/documents/Jefferson/99-01-02-0756

Claiborne, W. C. (1805, March 18). *To James Madison from William C. C. Claiborne.* Retrieved December 13, 2019, from Founders Online: https://founders.archives.gov/documents/Madison/02-09-02-0151

Claiborne, W. C. (1805, August 6). *To James Madison From William C. C. Claiborne, 6 August 1805.* Retrieved April 4, 2019, from Founders Online: https://founders.archives.gov/documents/Madison/02-10-02-0157

Claiborne, W. C. (1806, July 15). *To Thomas Jefferson from William C. C. Claiborne, 15 July 1806.* Retrieved November 1, 2019, from Founders Online: https://founders.archives.gov/documents/Jefferson/99-01-02-4036

Claiborne, W. C. (1810, March 4). *To James Madison from William C. C. Claiborne.* Retrieved November 13, 2020, from Founders Online: https://founders.archives.gov/documents/Madison/03-02-02-0320

Clark, D. (1809). *Proofs of the corruption of Gen. James Wilkinson and of his connection with Aaron Burr : with a full refutation of his slanderous allegations in relation to the character of the principal witness against him.* Philadelphia: Wm. Hall, Jr. & Geo. W. Pierie.

Clark, E. (2013). *The Strange History of the American Quadroon: Free Women of Color in the Revolutionary Atlantic World.* Chapel Hill: University of North Carolina Press.

Claye, J. (1878). *Gazette des beaux-arts.* Paris.

Cochran, E. M. (1963). *The Fortier Family and Allied Families.* Estelle M. F. Cochran.

Cohen, H. (1854). *Cohen's New Orleans Directory.* New Orleans: Picayune.

Collins, P. (2014). *Duel with the Devil: The True Story of How Alexander Hamilton and Aaron Burr Teamed Up to Take on America's First Sensational Murder Mystery.* New York: Broadway Books.

Colodon, D. (1893, January 1). Souvenirs et mémoires: autobiographie.

Cooper, S. (n.d.). *Norbert Rillieux, Thermodynamics and Chemical Engineering.* Retrieved December 4, 2015, from American Chemical Society: https://www.acs.org/content/dam/acsorg/education/whatischemistry/landmarks/norbertrillieux/rillieux-thermodynamics-engineering-landmark-lesson-plan.pdf

Cormier, S. A. (2019, November 6). *Acadians in Gray.* Retrieved November 6, 2019, from http://www.acadiansingray.com/Acadians%20of%20LA%20-Intro-4a.html#new_six

Correspondence Between the Treasury Department in Relation to the Cuban Expedition and William Freret, Late Collector. (1851). New Orleans: Alex Levy and Co.

Crescent City Club. Its Complete Reorganization as a White League. (1874, July 1). *Times Picayune,* p. 1.

Cruzat, H. H. (1919, January). The Ursulines of Louisiana. *Louisiana Historical Quarterly, 2*(1).

Currie, C. R. (1995). *Sugar at LSU: Cultivating a Sweeter Future.* Retrieved July 8, 2017, from LSU Library: http://www.lib.lsu.edu/sites/all/files/sc/exhibits/e-exhibits/sugar/contents.html

Dardar, T. M. (2004, September). *Louisiana Indians.* Retrieved January 24, 2019, from Snowowl: http://www.snowwowl.com/peoplelouisiana4.html

Davis, J. (1906). History of the Thoroughbred, Together with Personal Reminiscences by the Author Who in Turn Has Been Jockey, Breeder and Owner. New York, New York: John Polhemus Printing Company. Retrieved from https://archive.org/stream/americanturf00dai/americanturf00davi_djvu.txt

Davis, W. C. (2006). *The Pirates Lafitte: The Treacherous World of the Corsairs of the Gulf.* Mariner Books.

Davis, W. C. (n.d.). *Jean and Pierre Lafitte.* Retrieved April 15, 2020, from 64 Parishes: https://64parishes.org/entry/jean-and-pierre-laffite

Denmark Vesey, Forgotten Hero. (1999, December). *The Atlantic.* Retrieved from Denmark Vesey, Forgotten Hero

Desdunes, R. L. (1973). *Our People and Our History: Fifty Creole Portraits.* (D. O. Mcants, Ed., & D. O. Mcants, Trans.) Baton Rouge, Lousiana: LSU Press.

Dessen, N. (2015). *Creole City: A Chronicle of Early Americn New Orleans.* Gainsville: University Press of Florida.

Died. (1857, July 20). *New York Daily Tribune.*

Dillard, T. (2010). *Statesmen, Scoundrels, and Eccentrics: A Gallery of Amazing Arkansans.* University of Arkansas Press.

Din, G. C. (1988). *The Canary Islanders of Louisiana.* Baton Rouge: Louisiana State University Press.

Din, G. C., & Harkins, J. E. (1996). *New Orleans Cabildo: Colonial Louisiana's First City Government, 1769-1803.* Baton Rouge: LSU Press.

Direct Data Capture, c. (1999). *U.S., War of 1812 Service Records, 1812-1815.* (Ancestry.com Operations Inc) Retrieved December 10, 2016, from Ancestry.com: ancestry.com

Dormon, J. H. (1977, Autumn). The Persistent Specter: Slave Rebellion in Territorial Louisiana. Louisiana History: *The Journal of the Louisiana Historical Association, 18*(4), pp. 389-404.

Dred Scott v John F. A. Sanford (U. S. Supreme Court March 6, 1857).

Dudley, T. A. (2012). *Ownership, Engagement, and Entrepreneurship: The Gens de Couleur Libres and the Architecture of Antebellum New Orleans, 1820-1850.* Austin: University of Texas.

Dufour, C. L. (1967). *Ten Flags in the Wind: The Story of Louisiana.* New York: Harper and Row.

Dunbar Rowland, L. (Ed.). (1907). *Encyclopedia of Mississippi History: Comprising Sketches of Counties, Towns, Events, Institutions and Persons.* Madison, WI: Selwyn A. Brant.

Duplicates of Intendants of the Army and of the Royal Archive of the Indies. (1803). Retrieved December 31, 2018, from

Archivos Espanole: http://pares.mcu.es/ParesVusquedas20/catalogo/description/451305

Editors of Encyclopedia Britannica. (2000, February 10). *Mary Ann Duff Dyke*. Retrieved from Encyclopedia Britannica: https://www.britannica.com/biography/Mary-Ann-Dyke-Duff

Ellis, F. S. (1998). *St. Tammany Parish L'Autre Cote du Lac.* Gretna: Pelican Publishing Co.

Ellis, S. S. (2019, May 16). *The Flamboyant 19th-Century Creole Aristocrat Who Built New Orleans' First Suburb.* Retrieved August 29, 2019, from https://www.whatitmeanstobeamerican.org/identities/the-flamboyant-19th-century-creole-aristocrat-who-built-new-orleans-first-suburb/

Ensor, B., & Wilson, E. M. (1993). *Historic Resources Assessment of the Pascagoula River/Delta, Twin Oaks and Manhannah Farm Tract, Tennessee-Tombigbee Waterway Wildlife Mitigation Project, Mississippi H.* Tuscaloosa: Panamerican Consultants, Inc.

Erickson, P. A. (1986). The anthropology of Josiah Clark Nott. *Kroeber Anthropological Society papers,* pp. 103-120.

Evans, E. N. (1988). *Judah P. Benjamin: The Jewish Confederate.* New York: The Free Press.

Evans, T. (2011, August). *Edward Charles Howard and Norbert Rillieux – Sugar plantation slavery and the birth of chemical engineering.* Retrieved June 12, 2018, from https://www.thechemicalengineer.com/features/cewctw-edward-charles-howard-and-norbert-rillieux-sugar-plantation-slavery-and-the-birth-of-chemical-engineering/

Fabre, M. (2000). New Orleans Expatriates in France. In S. Kein (Ed.), *The History and Legacy of Louisiana's Free People of Color* (pp. 179-195). Baton Rouge, Louisiana: LSU Press.

Fandrich, J. (2005). *The Mysterious Voodoo Queen, Marie Laveaux: A Study of Powerful Female Leadership in Nineteenth Century New Orleans.* New York: Routledge.

Feigenbaum, G. (1999). Edgar Degas, Almost a Son of Louisiana. In G. Feigenbaum, *Degas and New Orleans: A French Impressionist in America.* New Orleans: New Orleans Museum of Art.

Fenner, E. D. (1850, January 1). General Report On the Medical Topography AND Meteorology of New Orleans, With an Account on the Prevalent diseases During the year 1849. *Southern Medical Reports,* 1. New Orleans, Louisiana: B.M. Norman.

Ferreiro, L. D. (2016, November 29). *The American Revolution Story Has a Hole the Size of Spain:.* (S. Kercher, & A. Martine, Editors) Retrieved December 29, 2017, from What It Means to be an American: http://www.whatitmeanstobeamerican.org/encounters/the-american-revolution-story-has-a-hole-the-size-of-spain/

Fessenden, M. (2016, January 8). *How a Nearly Successful Slave Revolt Was Intentionally Lost to History.* Retrieved June 25, 2020, from SMITHSONIANMAG.COM: https://www.smithsonianmag.com/smart-news/its-anniversary-1811-louisiana-slave-revolt-180957760/

Finkelman, P. (2011). *Millard Fillmore: The American Presidents Series: The 13th President, 1850-1853.* Macmillan.

Fire at Freret Press. (1830, Aug 7). *Natchez Democrat,* p. 7.

Flemming, T. (1982, April/May). Bernardo De Gálvez: The Forgotten Revolutionary Conquistador Who Saved Louisiana. *American Heritage, 33*(3). Retrieved October 8, 2019, from https://www.americanheritage.com/bernardo-de-galvez

Follet, R. J. (1997). *The Sugar Masters: Slavery, Economic Development, and Modernization on Louisiana Sugar Plantations, 1820-1860.* Baton Rouge, Louisiana: Louisiana State University LSU Digital Commons. Retrieved from http://digitalcommons.lsu.edu/cgi/viewcontent.cgi?article=7539&context=gradschool_disstheses

Ford, E. (2016, July 17). *The Last Moments of Girod St. Cemetery.* Retrieved September 7, 2019, from https://www.oakandlaurel.com/blog/the-last-moments-of-girod-street-cemetery

Fornal, J. (2016, October 5). *Nat Turner's Slave Uprising Left Complex Legacy.* (National Geographic Partners, LLC) Retrieved from National Geographic: http://news.nationalgeographic.com/2016/10/nat-turner-slave-rebellion-legacy/

Fortier, A. (2012 (originally published 1904), February 24). A History of Louisiana Vol. 2. New Orleans, Louisiana: Cornerstone Book Publisher.

Founding of Liberia, 1847. (n.d.). Retrieved July 10, 2017, from United States Department of State, Office of the Historian: https://history.state.gov/milestones/1830-1860/liberia

(1827). *France Patent No. 1BA2362.* Retrieved November 10, 2016, from http://bases-brevets19e.inpifr/Thot/FrmFicheDoc.asp?idfiche=0017446&refFiche=0017128

Francis, H. J. (2011). *Investing in Citizenship: Free Men of Color and the case against Citizens Bank - Antebellum Louisiana.* New Orleans, Louisiana: University of New Orleans. Retrieved from http://scholarworks.uno.edu/cgi/viewcontent.cgi?article=2410&context=td

Frasier, J. (2003). *The French Quarter of New Orleans.* Jackson: University of Mississippi Press.

Frasier, J., & Freeman, W. (2012). T*he Garden District of New Orleans.* Jackson: University Press of Mississippi.

Free People of Color in Louisiana: Revealing an unknown past. (n.d.). Retrieved from Louisiana Digital Library: http://www.louisianadigitallibrary.org/cdm/ref/collection/p16313coll51/id/35121

Freeman, J. B. (2002). *Affairs of Honor: National Politics in the New Republic.* Yale University Press.

Fricker, J. (2013). *Louisiana in 1803.* Retrieved April 30, 2017, from Preservation Resource Center of New Orleans: http://prcno.org/programs/preservationinprint/piparchives/2003%20PIP/March%202003/12.html

Gallatin, A. (1804, August 20). *Gallatin to Jefferson 20th August 1804.* Retrieved February 7, 2019, from Online Library of Liberty: https://oll.libertyfund.org/titles/gallatin-the-writings-of-albert-gallatin-vol-1/simple

Galloway, J. (1989). *The Sugar Cane Industry: An Historical Geography from its Origins to 1914.* Cambridge: Cambridge University Press.

Galván, J. A. (2004). Sugar and Slavery: the Bittersweet Chapter in the 19th Century Cuba, 1817-1886. *Revista de Humanidades: Tecnológico de Monterrey, 16,* pp. 211-231. Retrieved from http://www.redalyc.org/pdf/384/38401609.pdf

Garcia, A. S., Garcia, M., & Luis, M. (2005). Los ingenios : colección de vistas de los principales ingenios de azúcar de la isla de Cuba. In A. S. Garcia, M. Garcia, & M. Luis, *Donde cristaliza la esperanza: lectura de Los ingenios* (pp. 9-61). Ediciones Doce Calles.

Garcia, C. (2013, September 13). *Edward Livingston.* (D. Johnson, Editor) Retrieved April 18, 2019, from 64 Parishes: https://64parishes.org/entry/edward-livingston

Gareis, J. v. (2001). Insurgencia y contrainsurgencia en el golfo de México, 1812-1820. In *La Independencia de México y el proceso autonomista novohispano 1808-1824* (pp. 185-228). Universidad Nacional Autónoma de México .

Garrigoux, J. (2017). *A Visonary Adventurer: Arsene Lacarriere Latour 1778-1837 The Unusual Travels of a Frenchman in the Americas.* (G. S. Brown, Trans.) Lafayette: University of Louisiana at Lafayette Press.

Garvey, J., & Widmer, M. L. (2012). *Beautiful Crescent: A History of New Orleans.* New Orleans: Pelican Publishing Co. Inc.

German Settlers in Louisiana and New Orleans. (n.d.). Retrieved November 13, 2020, from The Historic New Orleans Collection: https://www.hnoc.org/research/german-settlers-louisiana-and-new-orleans

Gick, J. (2013). *Epidemics.* Retrieved May 3, 2017, from New Orleans Pharmacy Museum: http://www.pharmacymuseum.org/epidemics

Gilman, S. H. (1886, April 15). Letter to the Editor. *The Times Picayune.*

Gradual Increase of African Slavery in Lousiana. (1868, July). *DeBow's Review, 5*(7), pp. 596-598.

Guillermo Prieto. (2010). *Viaje a los Estados-Unidos Vol. 2 [digital version].* Rice University. Houston: Instituto de Investigaciones Jose Maria Luis Mora. Retrieved from https://scholarship.rice.edu/jsp/xml/1911/27453/1/m002b.tei.html

Haber, L. (1970). *Black Pioneers of Science and Invention.* New York: Houghton Mifflin Harcourt.

Hamilton C. Horton, J. (1965, December). Judah P. Benjamin: Lawyer Under Three Flags. *American Bar Association Journal, 51,* pp. 1149-1153.

Harris, S.-A. (1999-2015). *The Evolution of the Isleño Identity.* Retrieved February 23, 2018, from Louisiana Folk Life: http://www.louisianafolklife.org/LT/Articles_Essays/islenos.html

Harvey, E. J. (2020, March 24). *Who was Alexander von Humboldt?* Retrieved August 28, 2020, from Smithsonian Magazine: https://www.smithsonianmag.com/smithsonian-institution/who-was-alexander-von-humboldt-180974473/

Hatch, W. C. (1893). *A History of the Town of Industry, Franklin County, Maine.* Farmington: Knowlton, McLeary & Co.

Heitmann, J. A. (1987). *The Modernization of the Louisiana Sugar Industry 1830-1910.* Baton Rouge: LSU Press.

Hemard, N. (2012). *He fought Pakenham Twice.* Retrieved April 17, 2020, from New Orleans Nostalgia: https://www.neworleansbar.org/uploads/files/HeFoughtPakenhamTwiceArticle.3-28.pdf

Historic New Orleans Collection. (n.d.). The Collins C. Diboll Vieux Carré Digital Survey. New Orleans, Louisiana. Retrieved from The Collins C. Diboll Vieux Carré Digital Survey

History of the City. (2020). (City of Mandeville) Retrieved April 17, 2020, from https://www.cityofmandeville.com/history/

History.com. (2009). *War of 1812.* (A&E Networks) Retrieved May 4, 2017, from History.com: http://www.history.com/topics/war-of-1812

Horsin-Deon, P. (1894, November 24). *Louisiana Planter and Sugar Manufacturer,* p. 331.

Horsin-Deon, P. (1894). *Le Sucre et L'Industrie Sucrier.* Paris: Bailliere et Fills.

Horsin-Deon, P. (1902). *Traité Théorique et Pratique de la Fabrication du Sucre de Betterave.*

Houdaille, J. (1956, July). Frenchmen and Francophiles in New Spain from 1760 to 1810. *The Americas, 13*(1), pp. 1-29. Retrieved April 8, 2020, from https://www.jstor.org/stable/979211

Hough, G., & Hough, N. C. (2000). Spanish Borderland Studies. *Spain's Louisiana Patriots in tis 1779-1783 War with England During the American Revolution.* Laguna Hills, California: SHHAR Press. doi:somosprimos.com/hough/louisiana.pdf

Huberich, C. H. (1947). *The political and legislative history of Liberia: a documentary history of the constitutions, laws and treaties of Liberia from the earliest settlements to the establishment of the Republic, a sketch of the activities of the American colonization soci.* New York: Cental Book Co.

Humboldt, A. v. (1804, May 24). To Thomas Jefferson from Alexander von Humboldt, 24 May 1804. *Letter.* Philadelphia: Founders Online. Retrieved August 31, 2020, from https://founders.archives.gov/documents/Jefferson/01-43-02-0369

Humboldt, A. v., & Bonpland, A. (1822). *Personal Narrative of Travels to the Equinoctial Regions of the New Continent During the Years 1799-1804: Volumes 1-2.* London: Longman, Hurst, Rees, Orme, and Brown.

Hylan, W. d. (1984, May 25). A Reminiscense of Bernard de Marigny, Founder of Mandeville. *Speech.* Mandeville.

Important from Havana: Rumored Revolution. (1851, July 23). *The New Orleans Bee.*

Insurrection of Blacks. (1811, March 4). *The Washingtonian,* p. 3.

Intitut National de la propriete industrielle. (1826). Retrieved November 11, 2016, from I: http://bases-brevets19e.inpi.fr/index.asp?page=rechercheRapide

Ireland, J. N. (1882). *Mrs. Duff (American Actor Series).* London: David Bogue.

Iroquois Research Institute. (1982). *Cultural Resources Survey of Fourteen Mississippi River Levee.* Fairfax: Department of the Army Corps of Engineers - New Orleans District.

J. David Hacker, L. H. (2010, February). The Effect of the Civil War on Southern Marriage Patterns. *Journal of Southern History, 76*(1), 39-70.

J.D.B. DeBow. (n.d.). (U.S. Department of Commerce) Retrieved from United States Census Bureau: https://www.census.gov/main/.in/php_module/lightbox/media.php?I_93a103fa87b4d1030f0a4c5d753dd6f4

James F. Barnett, J. (2007). *The Natchez Indians*. Jackson: University Press of Mississippi.

James F. Barnett, J. (2007). *The Natchez Indians: A History to 1735*. Jackson: University of Mississippi Press.

James Starrs, K. G. (2012). *Death of Meriwether Lewis: A Historic Crime Scene Investigation*. River Junction Press LLC.

Jefferson, T. (1804, May 28). From Thomas Jefferson to Alexander von Humboldt, 28 May 1804. *Letter*. Washington D.C.: Founders Online. Retrieved August 31, 2020, from https://founders.archives.gov/documents/Jefferson/01-43-02-0389

Jefferson, T. (1804, August 30). *From Thomas Jefferson to William C. C. Claiborne*. Retrieved May 5, 2019, from Founders Online: https://founders.archives.gov/documents/Jefferson/99-01-02-0296

Jefferson, T. (1804, July 1). *Notes on New Orleans Characters, 1 July 1804*. Retrieved April 11, 2019, from Founders Online: https://founders.archives.gov/documents/Jefferson/99-01-12-0008

Jefferson, T. (1804, August 16). *To James Madison from Thomas Jefferson 16 August 1804*. Retrieved April 18, 2019, from Founders Online: https://founders.archives.gov/documents/Madison/02-07-02-0586

Jewish Virtual Library. (1998 - 2017). *Virtual Jewish World: Charleston, South Carolina.* (American-Israeli Cooperative Enterprise) Retrieved July 16, 2017, from Jewish Virtual Library: http://www.jewishvirtuallibrary.org/charleston-south-carolina-jewish-history-tour

John Frederick Drinkwater, J. D. (2017, June 17). *France.* (Encyclopædia Britannica, inc.) Retrieved June 28, 2017, from Encyclopædia Britannica: https://www.britannica.com/place/France/Napoleon-and-the-Revolution

Johnson, A. (2014, March 3). *A Legacy of Triumph: More Stories of Duncan F. Kenner and Abe Hawkins.* Retrieved from Antebellum Turf Times: http://www.antebellumturftimes.com/2014/03/a-legacy-of-triumph-more-stories-of-duncan-f-kenner-and-abe-hawkins-at-ashland-plantation/

Johnson, A. (2014, March 3). *A Legacy of Triumph: The Red Fox of the South & Old Abe of Ashland Plantation.* Retrieved from Deep South Magazine: http://deepsouthmag.com/2014/03/03/a-legacy-of-triumph-the-red-fox-of-the-south-old-abe-of-ashland-plantation/

Johnson, C. L. (1939, Winter). A Brief Chronology of the Tchefunte Park Area. *Louisiana Conservation Review,* p. 47.

Jones, E. (1801, August 10). *To James Madison From Evan Jones, [10 August] 1801.* Retrieved April 18, 2019, from Founders Online: https://founders.archives.gov/documents/Madison/02-02-02-0038

Jones, E. (1801, May 15). *To James Madison from Evan Jones, 15 May 1801.* Retrieved April 18, 2019, from Founders Online: http://founders.archives.gov/documents/Madison/02-01-02-0243

Jones, H. (2009). *Crucible of Power: A History of American Foreign Relations to 1913.* Lanham, MD: Rowman & Littlefield.

Josefowicz, D. G. (2017). *The Zodiac at Dendera and the debate over the age of the earth.* Retrieved from The Victorian Web: http://www.victorianweb.org/science/denderazodiac.html

Judith Longest Bethea. (n.d.). Manuscript Collection Louisiana Division New Orleans Public Library.

Kane, H. T. (1945). *Plantation Parade, The Grand Manner in Louisiana.* New York: William Morrow and Company. Retrieved March 28, 2018, from The USGenWeb Archives Project: files.usgwarchives.net/la/ascension/bios/bringier.txt

Kapplan-Levenson, L. (2016, September 22). *TriPod Mythbusters: Quadroon Balls And Plaçage.* Retrieved from New Orleans Public Radio: http://wwno.org/post/tripod-mythbusters-quadroon-balls-and-pla-age

Kelley, L. D. (2011, January 16). Yellow Fever. *knowlouisiana. org Encyclopedia of Louisiana.* (D. Johnson, Ed.) Louisiana: Louisiana Endowment for the Humanities. Retrieved June 2, 2017, from http://www.knowlouisiana.org/entry/yellow-fever-in-louisiana

Kendall, J. (1922). *History of New Orleans.* New York, Chicago: The Lewis Publishing Company.

Kendell, J. (1922). *History of New Orleans.* Chicago: Lewis Publishing.

King, G. (1921). *Creole Families of New Orleans.* New York: Macmillan.

Klein, U. (2012). The Prussian Mining Official Alexander von Humboldt. *Annals of Science, 69,* 27-68.

Knight, F. W., & Levinson, S. H. (2017, July 19). *Cuba.* (Encyclopædia Britannica, inc.) Retrieved August 7, 2017, from Encyclopædia Britannica: https://www.britannica.com/place/Cuba/Sugarcane-and-the-growth-of-slavery

Kolb, F. B. (2007, April). *Acadian Settlement in Louisiana: Colonial Populations and Imperial Policy (Senior Honors Thesis)*. College Station, TX: Texas A & M.

Kolb, F. B. (2014). *Contesting Borderlands: Policy and Practice in Spanish Louisiana, 1765-1803.* Nashville: Vanderbilt University.

Koppeschaar, E. (1914). *Evaporation in the Cane and Beet Sugar Factory.* London: Norman Roger.

Krichtal, A. (2013). *Liverpool and the Raw Cotton.*

Kukla, J. (2009). *A Wilderness so immens: The Louisiana Purchase and the Destiny of America.* Knopf Doubleday Publishing Group.

Lachance, P. (1982, Summer). Intermarriage and French Cultural Persistence in Late Spanish and Early American New Orleans. *Social History, 15,* pp. 47-81.

Lady and Two Masked Men. (1911, November 2). *Belfast Telegraph.*

Lafayette College's Special Collections and Digital Scholarship Services. (n.d.). (L. C. Services, Producer) Retrieved February 17, 2017, from The McDonough Project: http://exhibits.lafayette.edu/mcdonogh/items/show/2484

Larned, J. N. (1895). *History for Ready Reference: Greece-Nibelungenlied.* C.A. Nichols Company.

Laussat, P. C. (1978). *Memoirs of My Life.* (R. D. Bush, Ed.) Baton Rouge: LSU Press.

Leclant, J. (2017). *Academie des Inscriptions et Belles-Lettres: History Since 1816.* Retrieved October 12, 2017, from Academie des Inscriptions et Belles-Lettres: http://www.aibl.fr/introduction-76-301/history-since-1816/?lang=en

Leonard, A. B., & Pretel, D. (2016). *The Caribbean and the Atlantic World Economy: Circuits of trade, money and knowledge, 1650-1914.* Springer.

Letter to the Editor. (1860, November 10). *Baton Rouge Tri-Weekly Gazette,* p. 1.

Lexa, J. (1893, December 9). *Louisiana Planter and Sugar Manufacturer, 11.*

Linklater, A. (2009). *An Artist in Treason: The Extraordinary Double Life of General James Wilkinson.* New York: Walker Publishing Co.

Lisle, J. B. (2017, February 11). *Dr. Placide Jules Armand Mercier.* Retrieved from Welcome to Stedman Family Organization Genealogies: http://johnlisle.us/genealogy/register.php?personID=I45469&tree=stedman_main&generations=

Long, C. M. (2011, January 11). *Eulalie Mandeville.* Retrieved February 24, 2018, from http://www.knowlouisiana.org/entry/eulalie-mandeville

Long, C. M. (2012). *Madame Lalaurie: Mistress of the Haunted House.* Gainseville: University of Florida Press.

Long, C. M. (n.d.). The "Octoroon Mistress" in William Faulkner.

Long, C. M. (n.d.). The "Octoroon Mistress" in William Faulkner's Absalom Absalom! *Academia.* Retrieved from https://www.academia.edu/33041976/The_Octoroon_Mistress.doc

Louisiana as a Spanish Colony. (n.d.). Retrieved October 15, 2019, from Library of Congress: https://www.loc.gov/collections/louisiana-european-explorations-and-the-louisiana-purchase/articles-and-essays/louisiana-as-a-spanish-colony/#fn7r

Louisiana as a Spanish Colony. (2017). Retrieved from Library of Congress: https://www.loc.gov/collections/louisiana-european-explorations-and-the-louisiana-purchase/articles-and-essays/louisiana-as-a-spanish-colony/

Louisiana Department of Culture Recreation and Tourism. (2017). *Louisiana State Museum Online Exhibits The Cabildo: Two Centries of Louisiana History - Antebellum Louisiana II: Agrarian Life.* Retrieved from Louisiana Department of Culture Recreation and Tourism: http://www.crt.state.la.us/louisiana-state-museum/online-exhibits/the-cabildo/antebellum-louisiana-agrarian-life/

LOUISIANA DEPARTMENT OF CULTURE RECREATION AND TOURISM. (2107, April 30). *ANTEBELLUM LOUISIANA II: AGRARIAN LIFE.* Retrieved from LOUISIANA STATE MUSEUM: Online Exhibits The Cabildo: Two Centuries of Louisiana History: http://www.crt.state.la.us/louisiana-state-museum/online-exhibits/the-cabildo/antebellum-louisiana-agrarian-life/

Louisiana Division New Orleans Public Library. (n.d.). *Administrations of the Mayors of New Orleans William Freret 1799 - 1864.* Retrieved January 22, 2020, from http://nutrias.org/~nopl/info/louinfo/admins/freret.htm

Louisiana Division/City Archives & Special Collections Administrations of Mayors of New Orleans. (n.d.). Retrieved May 3, 2017, from New Orleans Public Library: http://nutrias.org/info/louinfo/admins/macarty.htm

Louisiana Life in Colonial Days. (1909, June 27). *Times Picayune,* p. 38 & 41.

Louisiana Soldiers in the War of 1812. (1998). *Ancestry.com.* Provo, Utah: Louisiana Genealogical and Historical Society.

Louisiana State Museum Online Exhibts: The Cabildo: Two Centuries of Lousiana History - The Battle of New Orleans. (2017). Retrieved January 11, 2018, from Louisiana Department of Culture Recreation and Tourism: https://www.crt.state.la.us/louisiana-state-museum/online-exhibits/the-cabildo/the-battle-of-new-orleans/index

Louisiana Sugar Planters' Association: Presentations to the Association of the Portraits of Etienne de Bore and of the Past Presidents of the Associa tion. (1909, January 23). *Louisiana Planter and Sugar Manufacturer, 42.*

Louisiana: European Explorations and the Louisiana Purchase. (n.d.). (Library of Congress) Retrieved October 21, 2019, from Library of Congress: https://www.loc.gov/collections/louisiana-european-explorations-and-the-louisiana-purchase/articles-and-essays/the-louisiana-purchase/

Lousiana Legislature. (1835). *Acts Passed at the First Session of the Twelfth Legislature of the State of Louisiana Began and Held in the City of New Orleans.* New Orleans.

Ludlow, N. M. (1880). *Dramatic Life as I Found it, A Record of Personal Experience ; with an Account of the Rise and Progress of the Drama in the West and South, with Anecdotes and Biographical Sketches of the Principal Actors and Actresses who Have at Times Appeared Upon the.* St. Louis: G. I. Jones and Company.

Lyceum Lectures. (1852, January 21). *New Orleans Crescent,* p. 2.

Mackenzie, G. N., & Rhoades, N. O. (Eds.). (1995). *Colonial Families of the United States of America: in Which is Given the History, Genealogy and Armorial Bearings of Colonial Families Who Settled in the American Colonies From the Time of the Settlement of Jamestown, 13th May, 1607, to the Battle of Lexi.* Baltimore: Genealogical Publishing Co., Inc.

MacMillan, C. (2015, March). Judah Benjamin: Marginalized Outsider or Admitted Insider? (P. A. Thomas, Ed.) *Journal of Law and Society, 42*(1), 150-172.

Madureira, N. L. (2014). *Key Concepts in Energy.* Heidelberg: Springer International Publishing.

Manassa, C., & Wolfe, S. J. (2018). *Unwrapping the Past.* (Peabody Museum of Natural History, Yale University) Retrieved January 17, 2018, from Echoes of Egypt: https://echoesofegypt.peabody.yale.edu/mummy-mania/unwrapped-egyptian-mummy-female-fragments-linen-wrapping

Marquis de Lafayette. (1996, October). (The Jefferson Foundation, Inc.) Retrieved June 17, 2017, from Monticello: https://www.monticello.org/site/jefferson/marquis-de-lafayette

Martyn, B. C. (1979). *Racism in the United States: A History of the Anit-Miscegenation Laws and Litiagtion.* Los Angeles, CA: Universtity of Southern California.

Mass Meeting. The Assemblage at Clay Statue. (1874, September 15). *Times Picayune,* p. 1.

McCarthy, K. M. (2004). *Apalachicola Bay.* Pinapple Press.

McCarthy, S. (2014). *175 Faces of Chemistry - Celebrating Diversity in Science: Norbert Rillieux.* Retrieved July 24, 2017, from Royal Society of Chemistry: http://www.rsc.org/diversity/175-faces/all-faces/norbert-rillieux

McCulloh, R. S., & Bache, A. D. (1848). *Reports from the Secretary of the Treasury: of scientific investigations in relation to sugar and hydrometers, made under the superintendence of Professor R. S. McCulloh.* Wendell and Van Benthuysen, Printers.

McCullough, D. (2011). *The Greater Journey: Americans in Paris.* New York: Simon and Schuster.

McFarland, C. V. (2012). *Americans in Egypt, 1770-1915: Explorers, Consuls, Travelers, Soldiers, Missionaries, Writers, and Scientists.* Jefferson, North Carolina: McFarland & Company, Inc.

McGrayne, S. B. (2001). *Prometheans in the Lab: Chemistry and the Making of the Modern World.* McGraw-Hill Companies.

Meade, G. P. (1946). A Negro Scientist of Slavery Days. *Scientific Monthly, LXII,* pp. 317-326.

Melish, J. (1816). *A geographical description of the United States, with the contiguous British and Spanish possessions, intended as an accompaniment to Melish's map of these countries.* Philadelphia: John Melish.

Meullion, J. B. (1839, March 20). Baptiste Meullion letter, 1839 March 20; Folder 01-23, 1839 March-July. *Jean Baptiste Meullion papers.* Louisiana Digital Library. Retrieved June 7, 2018, from http://louisianadigitallibrary.org/islandora/object/fpoc-p16313coll51%3A39454

Miller, E. L. (2004). *New Orleans and the Texas Revolution.* Texas A&M University Press.

Miller, J. (2014, Sepember 22). Eccentrics. *Vanity Fair.* Retrieved from https://www.vanityfair.com/hollywood/2014/09/nicolas-cage-memories

Millmore, M. (2017). *Mystery of the Rosetta Stone.* Retrieved from Discovering Ancient Egypt: https://discoveringegypt.com/egyptian-video-documentaries/mystery-of-the-rosetta-stone/

Morton, S. G. (1844). *Crania Aegyptiaca: Or, Observations on Egyptian Ethnography, Derived from Anatomy, History, and the Monuments.* Philadelphia: John Pennington.

Mott, F. L. (1938). *A History of American Magazines 1850-1865.* Cambridge: Harvard University Press. Retrieved from All Poetry: https://allpoetry.com/Elizabeth-Oakes-Smith

Mr. Gliddon's Lectures. (1852, January). *Times Picayune.*

Mrs. Duff. (1838, March 13). *Times Picayune,* p. 2.

Murrin, J. M., & James M. McPherson, P. E. (2005). *Liberty, Equality, Power: A History of the American People, Volume 1: to 1877.* Thompson.

New Orleans annual and commercial register of 1846. (1845). E.A. Michel. Retrieved from https://archive.org/details/neworleansannual00mich

Nolan, B. (2012, February 1). Black Catholics: The Times-Picayune covers 175 years of New Orleans history. *The Times Picayune.*

Norbert Rillieux. (1887, December 17). *Scientific American Supplement, XXIV*(624), pp. 770-771.

Norbert Rillieux. (1894, September 2). *LA Sucrerie INDIGÈNE ET COLONIALE*, pp. 470-471.

Norbert Rillieux. (1894, October 23). *La Sucrerie Indigene & Coloniale,* 470-471.

Norbert Rillieux Biography. (1887, December 17). *Scientific American Supplement,* 24(624).

Norbert Rillieux Commémoration du Centenaire de la mise en marche de la première installation d'évaporation dans le vide a triple effet á la Louisiane en 1834. (1834). Amsterdam, Netherlands.

Norbert Rillieux: Commemoration du Centenaiire de la mise en marche de la premiere installation d'evaporation dans le vide a triple effet a la Louisiane en 1834. (1934). Amsterdam.

Nott, J. C. (1849). *Two Lectures on the Connection Between the Biblical and Physical History of Man: Delivered by Invitation from the Chair of Political Economy, Etc., of the Louisiana University, in December 1848.* New York: Bartlett and Welford.

Nott, J. C., & Gliddon, G. R. (1854). *Types of Mankind: Or, Ethnological Researches, Based Upon the Ancient Monuments, Paintings, Sculptures, and Crania of Races, and Upon Their Natural, Geographical, Philological and Biblical History.* Philadelphia: Lippincott, Grambo & Company.

Nystrom, J. (2017, August). *The Battle of Liberty Place.* Retrieved from knowlouisiana.org Encyclopedia of Louisiana: http://www.knowlouisiana.org/entry/the-battle-of-liberty-place

Nystrom, J. A. (2010). *New Orleans after the Civil War: Race, Politics, and a New Birth of Freedom.* John Hopkins University Press.

O., J. E., & Vincent, K. (1997). *Myths, Misdeeds, and Misunderstandings: The Roots of Conflict in U.S.-Mexican Relations.* Rowman & Littlefield Publishers, Inc.

Obituary of Vincent Rillieux. (1833, July 17). *The New Orleans Bee.*

O'Connell, D. (2006). *Furl the Banner: The Life of Abram J. Ryan, Poet-priest of the South.* Mercer University Press.

O'Connor, T. (1895). *The History of the Fire Department of New Orleans.* New Orleans.

Onebane, D. M. (2014). *The House That Sugarcane Built.* University Press of Mississippi.

Ouchley, K. (2014, January 23). *Natchez Revolt of 1729.* (D. A. Johnson, Editor, & Louisiana Endowment for the Humanities, 2010) Retrieved September 16, 2019, from 64 Parishes: https://64parishes.org Encyclopedia of Louisiana

Pack, E. (1996-2006). *Massacre at Fort Rosalie - November 28, 1729: Natchez, Adams Co., MS.* Retrieved September 17, 2019, from Adams Co, MS Genealogical and Historical Research : http://www.natchezbelle.org/adams-ind/massacre.htm

Packwood, T. (1844, February 17). Letter to the Editor. *Times Picayune.*

Panorama of the Nile. (1852, March 28). *Times Picayune,* p. 4.

Paquette, R. L. (2011, January 10). *Slave Insurrection of 1811.* (D. Johnson, Editor, & Louisiana Endowment for the Humanities) Retrieved March 28, 2018, from Knowlouisiana.org Encyclopedia of Louisiana: http://www.knowlouisiana.org/entry/slave-insurrection-of-1811

Pasquier, M. T. (n.d.). *Tunica Tribe.* (L. E. Humanities, Producer) Retrieved April 2020, 2020, from 64 Parishes: https://64parishes.org/entry/tunica-tribe

Passenger Lists of Vessels Arriving at New Orleans, Louisiana, 1820-1902; NAI Number: 2824927; Record Group Title: Records of the Immigration and Naturalization Service; Record Group Number: 85. (2006). *The National Archives at Washington, D.C.; Washington, D.C.* Provo, Utah: Ancestry.com Operations, Inc.

Paul Horsin-Deon. (1902, November 22). *Louisiana Planter and Sugar Manufacturer, 30*(21).

Peterson, A. H. (1964). *The Administration of Public Schools in New Orleans, 1841 - 1861.* Baton Rouge, Louisiana: LSU.

Philadelphia Ward 8, Philadelphia, Pennsylvania. (1860). *1860 United States Federal Census.* Ancestry.com Operations, Inc.

Pickering, T. (1799, April 12). *To John Adams from Timothy Pickering, 12 April 1799.* Retrieved April 11, 2019, from Founders Online: https://founders.archives.gov/documents/Adams/99-02-02-3429

Pierce, B. (1906). *Judah P. Benjamin.* Philadelphia: George Jacobs and Co.

Plaquette, R. L. (2009, March). "A Horde of Brigands?" The Great Louisiana Slave Revolt Reconsidered. *Historical Reflections, 35*(1), pp. 72-96.

Pollock, M. (2011, July 10). Dubious Death Site. *New York Times New York edition,* p. MB9.

Pope, W. F. (1895). *Early Days in Arkansas: Being for the Most Part the Recollections of and Old Settler.* Little Rock: Southern Historical Press.

Powell, L. N. (2012). *The Accidental City: Improvising New Orleans.* President and Fellows of Harvard College.

Prieto, G. (1878). *Viaje a los Estado - Unidos.* Mexico: Dublan Y Chavez.

Pritchard, W. (1939). The Effects of the Civil War on the Louisiana Sugar Industry. *The Journal of Southern History, 5*(3), pp. 315-332. Retrieved from www.jstor.org/stable/2191497

Proceedings of the Convention of the Republican Party of Louisiana Held at Economy Hall, New Orleans, September 25, 1865: And of the Central Executive Committee of the Friends of Universal Suffrage of Louisiana, Now the Central Executive Committee of the. (1865). New Orleans: New Orleans Tribune.

Proposition to Erect Not One, but a Hundred Monuments to a Great Inventor. (1886, July 12). *Times Picayune.*

Pryor, E. S. (2016). *Colored Travelers, Mobility and the Fight for Citizenship before the Civil War.* Chapel Hill: The University of North Carolina Press.

Pryor, E. S. (2016). *Colored Travlers: Mobility and the Fight for Citizenship Before the Civil War.* Chapel Hill: UNC Press Books.

R. Christopher Goodwin & Associates, Inc. (1989). Significance Assessment of 16AN26, New River Bend Revetment, Ascension Parish Louisiana. *Cultural Resources Series.* New Orleans, Louisiana.

R. Christopher Goodwin and Associates. (1989, September). Cultural Resources Investigations of the West Bank Hurricane Protection Project, Jefferson Parish Louisiana. New Orleans, Louisiana: US Army Corps of Engineers - New Orleans District. Retrieved from http://www.dtic.mil/dtic/tr/fulltext/u2/a225278.pdf

Radicalism Outdone. (1873, June 21). *Ouachuta Telegraph.*

Rankin, D. C. (1974, August). The Origins of Black Leadership in New Orleans During Reconstruction. *The Journal of Southern History, 40*(3), 417-440. Retrieved September 9, 2016, from http://www.jstor.org/stable/2206492

Rasmussen, D. (2011). *American Uprising: The Untold Story of America's Largest Slave Revolt.* New York: Harper Collins.

Reeves, S. K., & Reeves, W. D. (1983). *Archival Evaluation of Floodwall Alignments.* New Orleans: U. S. Army Corps of Engineers.

Reinders, R. c. (1965, Summer). The Free Negro in the New Orleans Economy, 1850-1860. *Louisiana History: The Journal of the Louisiana Historical Association, 6*(3), 273-285. Retrieved from http/:www.jstor.org/stable/4230851

Renaux, J. (1833, February 10). Brown Gas Machines. *L'Echo de la Fabrique,* p. 47.

(1870). *Reports of Cases Argued and Determined in the Supreme Court of Louisiana Vol. 22.* New Orleans: State of Louisiana.

Republican Party of Lousiana . (1865). *Proceedings of the convention of the Republican Party of Louisiana held at Economy Hall, New Orleans, September 25, 1865: and of the Central Executive Committee of the Friends of Universal Suffrage of Louisiana, now the Central Executive Committee of the.* New Orleans: New Orleans Tribune.

Resistance. (2015). Retrieved March 20, 2018, from Whitney Plantation: http://whitneyplantation.com/resistance.html

Reynolds, D. E. (1964, Winter). The New Orleans Riot of 1866, Reconsidered. *Louisiana History: The Journal of the Louisiana Historical Association, 5*(1), pp. 5-27.

Richey, E. C., & Kean, E. P. (1915). *The New Orleans Book.* New Orleans: The L. Graham Co. Ltd. Printers. Retrieved June 6, 2018, from https://archive.org/details/neworleansbook01rich

Rightor, H. (1900). *Standard History of New Orleans, Louisiana.* New Orleans: Lewis Publishing Company.

Rillieux, N. (1850, January). Letter to R. S. McCulloh. (J. D. Bow, Ed.) *DeBow's Commercial Review of the South and West, 7,* pp. 56-59.

Rillieux, N. (1886, July 12). Letter to the Editor. *Times Picayune.*

Rillieux, N. (1886, October 11). Letter to the Editor. *Times Picayune.*

Riquelmy, C., & Currie, D. (1995). *LSU Library.* (L. S. Libraries, Producer) Retrieved July 8, 2107, from Sugar at LSU: Cultivating a Sweeter Future: http://www.lib.lsu.edu/sites/all/files/sc/exhibits/e-exhibits/sugar/contents.html

Rittiez, F. (1855). *Histoire du règne de Louis-Philippe ier, 1830 à 1848, précis, faisant suite à l'Histoire de la Restauration.* (V. Lecou, Ed.) Paris: Libraire de la Societe des Gens Lettres.

Robbins, H. (1928, March 4). When a Future King: The Pilgrimage of Louis Philippe to New Orleans. *Times Picayune.*

Robinson, A. (2012). *Cracking the Egyptian Code, The Revolutionary Life of Jean-François Champollion.* Oxford University Press.

Robinson, A. (2012). *Cracking the Egyptian Code, The Revolutionary Life of Jean-François Champollion.* Oxford University Press.

Robinson, A. (n.d.). *Historic New Orleans Collection: Narciso López.* Retrieved January 30, 2018, from Historic New Orleans Collection: https://www.hnoc.org/narciso-l%C3%B3pez-gefe-de-los-piratas-invasores

Rodriguez, J. P. (2002). *The Lousiana Purchase: A Historical and Geographical Encyclopedia.* ABC-CLIO.

Rogers, J. D. (2006). *History of the New Orleans Flood Protection System - Chapter 4.* Preliminary Report on the Performance of the New Orleans Levee Systems in Hurricane Katrina on August 29, 2005, Independent Levee Investigation team, New Orleans. Retrieved from https://web.mst.edu/~rogersda/levees/Ch%204-HISTORY%20OF%20THE%20NEW%20ORLEANS%20FLOOD%20PROTECTION%20SYSTEM-5-20-06-embedded_figures.pdf

Rood, D. (2017). *The Reinvention Of Atlantic Slavery: Technology, Labor, Race, And Capitalism In The Greater Caribbean.* New York: Oxford University Press.

Roth, D. (2010). *Louisiana Hurricane History.* Camp Spring MD: National Weather Service. Retrieved from wpc.ncep.noaa.gov/research/lahur.pdf

Roudané, M. C. (2014). *The New Orleans Tribune: An Introduction to America's First Black Daily Newspaper.* Mark Charles Roudané.

Rubenstein, A. G. (1994). Mary Ann Dyke Duff. In J. B. Litoff, & J. McDonnell (Eds.), *A Guide to European Immigrant Women in the United States: A Biographical Dictionary* (pp. 84-85). New York: Garland Publishing.

Samuel Wilson, J. (1992). *The Pitot House on Bayou St. John.* New Orleans: Louisiana Landmark Society.

Sarrans, B. (1833). *Memoirs of General Lafayette: And of the French Revolution of 1830, Volume 1.* Boston: Lilly, Wait, Colman, and Holden.

Scarborough, W. K. (2006). *Masters of the Big House: Elite Slaveholders of the Mid-Nineteenth-Century South.* Baton Rouge: LSU Press.

Schermerhorn, C. (2015, March 19). Intertwined trades in sugar, slavery. *The Virginian-Pilot.* Retrieved from https://pilotonline.com/opinion/columnist/guest/schermerhorn-intertwined-trades-in-sugar-slavery/article_e024414d-3568-53de-ad98-cc6fb7dee717.html

Schermerhorn, C. (2015). *The Business of Slavery and the Rise of American Capitalism, 1815-1860.* New Haven: Yale University Press.

Schouler, J. (1882). *A Treatise on the Law of the Domestic Relations, Embracing Husband and Wife, Parent and Child, Guardian and Ward, Infancy, and Master and Servant.* Boston: Little, Brown and Company.

Schulman, M. (1996-2015). *The Panic of 1837.* (Multieducator) Retrieved July 9, 2017, from History Central: http://www.historycentral.com/Ant/1837.html

Sharer, R. J., & Traxler, L. P. (2006). *The Ancient Maya.* Standford University Press.

Shen, K. (2015, October 27). *Brown University Library.* Retrieved from Brown Universtiy Department of African Studies: History of Haiti 1492-1805 : http://library.brown.edu/haitihistory/8.html

Sidelights on Louisiana History Section: ""Data Concerning the Natchez Massacre 1729-1730. (1918, January). *Louisiana Historical Quarterly, 1*(3), pp. 87-183.

Smithsonian Institution. (2014). *Patent Model for Multiple Effect Vacuum Evaporator.* Retrieved December 12, 2016, from Smithsonian Institution: Anacostia Community Museum: http://anacostia.si.edu/exhibits/online_academy/Academynf/artifacts/objects/object_2_frame.htm

Snellings, G. (1860, April). Louisiana Law on Nullity of Marriage. *Louisiana Law Review, 20.* Retrieved from http://digitalcommons.law.lsu.edu/lalrev/vol20/iss3/7

Societe des Amis du Peuple. (1832). *Proces Des Quinze*. Paris: Auguste Mie.

Sons of the American Revolution. (1920). *Year book of the Louisiana Society Sons of the American Revolution.* New Orleans: Sons of the American Revolution, Louisiana Society.

Southern Mississippi Planning and Development District. (1991). Gautier waterfront opportunities 1990. Gulfport, Mississippi. Retrieved April 22, 2017, from https://www.gpo.gov/fdsys/pkg/CZIC-ht168-g38-g38-1991/content-detail.html

Spady, J. G. (1989). Dr. Cheikh Anta Diop and the Background of Scholarship on Black Interest in Egyptology and Nile Valley Civilizations. *Presense Africaine, Nouvelle serie, 292*-312. Retrieved October 10, 2015, from http://www.jstor.org/stable24351992

Sponsel, A. (2020). *Alexander von Humbolt: Darwin Correspondence Project.* Retrieved August 28, 2020, from University of Cambridge: https://www.darwinproject.ac.uk/alexander-von-humboldt

Starr, J. B. (1976). *Tories, Dons, and Rebels: The American Revolution in British West Florida.* Gainseville: University of West Florida.

State of Louisiana. (2017, March 24). Retrieved from Culture Recreation and Tourism: http://www.crt.state.la.us/dataprojects/museum/spanishcolonial/02_Jan_9_1771_to_Dec_11_1771.pdf

Stockwell, M. (n.d.). *Marquis de Lafayette*. Retrieved June 7, 2017, from George Washington's Mount Vernon: http://www.mountvernon.org/digital-encyclopedia/article/marquis-de-lafayette/

Stone, A. H. (1915, April). The Cotton Factorage System of the Southern States. *The American Historical Review, 20*(3), pp. 557-565. Retrieved December 14, 2019, from https://www.jstor.org/stable/1835857

Sugar Planter' Association. (1886, July 9). *Times Picayune,* p. 8.

Summary of 1811-1812 New Madrid Earthquakes Sequence. (n.d.). Retrieved September 24, 2020, from https://www.usgs.gov/natural-hazards/earthquake-hazards/science/summary-1811-1812-new-madrid-earthquakes-sequence?qt-science_center_objects=0#qt-science_center_objects

Swift, J. (2017, April 19). *Siege of Paris.* Retrieved from Encyclopædia Britannica: https://www.britannica.com/topic/Siege-of-Paris-1870-1871

Taylor, B. (1869). *A Journey to Central Africa; or Life and Landscapes from Egypt to the Negro Kingdoms of the White Nile.* New York: G.P. Putnam and Son.

Taylor, M. (n.d.). Contexts: Free People of Color in the Americas, 1492-1830. *Free People of Color: Revealing an Unknown Pas*t. Baton Rouge, Louisiana: Louisiana State University. Retrieved from http://lib.lsu.edu/sites/all/files/sc/fpoc/history.html#historycontexts

Thayer, W. (2017). Bill Thayer's website. *Galvez' Administration 1777 - 1783, Mirro's Administration 1784-1785.* Retrieved April 18, 2017, from http://penelope.uchicago.edu/Thayer/E/Gazetteer/Places/America/United_States/Louisiana/_Texts/GAYHLA/4/3*.html

The Aaron Burr Association. (2015). Retrieved August 14, 2019, from www.aaronburrassociation.org/chronology.htm

The Atlanta, 16 U.S. 409 (U. S. Supreme 1818).

(n.d.). *The Census Tables for the French Colony of Louisiana 1699-1732*. Census. Retrieved April 19, 2018, from https://www.ancestry.com/interactive/48009/CensusTablesLA-000605-62

The Collectorship. (1851, September 27). *The Daily Delta*, p. 2.

The Collins C. Diboll Vieux Carré Digital Survey. (n.d.). New Orleans, Louisiana. Retrieved April 20, 2017, from http://www.hnoc.org/vcs/index.php

The Collins C. Diboll Vieux Carré Digital Survey. (n.d.). Retrieved April 18, 2020, from https://www.hnoc.org/vcs/

The Collins C. Diboll Vieux Carre Digital Survey: A Project of the Historic New Orleans Collection. (n.d.). Retrieved April 19, 2018, from Historic New Orleans Collection: https://www.hnoc.org/vcs/property_info.php?lot=22782-30

The Commissioners of Patents' Journal Great Britain. (1878). London.

The Commissioners of Patents' Journal Great Britain. (1880). London.

The Declaration of the Rights of Man 1789. (2008). (L. G.-Y. School, Producer) Retrieved June 7, 2017, from The Avalon Project: http://avalon.law.yale.edu/18th_century/rightsof.asp

The Editors of Encyclopædia Britannica. (2015, December 11). *Franco-German War.* Retrieved from Encyclopædia Britannica: https://www.britannica.com/event/Franco-German-War

The Greatest Demonstration. Republican Mass Meeting. (1868, April 15). *The New Orleans Republican*, p. 1.

The Introduction of Cotton into the Mississippi Valley. (1858, September 18). Times Picayune, p. 1.

The Mummy Last Night. (1852, February 29). *Times Picayune*, p. 3.

The National Archives of the UK; Kew, Surrey, England; General Register Office: Registers of Births, Marriages and Deaths Surrendered to the Non-Parochial Registers Commissions of 1837 and 1857; Class Number: RG 4; Piece Number: 4594. (n.d.). *Ancestry.com. England & Wales, Non-Conformist and Non-Parochial Registers, 1567-1936 [database on-line].* Provo: Ancestry.com.

The Rillieux Patents. (1889, June 22). *Louisiana Planter and Sugar Manufacturer,* p. 301.

THE UNITED STATES, APPELLANTS, v . THE HEIRS OF VINCENT RILLIEUX, DECEASED, 55 U.S. 189 (United States Supreme Court January 1, 1852).

The White League. Its Platform in Full. A Manly and Straightforward Document. (1874, July 2). *Times Picayune,* p. 1.

Thompson, J. (2015). *Wonderful Things: A History of Egyptology 1: From Antiquity to 1881, Volume 3.* The American University in Cairo Press.

Thompson, T. P. (1915). Early Financing in New Orleans. 1831 - Being the Story of the Canal Bank - 1915. *In Publications of the Louisiana Historical Society: Volumes 7-9* (pp. 1 - 61). New Orleans: Louisiana Historical Society.

Tidrick, D. (2003, December). St. Tammany Parish Cronological History. *STAR St. Tammany Ancestral Roots: The Quarterly Newsletter of the St. Tammany Genealogical Society.* Covington, Louisiana: St. Tammany Genealogical Society. Retrieved from textlab.io/doc/810714/stgs-vol-xv-no.-4.pub

Tinker, E. L. (1933). *Craps.* Retrieved September 1, 2019, from Que la fête commence! The French Influence on the Good Life in New Orleans An Exhibit from the New Orleans Public Library: http://nutrias.org/exhibits/french/craps.htm

Trafton, S. (2004). *Egypt Land: Race and the Nineteenth-Century.* Durham: Duke University.

Trickey, E. (2017, January 13). *The Little Remembered Ally Who Helped America Win the Revolution.* Retrieved October 3, 2019, from https://www.smithsonianmag.com/history/little-remembered-ally-who-helped-america-win-revolution-180961782/

Trist, E. (1808, April 18). *To Thomas Jefferson from Elizabeth House Trist, 18 April 1808.* Retrieved July 25, 2019, from Founders Online: https://founders.archives.gov/documents/Jefferson/99-01-02-7853

Troop Roster: Battle of New Orleans. (n.d.). Retrieved February 23, 2018, from National Park Service: https://www.nps.gov/jela/learn/historyculture/upload/CHALTroopRoster.pdf

U.S. Department of Interior. (1860). 8th Census United States. - 1860; Instructions to U.S. Marshalls. Instructions to Assisstants. Washington: George W. Bowman. Retrieved from https://www.census.gov/history/pdf/1860instructions.pdf

Ulentin, A. (2012). *Shade of Grey: Slaveholding Free Women of Color (dissertation).* Baton Rouge, LA: Louisiana State University.

Ulentin, A. (2012). *Shades of grey: slaveholding free women of color in antebellum New Orleans, 1800-1840 LSU Doctoral Dissertation.* Baton Rouge: LSU.

United States Commissioner of Patents. (1849). *House Documents, Otherwise Publ. as Executive Documents: 13th Congress, 2d Session-49th Congress, 1st Session, Volume 6.* Washington D.C.: Wendell and Benthuysen.

United States Congressional Serial Set: Volulme 495. (1846). Washington D.C.: U.S. Government Printing Office.

United States Department of State, Office of the Historian. (2017, July 10). *Founding of Liberia, 1847.* Retrieved from United States Department of State, Office of the Historian: https://history.state.gov/milestones/1830-1860/liberia

United States v. Heirs of Rilleiux, 55 U.S. 189 (U. S. Supreme 1852).

Urban, C. S. (1957, February). The Africanization of Cuba Scare, 1853-1855. *The Hispanic American Historical Review, 37*(1), pp. 29-45.

Uzee, P. D. (1971, Summer). The Beginnings of the Louisiana Republican Party. *Louisiana History: The Journal of the Louisiana Historical Association, 12*(3), pp. 197-211.

Valencius, C. B. (2013). *The Lost History of the New Madrid Earthquakes.* Chicago: University of Chigaco Press.

Van Zante, G. A. (2008). *New Orleans 1867: Photographs by Theodore Lilienthal.* New York: Merrell Publishers Limited.

Vanney, A. (2014). *Images of America: Slidell.* Charleston: Arcadia Publishing.

Vassoler, I. (2004). The Mexican Mining Bubble That Burst. In *Alexander von Humboldt: From the Americas the Cosmos* (pp. 427 - 435). New York, New York: Bildner Center for Western Hemisphere Studies.

Vaughan, E. (2003). *Louisiana Sugar: a Geohistorical Perspective (Dissertation).* Baton Rouge: Louisiana State University and Agricultural and Mechanical College. Retrieved June 6, 2018, from https://digitalcommons.lsu.edu/cgi/viewcontent.cgi?referer=https://www.google.com/&httpsredir=1&article=4692&context=gradschool_dissertations

Vella, C. (1997). *Intimate Enemies: The Two Worlds of the Baroness Pontalba.* Baton Rouge : LSU Press.

Vella, C. (1999). The Country for Men with Nerve. In G. Feigenbaum, *Degas and New Orleans: A French Impressionist in America.* New Olreans: New Orleans Museum of Art.

Vernet, J. (2013). *Strangers on Their Native Soil: Opposition to United States' Governace in Louisiana's Orleans Territory, 1903-1809.* University Press of Mississippi.

Vidrine, J. (1991). *A Man Can Stand, Yeah: Ranching Traditions in Louisiana.* Retrieved from Folk Life in Louisiana: http://www.louisianafolklife.org/LT/Articles_Essays/creole_art_ranching_trad.html

Walder, J. E. (1987). Racism, Slavery, and Free Enterprise: Black Entrepreneurship in the United States before the Civil War. *The Business History Review, 60*(3), 343-382. Retrieved from http://www.jstor.org/stable/3115882

Walker, J. K. (2009). *The History of Black Business in America: Capitalism, Race, Entrepreneurship, Volume 1.* Chapel Hill: UNC Press Books.

Wallasey. (2017, August). Retrieved from WeRelate.org: https://www.werelate.org/wiki/Place:Wallasey%2C_Cheshire%2C_England

Washington, G. (1939). *The Writings of George Washington from the Original Manuscript Sources: 1745-1799.* (J. C. Fitzpatrick, Ed.) Washington D. C. : United States Congress.

Weissbach, M. M. (1999). *Unlocking the Civilization of Ancient Egypt: How Champollion.* Retrieved from The Schiller Institute: https://www.schillerinstitute.org/fid_97-01/993_champollion.html

White, L. C. (Ed.). (2006). Connecticut Town Birth Records, pre-1870 (Barbour Collection). *Connecticut Town Birth Records, pre-1870 (Barbour Collection).* Provo, Utah.

Whitten, D. O. (1995). *Andrew Durnford: a Black sugar planter in the antebellum South.* New Brunswick: Transaction Publishers.

Wilkins, W. W. (1963). *Historic; American Buildings Survey: ROBERT A. GRINNAN HOUSE.* Philadelphia: National Park Service Eastern Office Design and Construction.

Wilkinson, J. (1811). *Burr's Conspiracy Exposed ; and General Wilkinson Vindicated Against the Slanders of His Enemies on that Important Occasion.* James Wilkinson.

Williams, T. H. (1945, August). The Louisiana Unification of 1873. *The Journal of Southern History, 11*(3), pp. 349-369. Retrieved from http://www.jstor.org/stable/21978121

Williams, W. D. (1989, Summer). Louis Bringier and HIs Description of Arkansas 1812. *The Arkansas Historical Quarterly, 48*(2), pp. 108 - 136. Retrieved April 04, 2020, from https://www.jstor.org/stable/40030789

Wisniak, J. (2012, April). Edward Charles Howard. Explosives, meteorites, and sugar. *Educación Química, 23*(2), pp. 230-239. Retrieved June 7, 2018, from https://www.sciencedirect.com/science/article/pii/S0187893X17301143

Wolfe, S. J. (2011). *The Great Gliddon Mummy Unwrappings.* Retrieved September 12, 2017, from pastispresent.org

Wright, T. F. (2013). *The Cosmopolitan Lyceum: Lecture Culture and the Globe in Nineteenth-Century America.* (T. F. Wright, Ed.) University of Massachusetts Press.

Zielinski, S. (2014, April 14). Ten Ancient Stories and the Geological Events That Might Have Inspired Them. *Smithsonian Magazine.*

About The Author

Michelle Freret Prather was born in New Orleans, Louisiana, and now lives in Covington, just across Lake Pontchartrain from the city of her birth. She is an eighth generation Louisianian and is fascinated with her state's complex and unique history. Michelle taught English and American history for twenty-five years and has a Master of Education in Curriculum and Instruction. She is now an independent researcher, writer, and consultant. Michelle is passionate about the stories of history at the granular level. She is interested in how time, place, culture, events, and personality steep together to produce the potent concoction that is our human story. She has honed her writing and research skills by attending workshops and seminars by noted authors and publishers including Anne Lamott, Edward Ball, and John J. Geoghegan.

End Notes

1 (The Census Tables for the French Colony of Louisiana 1699-1732)

2 Ancestry.com. U.S. and Canada, Passenger and Immigration Lists Index, 1500s-1900s [database on-line]. Provo, UT, USA: Ancestry.com Operations, Inc, 2010; (Vanney, 2014) Introduction; (Ellis F. S., 1998) p.39

3 (Ensor & Wilson, 1993)

4 (Southern Mississippi Planning and Development District, 1991)

5 (Pasquier, n.d.)

6 (United States v. Heirs of Rillieux, 1852)

7 http://www.crt.state.la.us/dataprojects/museum/spanishcolonial/02_Jan_9_1771_to_Dec_11_1771.pdf Accessed 03/24/2017

8 Tronquette - Her formal name according to her husband's will was Dona Catalina Larose (Will of Don Vicente Rillieux City of New Orleans, 4th of September 1797 – translated copy in the Douglass Freret Papers.)

9 Vincent Rillieux's will written in 1797, lists eight children and their ages: Vincent 19, Maria Eugenia 17 1/2, Maria 14,

Marianotinete 12 1/2, Miguel Vincente 9, Eloysa 7, Desiré 3, Juan 7 mos.

[10] (St. Tammany Parish Government, 2017)

[11] (Vidrine, 1991)

[12] (Ferreiro, 2016)

[13] (Ferreiro, 2016)

[14] *See section on Evan Jones*

[15] (Powell, 2012)

[16] Ibid

[17] (Ellis F. S., 1998)

[18] (Thayer, 2017); (Ellis F. S., 1998); (Former, 2012 (originally published 1904))

[19] (Frasier, The French Quarter of New Orleans, 2003)

[20] (Samuel Wilson, 1992)

[21] (Louisiana Landmark Society Pitot House, 2017)

[22] (Ancestry.com, U.S. Newspaper Extractions from the Northeast, 1704-1930, 2014)

[23] (The Collins C. Diboll Vieux Carré Digital Survey)

[24] (Ancestry.com, Louisiana, Wills and Probate Records 1756-1984, 2015) A Faubourg is a neighborhood that lies outside of the city proper.

[25] (Frasier & Freeman, The Garden District of New Orleans, 2012)

[26] (THE UNITED STATES, APPELLANTS, v . THE HEIRS OF VINCENT RILLIEUX, DECEASED, 1852)

[27] According to the guide for navigating and searching the Collins C. Dibdoll Vieux Carré Digital Survey, in legal documents f.w.c was used after the name of a free woman of color or f. c. l. for femme de couleur libre. See https://www.hnoc.org/vcs/navigamng_the_survey.php

[28] 1820 U S Census; Census Place: New Orleans, New Orleans City, Louisiana; Page: 81; NARA Roll: M33_32; Image: 93

[29] (LOUISIANA DEPARTMENT OF CULTURE RECREATION AND TOURISM, 2017)

[30] (Balcourt, 1820)

[31] (Richey & Kean, 1915, p. 30)

[32] (Fricker, 2013) (Vella, Intimate Enemies: The Two Worlds fo the Baroness Pontalba, 1997)

[33] (Vella, Intimate Enemies: The Two Worlds fo the Baroness Pontalba, 1997)

[34] (Gick, 2013)

[35] (Vella, Intimate Enemies: The Two Worlds fo the Baroness Pontalba, 1997)

[36] (A Visior's Guide to New Orleans 1875, New Orleans)

[37] (Fenner, 1850)

[38] (Norbert Rillieux, 1887) (Direct Data Capture, 1999)

[39] (History.com, 2009)

[40] (Louisiana Soldiers in the War of 1812, 1998)

[41] (Louisiana State Museum Online Exhibits: The Cabildo: Two Centuries of Louisiana History - The Battle of New Orleans, 2017)

[42] (Louisiana Division/City Archives & Special Collections Administrations of Mayors of New Orleans, n.d.) (Richey & Kean, 1915)

[43] (Rogers, 2006)

[44] (Dudley, 2012)

[45] (Meullion, 1839)

[46] (Ancestry.com, Louisiana, Wills and Probate Records 1756-1984, 2015)

[47] Ibid

[48] (Garvey & Widmer, 2012)

[49] (Kapplan-Levenson, 2016)

[50] (Ancestry.com, Louisiana, Wills and Probate Records 1756-1984, 2015)

[51] (Ancestry.com, Louisiana, Wills and Probate Records 1756-1984, 2015)

[52] (Clark E., 2013, p. 92) (Bell, 1997)

[53] (Clark E., 2013, p. 148)

[54] (Kapplan-Levenson, 2016)

[55] (Vella, Intimate Enemies: The Two Worlds fo the Baroness Pontalba, 1997)

[56] (Louisiana Division/City Archives & Special Collections Administrations of Mayors of New Orleans, n.d.)

[57] (Benfey, Degas in New Orleans: encounters in the Creole world of Kate Chopin and George Washington Cable, 1997)

[58] (Chambers, 2010)

[59] (Ancestry.com, Louisiana, Wills and Probate Records 1756-1984, 2015)

[60] Jean Baptiste Meullion papers, Manuscripts Collection 713, Louisiana Research Collection, Howard-Tilton Memorial Library, Tulane University, New Orleans; 1792 Opelousas Census of Free People of Color

[61] (Clark E., 2013, p. 154)

[62] (Clark E., 2013, p. 92)

[63] (Ulentin, Shades of grey: slaveholding free women of color in antebellum New Orleans, 1800-1840 LSU Doctoral Dissertation, 2012)

[64] (Reinders, 1965)

[65] (Historic New Orleans Collection)

[66] (Wilkins, 1963)

[67] (Ulentin, Shade of Grey: Slaveholding Free Women of Color (dissertation), 2012)

[68] Hall, Gwendolyn Midlo, comp. Louisiana, Slave Records, 1719-1820 [database on-line]. Provo, UT, USA: Ancestry.com Operations Inc, 2009. Original data: Hall, Gwendolyn Midlo, comp. Afro-Louisiana History and Genealogy, 1719-1820. Database downloaded from http://www.ibiblio.org/laslave/, 2003

[69] http://www.crt.state.la.us/dataprojects/hp/nhl/aZachments/Parish44/Scans/44008001.pdf

[70] (Troop Roster: Battle of New Orleans)

[71] (Ulentin, Shades of grey: slaveholding free women of color in antebellum New Orleans, 1800-1840 LSU Doctoral Dissertation, 2012)

[72] (Ulentin, Shades of grey: slaveholding free women of color in antebellum New Orleans, 1800-1840 LSU Doctoral Dissertation, 2012) (Harris, 1999-2015)

[73] (Nolan, 2012)

[74] (Kapplan-Levenson, 2016)

[75] (Fandrich, 2005)

[76] (Clark E., 2013, p. 85)

[77] (Clark E., 2013, p. 87)

[78] (Snellings, 1860) (Clark 2013, 87)

[79] (German Settlers in Louisiana and New Orleans)

[80] (Claiborne W. C., 1810)

[81] (Plaquette, 2009)

[82] (Rasmussen, 2011)

[83] (Fessenden, 2016) Maroons were enslaved people who escaped and lived in small hidden communities.

[84] (Rasmussen, 2011)

[85] (Paquette, 2011)

[86] Ibid

[87] (Insurrection of Blacks, 1811) (Rasmussen, 2011) (Paquette, 2011) (Pittsburgh Weekly Gazette, 1811)

[88] (Rasmussen, 2011)

[89] Ibid [90] Ibid [91] (Baptist, 2016)

[92] Ibid

[93] (Resistance, 2015)

[94] (Dormon, 1977)

[95] (Baptist, 2016)

[96] (Paquette, 2011) (Rasmussen, 2011)

[97] (Rasmussen, 2011)

[98] (Dormon, 1977) (Buman N. A., 2008)

[99] (Dudley, 2012) (Ancestry.com, Louisiana, Wills and Probate Records 1756-1984, 2015)

[100] (Le Gaulois, 1894) (France Patent No. 1BA2362, 1827) (A Proposition to Erect Not One, but a Hundred Monuments to a Great Inventor, 1886)

[101] (McCullough, 2011)

[102] (Kelley, 2011)

[103] (Taylor M.) (Fabre, 2000)

[104] (Vella, Intimate Enemies: The Two Worlds fo the Baroness Pontalba, 1997) (Admittance and Seating Policies for the American Theatre in New Orleans in 1820, 2007)

[105] (Admittance and Seating Policies for the American Theatre in New Orleans in 1820, 2007)

106 (Taylor M.)

107 (Berlin, 1974)

108 (Fabre, 2000)

109 (Taylor M.)

110 (Desdunes, 1973)

111 (Dufour, 1967)

112 (McCullough, 2011)

113 (Vella, Intimate Enemies: The Two Worlds fo the Baroness Pontalba, 1997) (Ancestry.com, Louisiana, Wills and Probate Records 1756-1984, 2015)

114 (Colodon, 1893)

115 (Intitut National de la propriete industrielle, 1826)

116 (Norbert Rillieux Biography, 1887)

117 (Renaux, 1833)

118 (Colodon, 1893)

119 (Norbert Rillieux Biography, 1887)

120 (American Chemical Society National Historic Chemical Landmarks. Norbert Rillieux and a Revolution in Sugar, 2002)

121 (Britannica, Ultra French History, n.d.)

122 (Sarrans, 1833)

123 (Norbert Rillieux, 1894)

124 (Stockwell, n.d.)

[125] (Sarrans, 1833) – Much of the retelling of the July Revolution comes from the writings of Bernard Sarrans, Lafayette's secretary.

[126] The Duke visited Louisiana as well and dined at the home of Marius Pons Bringier. See the chapter on the Bringiers.

[127] (McCullough, 2011); (Sarrans, 1833)

[128] (Allison, 1923)

[129] (Societe des Amis du Peuple, 1832)

[130] (Rillieux, Letter to R. S. M"Culloh, 1850)

[131] (Rillieux, Letter to the Editor, 1886)

[132] (M"Culloh & Bache, 1848)

[133] (Burke, 2014)

[134] (Colodon, 1893)

[135] Ibid

[136] See sectoon on Edmond Rillieux

[137] (Cane Sugar, 1907) (United States Congressional Serial Set: Volume 495 , 1846)

[138] (Rillieux, Letter to R. S. M"Culloh, 1850) William Freret was Norbert Rillieux's first cousin on his father's side. William was the son of James Freret and Eugenie Rillieux, Vincent Rillieux, Jr.'s sister.

[139] (Obituary of Vincent Rillieux, 1833) Some claim that that Vincent was killed in a duel. However, it is possible that as the story was passed down in family lore, that Vincent was confused with his brother Michel Vincent who was killed in a duel according to accounts in a northern newspaper.

[140] (Clark E. , 2013)

[141] (Bell, 1997)

[142] (Ancestry.com, Louisiana, Wills and Probate Records 1756-1984, 2015)

[143] (Smithsonian Institution, 2014)

[144] (Rillieux, Letter to the Editor, 1886)

[145] See the section on Edmond Rillieux for further details on his disappearance.

[146] (Meade, 1946)

[147] (Schulman, 1996-2015)

[148] (Rillieux, Letter to the Editor, 1886)

[149] (Rillieux, Letter to the Editor, 1886)

[150] (White, 2006)

[151] (Dessen, 2015, pp. 167-169)

[152] (Buman N. , 2013)

[153] (Boiling Sugar, 1842)

[154] (Follet, 1997)

[155] (Rillieux, Letter to the Editor, 1886)

[156] (Norbert Rillieux Biography, 1887)

[157] (Packwood, 1844)

[158] (United States Commissioner of Patents, 1849)

[159] (Follet, 1997)

[160] (Norbert Rillieux Biography, 1887)

[161] (McCulloh & Bache, 1848)

[162] (New Orleans annual and commercial register of 1846, 1845)

[163] (Pierce, 1906)

[164] (Norbert Rillieux: Commemoration du Centenaiire de la mise en marche de la premiere installation d'evaporation dans le vide a triple effet a la Louisiane en 1834, 1934) (Horsin-Deon, Louisiana Planter and Sugar Manufacturer, 1894)

[165] (Evans E. N., 1988) (Scarborough, 2006)

[166] (Iroquois Research Institute, 1982)

[167] (Evans E. N., 1988)

[168] (Horsin-Deon, Louisiana Planter and Sugar Manufacturer, 1894)

[169] (Kendell, 1922)

[170] (Lousiana Legislature, 1835)

[171] (Horsin-Deon, Louisiana Planter and Sugar Manufacturer, 1894)

[172] A hogshead is a barrel that holds approximately 1,000 lbs.

[173] (Louisiana Department of Culture Recreation and Tourism, 2017)

[174] (Barbados Today, 2017)

[175] (Koppeschaar, 1914) (Alfred, 1904)

[176] (Norbert Rillieux Biography, 1887)

[177] (Rillieux, Letter to the Editor, 1886)

[178] (McCulloh & Bache, 1848)

[179] (Heitmann, 1987) (McCulloh & Bache, 1848)

[180] (Berlin, 1974)

[181] (Bell, 1997) (Taylor M.)

[182] (Reinders, 1965)

[183] (Walder, 1987)

[184] (Trafton, 2004) (Breeden, 1976) (Erickson, 1986)

[185] (Morton, 1844) (Manassa & Wolfe, 2018)

[186] (Wolfe, 2011) (McFarland, 2012) (Trafton, 2004)

[187] (The Mummy Last Night, 1852)

[188] (Lyceum Lectures, 1852)

[189] (Panorama of the Nile, 1852)

[190] (Erickson, 1986)

[191] (Times Picayune, 1886)

[192] (Nott J. C., 1849)

[193] (Nott & Gliddon, 1854)

[194] (Bourbourg, 1868)

[195] (Bourbourg, 1868)

[196] Académie des Inscriptions et Belle-LeZers is an organization concerned with French scholarship in the area of classics, Middle Eastern, and Asian studies and is a highly selective body of which Champollion was a member.

[197] (Norbert Rillieux, 1894)

[198] (Evening Star, 1857)

[199] (Benfey, Norbert Rillieux: Chemical Engineer and Free Black Cousin of Edgar Degas, 1998)

[200] (Dred Scott v John F. A. Sanford, 1857)

[201] (Pryor, Colored Travelers: Mobility and the Fight for Citizenship Before the Civil War, 2016)

[202] (Martyn, 1979)

[203] (New York Daily Times, 1857)

[204] Ibid

[205] Irma and Paul Milstein Division of United States History, Local History and Genealogy, The New York Public Library. "New York City directory" New York Public Library Digital Collections. Accessed August 21, 2018. hZp:// digitalcollecmons.nypl.org/items/d73e7cd0-529b-0134-92d5-00505686a51c - 1854

[206] (Davis J., 1906) See section Duncan Kenner.

[207] (Brooklyn Daily Eagle, 1911)

[208] (Mott, 1938)

[209] (Died, 1857)

[210] (A Greenwood Romance: The Secret of a Great Actress's Death Disclosed After Seventeen Years, 1874)

211 "United States Passport Applications, 1795-1925," database with images, FamilySearch (https://familysearch.org/ark:/61903/1:1:QGKJ-K2HC : 22 December 2017), Norbert Rillieux, 1862; citing Passport Application, United States, source certificate #, Passport Applications, 10/31/1795 - 12/31/1905., 108, NARA microfilm publications M1490 and M1372 (Washington D.C.: National Archives and Records Administration, n.d.)

212 "United States Passport Applications, 1795-1925," database with images, FamilySearch (https://familysearch.org/ark:/61903/1:1:QGKJ-K2HC : 22 December 2017), Norbert Rillieux, 1862; citing Passport Application, United States, source certificate #, Passport Applications, 10/31/1795 - 12/31/1905., 108, NARA microfilm publications M1490 and M1372 (Washington D.C.: National Archives and Records Administration, n.d.)

213 (Pryor, Colored Travelers, Mobility and the Fight for Citizenship before the Civil War, 2016)

214 (Dred Scott v John F. A. Sanford, 1857)

215 National Archives and Records Administration (NARA); Washington D.C.; NARA Series: Registers and Indexes for Passport Applications, 1810-1906; Roll #: 2; Volume #: Roll 2 - Index to Passport Applications, 11 May 1843-30 Sep 1846

216 (Pritchard, 1939)

217 (Meade, 1946)

218 (J.D.B. DeBow, n.d.)

219 (Sugar Planter' Association, 1886)

220 (Proposition to Erect Not One, but a Hundred Monuments to a Great Inventor, 1886)

221 (Barbados Today, 2017)

222 (The Rillieux Patents, 1889)

223 Wallasey 2017

224 Certified copy of an entry of marriage given at the general register office Application Number 1197369-1 April 27, 2009

225 (Schouler, 1882)

226 (Snellings, 1860) (J. David Hacker, 2010)

227 (Norbert Rillieux Commémoration du Centenaire de la mise en marche de la première installation d'évaporation dans le vide a triple effet á la Louisiane en 1834., 1834)

228 (Horsin-Deon, Louisiana Planter and Sugar Manufacturer, 1894)

229 (McGrayne, 2001) (McCarthy S., 2014)

230 (Lady and Two Masked Men, 1911) The Belfast Telegraph published the recounting of an assault and robbery of a Mme. Rillieux who was an octogenarian and was of English descent. This must have been Emily Rillieux as she would have been in her 80's and was of English descent.

231 (Norbert Rillieux: Commemoration du Centenaiire de la mise en marche de la premiere installation d'evaporation dans le vide a triple effet a la Louisiane en 1834, 1934)

232 (Austin, 2016)

233 (Benfey, Degas in New Orleans: encounters in the Creole world of Kate Chopin and George Washington Cable, 1997)

234 (Taylor M.) (Reinders, 1965)

235 (Constance Vivant listed as f.w.c. in a real estate transaction of 1818 - Hall, Gwendolyn Midlo, comp. Louisiana, Slave Records, 1719-1820 [database on- line]. Provo, UT, USA: Ancestry.com

Operations Inc, 2009.) (Vivant has no racial designation in a transaction with her mother, Louison Cheval, however Cheval is listed with f.w.c. behind her name. The Collins C. Diboll Vieux Carré Digital Survey n.d.) (Vivant is referred to as Constance Vivant f.d.c., femme de couleur, in her son Edmond's probate in 1832. Ancestry.com, Louisiana, Wills and Probate Records 1756-1984 2015)

[236] New Orleans, Louisiana Birth Records Index, 1790-1899; Volume: 6; Page Number: 709

[237] (U.S. Department of Interior, 1860)

[238] (Nystrom J. A., 2010)

[239] (Republican Party of Louisiana , 1865)

[240] (Rankin, 1974)

[241] Ibid [242] Ibid [243] (Uzee, 1971)

[244] Ibid

[245] (Proceedings of the Convention of the Republican Party of Louisiana Held at Economy Hall, New Orleans, September 25, 1865: And of the Central Executive Committee of the Friends of Universal Suffrage of Louisiana, Now the Central Executive Committee of the , 1865)

[246] (Reynolds, 1964)

[247] Ibid

[248] (Roudané, 2014)

[249] (The Greatest Demonstration. Republican Mass Meeting, 1868)

[250] (Williams T. H., 1945)

[251] Ibid

252 (New Orleans Times, 1873)

253 (Williams T. H., 1945)

254 (Radicalism Outdone, 1873)

255 (Williams T. H., 1945)

256 (Nystrom J. A., 2010)

257 The speeches were published in the July 16, 1873 edition of the *Daily Picayune*.

258 (Nystrom J. A., 2010)

259 (O'Connell, 2006)

260 (Williams T. H., 1945)

261 *Dernier Tribut* or *Last Tribute*

262 (Williams T. H., 1945)

263 Ibid

264 (Bell, 1997)

265 (Times Picayune, July 18, 1873)

266 (Williams T. H., 1945) (Times Picayune July 23, 1873)

267 (Williams T. H., 1945) (Nystrom J. A., 2010)

268 (Benfey, Degas in New Orleans: encounters in the Creole world of Kate Chopin and George Washington Cable, 1997) (Nystrom J. A., 2010)

269 (Nystrom J. A., 2010)

270 (Kendall, 1922)

271 (Nystrom J., 2017)

272 (The White League. Its Platform in Full. A Manly and Straightforward Document, 1874)

273 Ibid

274 (Mass Meeting. The Assemblage at Clay Statue, 1874)

275 Ibid

276 (Kendall, 1922)

277 (Nystrom J. A., 2010)

278 (Kendall, 1922) (Nystrom J. A., 2010)

279 (Benfey, Degas in New Orleans: encounters in the Creole world of Kate Chopin and George Washington Cable, 1997)

280 Ibid

281 (Benfey, Degas in New Orleans: encounters in the Creole world of Kate Chopin and George Washington Cable, 1997)

282 (Feigenbaum, 1999)

283 (Brown M. R., A Tale of Two Families: The De Gas-Musson Correspondence at Tulane University, 1999, p. 71)

284 (Vella, The Country for Men with Nerve, 1999)

285 (Beckert, 2014) 2

86 (Vella, The Country for Men with Nerve 1999)

287 Ibid

288 (Boggs J. S., 1999)

[289] (Benfey, Degas in New Orleans: encounters in the Creole world of Kate Chopin and George Washington Cable, 1997) (Johnson A., A Legacy of Triumph: More Stories of Duncan F. Kenner and Abe Hawkins, 2014)

[290] (James F. Barnett 2007)

[291] (James F. Barnett, The Natchez Indians 2007)

[292] Ibid

[293] (Dunbar Rowland, 1907)

[294] (James F. Barnett, The Natchez Indians: A History to 1735, 2007)

[295] (Bourgeois, 1957)

[296] (Sidelights on Louisiana History Section: ""Data Concerning the Natchez Massacre 1729-1730, 1918) (Bourgeois, 1957)

[297] (Chambon, 1908)

[298] (Ouchley, 2014)

[299] (Pack, 1996-2006)

[300] (Cruzat, 1919) (Powell, 2012)

[301] (Bourgeois, 1957)

[302] Ibid

[303] (Cormier, 2019)

[304] (Dufour, 1967)

[305] (Dufour, 1967) (Larned, 1895)

[306] (Powell, 2012)

[307] (Dufour, 1967)

[308] (Former, 2012 (originally published 1904))

[309] (Dufour, 1967) (Former, 2012 (originally published 1904))

[310] *Andre Verret was the brother of Nicolas Verret, who was married to Michel Cantrelle's sister Marie Marguerite Cantrelle.*

[311] (Chandler 1986)

[312] Ibid

[313] (Dufour, 1967) (Louisiana as a Spanish Colony, n.d.)

[314] (St. Louis Catholic Cathedral, Marriage Register 1777-1784, p. 60)

[315] (Trickey, 2017)

[316] (Roth, 2010)

[317] (Flemming, 1982)

[318] (Bradley, 2002)

[319] (Flemming, 1982)

[320] (Louisiana: European Explorations and the Louisiana Purchase, n.d.)

[321] (Laussat 1978, 20)

[322] (Laussat, 1978, p. 64) *See further discussion of the Bringier visit in section on the Bringier family.*

[323] (Laussat 1978, 68)

[324] (Dardar, 2004) *The three families had adjacent plantations and were related.*

[325] Ibid

[326] (Beauchamp, 2009)

[327] (Laussat, 1978, p. 68)

[328] (Dardar, 2004)

[329] (Laussat 1978, 124)

[330] (Claiborne W. C., To Thomas Jefferson from William C. C. Claiborne, 19 November 1804, 1804)

[331] *See the section on Evan Jones for further information.*

[332] (Bradley, 2002) (Claiborne W. C., To Thomas Jefferson from William C. C. Claiborne, 19 November 1804, 1804)

[333] (Bradley, 2002)

[334] (Claiborne W. C., To Thomas Jefferson from William C. C. Claiborne, 15 July 1806, 1806)

[335] (Claiborne W. C., To Thomas Jefferson from William C. C. Claiborne, 15 July 1806, 1806)

[336] (Carter, 1940) (Beauchamp, 2009) Note: *The Territorial papers include a pardon from Gov. Claiborne of Anselm Roman; however, genealogical research has not found an Anselm Roman. Michel Cantrelle's daughter Marie "Celeste" was married to Onézime Roman. It is unclear if Anselm and Onézime are the same person.*

[337] (Bradley, 2002)

[338] Louis Judice was married to Marie Jeanne Cantrelle, the sister of Nicolas Verret's wife.

[339] (Kolb F. B., 2007) (Brasseaux & Voorhies, 1989)

[340] For further discussion of the Insurrection of 1768 see the section on Jacques Cantrelle.

[341] (Bourgeois, 1957) (Cochran, 1963)

[342] (Cochran, 1963)

[343] (Bradley, 2002)

[344] (Bradley, 2002, p. 375)

[345] (Bradley 2002)

[346] (Starr, 1976) (Bradley, 2002)

[347] (Starr, 1976)

[348] (Kolb F. B., 2014)

[349] (Powell, 2012) (Kolb F. B., 2014) (Vernet, 2013)

[350] (Powell, 2012) (Kolb F. B., 2014)

[351] (Bradley, 2002)

[352] Ibid

[353] (Dufour, 1967) *Marie Marguerite Verret married Evan Jones in 1781. Her uncle, André Verret and her grandfather, Jacques Cantrelle, took part in the rebellion. For further details see the chapter on the Verret Family.*

[354] (Bradley, 2002)

[355] (Alexander, 2004)

[356] (Din, The Canary Islanders of Louisiana, 1988)

357 (Washington, 1939) *At the time of the letter, Philemon Dickinson was a major general commanding the New Jersey Militia and would later serve as a delegate from Delaware to the Continental Congress.*

358 (Kolb F. B., 2014)

359 (Din 1988)

360 (Freeman, 2002) (Collins, 2014) (Pollock, 2011)

361 (Pollock, 2011)

362 (Pickering, 1799)

363 (Adams J. , 1799)

364 (Din & Harkins, New Orleans Cabildo: Colonial Louisiana's First City Government, 1769--1803 , 1996) (Jones E. , To James Madison from Evan Jones, 15 May 1801, 1801)

365 (Din & Harkins, New Orleans Cabildo: Colonial Louisiana's First City Government, 1769--1803 , 1996) (Vernet 2013)

366 (Bradley, 2002)

367 (Vernet, 2013)

368 (Bradley, 2002)

369 (Bradley, 2002) *The treaty was secret and was not known to the citizens.*

370 (Jones E. , To James Madison from Evan Jones, 15 May 1801, 1801)

371 (Jones E. , To James Madison from Evan Jones, 15 May 1801, 1801)

372 (Laussat 1978, 75-76)

[373] (Claiborne W. C., To James Madison from William C. C. Claiborne, 2 January 1804, 1804)

[374] (Vernet, 2013)

[375] (Rightor, 1900)

[376] (Vernet, 2013)

[377] (Mackenzie and Rhoades 1995)

[378] (Vernet, 2013)

[379] (C. Garcia 2013)

[380] (Brown C. , 2009)

[381] (Carter, 1940)

[382] Ibid

[383] (Jefferson, Notes on New Orleans Characters, 1 July 1804, 1804)

[384] (Gallamn, 1804)

[385] (Jefferson, Notes on New Orleans Characters, 1 July 1804, 1804)

[386] (Jefferson, To James Madison from Thomas Jefferson 16 August 1804, 1804)

[387] (Jefferson, From Thomas Jefferson to William C. C. Claiborne, 1804)

[388] (Bradley, 2002, p. 37)

[389] (Vernet, 2013)

[390] Ibid

[391] (Bradley 2002, 37)

[392] (Bradley 2002, 38) (Vernet 2013, 79)

[393] (Claiborne W. C., To James Madison from William C. C. Claiborne, 1804)

[394] (Claiborne W. C., To James Madison from William C. C. Claiborne 13 October 1804, 1804)

[395] (Claiborne W. C., To James Madison from William C. C. Claiborne 5 November 1804, 1804)

[396] (Claiborne W. C., To Thomas Jefferson From William C. C. Claiborne, 2 December 1804, 1804)

[397] (Vernet, 2013)

[398] (Vernet, 2013, p. 85) Quoted from *Annuls of Congress*, 8th Congress, 2nd Session, 14:727-728.

[399] (Vernet, 2013)

[400] (Dufour, 1967)

[401] (Claiborne, To James Madison From William C. C. Claiborne, 6 August 1805 1805)

[402] (James Starrs, 2012)

[403] (Linklater 2009)

[404] Ibid

[405] (The Aaron Burr Association, 2015)

[406] (Vernet, 2013)

[407] Ibid

[408] Ibid

[409] (Wilkinson, 1811)

[410] (Bradley, 2002)

[411] (Dufour, 1967)

[412] (Rodriguez, 2002)

[413] (Christ Church Cathedral)

[414] (Hylan, 1984)

[415] (S. S. Ellis 2019)

[416] (Trist, 1808) *Elizabeth House Trist was an old friend of Thomas Jefferson's and was the grandmother of Nicholas Philip Trist who was married to Jefferson's granddaughter, Virginia Jefferson Randolph.*

[417] (C. L. Johnson 1939)

[418] (Acts Passed at the First Session of the Legislative Council of the Territory of Orleans: Begun and Held at the Principal, in the City of New-Orleans, on Monday the Third Day of December, in the Year of Our Lord One Thousand Eight Hundred and Four, and of , 1805)

[419] (Ellis S. S., 2019)

[420] (Trist, 1808)

[421] (King, 1921)

[422] *He dropped the Emmanuel and was referred to as Marius Pons or Marius.*

[423] (Kane, 1945) (King, 1921)

[424] (Bauer C. A., 2011)

[425] (Laussat, 1978)

[426] (Bauer C. A., 2011) (King, 1921)

[427] (Bauer C. A., 2011)

[428] (Kane, 1945) (Bauer C. A., 2011)

[429] (The Introduction of Cotton into the Mississippi Valley, 1858) For more information on Daniel Clark see Evan Jones.

[430] Françoise "Fanny" 1786, Elizabeth Louise "Betsy" 1788, Michel "Doradou" 1789, Françoise "Laure" 1792, and Melanie Elizabeth 1793

[431] (Kane, 1945)

[432] (Kane, 1945)

[433] (Kane, 1945)

[434] (Bauer C. A., 2011)

[435] (Bauer C. A., 2011) (Kane, 1945)

[436] (Bauer C. A., 2011) (Lachance, 1982) (Kane, 1945)

[437] (Bauer C. A., 2011) (Kane, 1945) (King, 1921)

[438] (Bradley, 2002)

[439] (McCarthy K. M., 2004)

[441] (Bauer C. A., 2011)

[442] Ibid

[443] Ancestry.com. *Louisiana, Wills and Probate Records, 1756-1984* [database on-line]. Provo, UT, USA: Ancestry.com Operations, Inc., 2015.Original data: Louisiana County, District and Probate Courts.

444 (Bauer C. A., 2011)

445 For detailed information about Michel Doradou Bringier see *Creole Genesis: The Bringier Family and Antebellum Plantation Life in Louisiana* by Craig A. Bauer and *Plantation Parade* by Harnett T. Kane.

446 (Bauer C. A., 2011)

447 (King, 1921)

448 (Bauer C. A., 1993)

449 Ibid

450 (Bauer C. A., 2011)

451 (Bauer C. A., 1993)

452 (R. Christopher Goodwin & Associates, Inc., 1989)

453 (Johnson A., A Legacy of Triumph: The Red Fox of the South & Old Abe of Ashland Plantation, 2014)

454 (Bauer C. A., 1993)

455 Ibid

456 (Louisiana Sugar Planters' Association: Presentations to the Association of the Portraits of Etienne de Bore and of the Past Presidents of the Association. 1909)

457 See the section about Norbert Rillieux.

458 For an extensive biography of Duncan Kenner see *A Leader Among Peers: The Life and Times of Duncan Farrar Kenner* by Craig A. Bauer.

459 (Kane, 1945)

[460] Ibid

[461] (Reports of Cases Argued and Determined in the Supreme Court of Louisiana Vol. 22, 1870)

[462] (Reports of Cases Argued and Determined in the Supreme Court of Louisiana Vol. 22, 1870) (Kane, 1945)

[463] (Bauer C. A., 2011)

[464] Colomb married Fanny Bringier, Louis's sister. See section on Marius Pons Bringier.

[465] (Letter to the Editor, 1860) The writer of the letter is identified only as C. His account in the *Baton Rouge Tri-Weekly Gazette* is based on the recollections told to him by Louis Bringier.

[466] (Sponsel, 2020)

[467] (Klein, 2012)

[468] Ibid

[469] (Brown C. A., 1944)

[470] (Brown C. A., 1944) (Harvey, 2020)

[471] (Brown C. A., 1944)

[472] (Vassoler, 2004) (Humboldt & Bonpland, Personal Narrative of Travels to the Equinoctial Regions of the New Continent During the Years 1799-1804: Volumes 1-2, 1822)

[473] (Humboldt, To Thomas Jefferson from Alexander von Humboldt, 24 May 1804, 1804)

[474] (Jefferson, From Thomas Jefferson to Alexander von Humboldt, 28 May 1804, 1804)

[475] (The Collins C. Diboll Vieux Carré Digital Survey)

476 (Bauer C. A., 2011) (Kane, 1945)

477 (Kane, 1945)

478 (Bauer C. A., 2011)

479 (Chavez, 2018)

480 (Houdaille, 1956)

481 (Williams W. D., 1989)

482 (Pope, 1895)

484 (Bennet, 1909) (Gradual Increase of African Slavery in Louisiana, 1868) (Bennet, 1909) Pierre Lafitte was in New Orleans as early as 1803, and Jean Lafitte according to Bennet was in New Orleans at least as early as 1806. See the section on Evan Jones for more on Daniel Clark.

485 (Davis W. C., Jean and Pierre Lafitte, n.d.)

486 (Bringier, otices of the Geology, Mineralogy, Topography, Productions, and Aboriginal inhabitants of the regions around the Mississippi and its confluent waters, 1821) It is possible that Louis had the exact date wrong. The major shocks of the New Madrid Earthquakes took place on December 16, 1811, January 23, 1812, and February 3, 1812.

487 (Valencius, 2013)

488 (Valencius, 2013)

489 (Bringier, otices of the Geology, Mineralogy, Topography, Productions, and Aboriginal inhabitants of the regions around the Mississippi and its confluent waters, 1821)

490 Ibid *Louis Bringier referenced a journal he kept while the Otomi tribe and noted that they did not speak Spanish.*

491 (Valencius, 2013)

492 *His precise knowledge of earth science was probably acquired during the expedition with von Humboldt.*

493 (Summary of 1811-1812 New Madrid Earthquakes Sequence, n.d.)

494 (Aurora General Advertiser, 1812) *The newspaper listed a letter for Louis Bringier at the Philadelphia Post Office.*

495 (Blaufarb, 2016)

496 (Myths, Misdeeds, and Misunderstandings: The Roots of Conflict in U.S.- Mexican Relations, 1997)

497 (Bennet, 1909)

498 (Blaufarb, 2016) (W. C. Davis, The Pirates Lafitte: The Treacherous World of the Corsairs of the Gulf 2006) (Gareis, 2001)

499 (Garrigoux, 2017)

500 See the section on Evan Jones

501 (Miller E. L., 2004)

502 (Garrigoux, 2017)

503 (Davis W. C., The Pirates Lafitte: The Treacherous World of the Corsairs of the Gulf, 2006)

504 Ibid

505 (Hemard, 2012) Humbert fought Pakenham in Ireland under Napoleon.

506 (Melish, 1816) (Williams W. D., 1989)

507 (Bringier & Darby, Prospectus of Historical and geographical tracts, with maps, on Louisiana by William Darby and Louis Bringier, New York)

508 (Williams W. D., 1989)

509 (Melish, 1816)

510 (Dillard, 2010)

511 (Williams W. D., 1989)

512 (Davis W. C., The Pirates Lafitte: The Treacherous World of the Corsairs of the Gulf, 2006)

513 (Blaufarb, 2016)

514 (Kane, 1945)

515 (Bauer C. A., 2011) (Williams W. D., 1989) (Kane, 1945)

516 (Bauer C. A., 2011)

517 (History of the City, 2020)

518 (Kane, 1945) (Bauer C. A., 2011)

519 (Ancestry.com, Louisiana, Wills and Probate Records 1756-1984, 2015)

520 It is probable that the young Mexican man was the son of the woman who Louis intended to marry in Mexico.

521 (Bauer C. A., 2011)

522 £200,000 pounds today

523 In all official documents from the Spanish period in New Orleans, James is referred to as Santiago.

524 (Stone, 1915)

525 Ibid

526 (Kukla, 2009)

527 See section on Vincent Rillieux

528 *As was the case with most males at that time in New Orleans, James was probably not practicing any religion, but knew that he had to profess Catholicism so he could marry.*

529 (The National Archives of the UK; Kew, Surrey, England; General Register Office: Registers of Births, Marriages and Deaths Surrendered to the Non- Parochial Registers Commissions of 1837 and 1857; Class Number: RG 4; Piece Number: 4594) James was baptized in April of 1773, a month aper he was born. This contradicts his testimony.

530 *This implies that he was not directly asked if he was Protestant or Roman Catholic, but how he took the oath.*

531 A transcript of the inquiry was found in the papers of Douglass Freret.

532 (Duplicates of Intendants of the Army and of the Royal Archive of the Indies, 1803)

533 (Rodriguez, 2002)

534 (Claiborne W. C., To James Madison from William C. C. Claiborne, 1805)

535 (Reeves & Reeves, 1983) (Guillermo Prieto, 2010)

536 (Kendall, 1922)

537 (Reeves & Reeves, 1983)

538 Ibid

539 (Fire at Freret Press, 1830)

540 (Reeves & Reeves, 1983)

541 (Rightor, 1900)

542 Rene Freret unpublished papers - correspondence

543 (Krichtal, 2013)

544 (The Atlanta, 1818)

545 (Krichtal, 2013)

546 Rene Freret unpublished papers - correspondence

547 (Reeves & Reeves, 1983)

548 (Cohen, 1854)

549 (Campanella 2016 *The Merchants' Exchange was located at 18 Royal St. – now 124 – 132 Royal*) (Acts Passed at the First Session of the Twelfth Legislature of the State of Louisiana 1835 *Other investors were John Hagan, J.B. Byrne, Peter Dubuys, Samuel J. Peters, Richard O. Pritchard, J.H. Caldwell, W. W. Montgomery, Maunsel White, Nath. Dick, Benj. Ha_, J.R. Sterrett, Benj. Levy, Wm Debuys, Jaonathan Montgomery, Thomas Barre,, Wm J. McLean, and Lucien Hermann*)

550 (Campanella, 2016)

551 (Campanella 2016) (Thompson T. P., 1915)

552 (Acts Passed at the Second Session of the Fourteenth Legislature of Louisiana, 1840)

553 *Most members of the Native American Association in N.O. were Whigs; however, there were a few Democrats.*

554 *At the time of the writing, residency requirements for naturalization was five years. The Native American Party advocated a period of twenty-one years for naturalized citizenship. The Native American Party also sought to prohibit foreign born people from running for elected office.)*

555 (Address of the Louisiana Native American Association to the Citizens of Louisiana and the Inhabitants of the United States, 1839) *William Freret signed the manifesto along with many influential, mostly Anglo-American, citizens of Louisiana.*

556 (Bevan, 2011)

557 (Kendall, 1922)

558 Ibid

559 (Administrations of the Mayors of New Orleans: William Freret, 2011)

560 (Kendell, 1922)

561 (O'Connor, 1895)

562 (Peterson, 1964)

563 Lafayette City of a section of the City of New Orleans.

564 (An Address to the Citizens of Louisiana on the Subject of the Recent Election in New Orleans, 1844)

565 (Galván, 2004)

566 (Knight & Levinson, 2017)

567 (Allahar, 1994)

568 Ibid

569 (Chaffin, 2011)

[570] (Murrin & James M. McPherson, 2005)

[571] (Caldwell, 1915)

[572] (Caldwell, 1915)

[573] (Robinson A., n.d.)

[574] (Robinson A., n.d.)

[575] (Chaffin, 2011)

[576] (Important from Havana: Rumored Revolution, 1851)

[577] (Finkelman, 2011)

[578] (Caldwell, 1915)

[579] (Caldwell, 1915) (Chaffin, 2011)

[580] (Caldwell, 1915) (Chaffin, 2011) (Murrin & James M. McPherson, 2005)

[581] (The New Orleans Bee, 1851)

[582] (Jones H., 2009) (Caldwell, 1915)

[583] (Jones H., 2009)

[584] (Correspondence Between the Treasury Department in Relation to the Cuban Expedition and William Freret, Late Collector, 1851)

[585] (Kendall, 1922)

[586] (Correspondence Between the Treasury Department in Relation to the Cuban Expedition and William Freret, Late Collector, 1851)

[587] (The Collectorship, 1851)

[588] (Stockwell, n.d.)

[589] (Urban, 1957) (Murrin & James M. McPherson, 2005)

[590] (Daily Delta, 1862)

[591] (Times Picayune, 1862)

[592] (Kendall, 1922)

[593] (Hatch, 1893)

www.ingramcontent.com/pod-product-compliance
Lightning Source LLC
Chambersburg PA
CBHW030255100526
44590CB00012B/411